Dedication

To all the Veterans who have served, or who are serving, our country in times of war and in times of peace, I honor and thank you.

To the Viet Nam Veterans who were children when I was also a child, I honor and thank you all for your service to our country. I was honored to listen to your stories, and I hope to bridge your lives to the lives of the civilians of our generation, and to others who never really knew you, until now.

To my Dad, Joseph Patrick Gordon McNeil, for a promise kept… I sent messages to the Universe, that I would one day be a writer of books, and the first one would be dedicated to you, Dad.

Introduction
FINALLY, A PARADE FOR YOU
by Molly Burton

It has been my intention to write a story about America's Viet Nam Veterans for over two decades. This was the war of my youth. It was the piece of history that colored the Sexual Revolution, "Women's Lib," and Civil Rights with the blood of those who sacrificed peace for service to our country. It was the age of Rock and Roll, the Cuban Missile Crisis, muscle cars, funny 'shrooms, and the assassination of President John F. Kennedy. Our parents were recovering from the privations of the Great Depression, World War II, and the Korean War. We, their children were coming of age in what everyone thought would be a time of prosperity, a good education and peaceful lives for all.

I was a senior in high school when I first heard about the Viet Nam conflict in a Modern Problems class. I remember telling my teacher, Mr. Nygaard, that I had a brother, Tim, who was a freshman, that I didn't want him to have to go to war. Mr. Nygaard replied that the problems would blow over in a few months. We all could not have been more wrong!

Years passed, and I had the opportunity to go to college... I had worked and saved for it during my childhood and teen years, and though my parents sent care packages and lots of love, they could not afford the tuition and expenses that college required. It was through scholarships and grants that I was able to realize my dream of becoming a teacher. I married in my junior year, and after graduation, and a few years of teaching, Oregon laws required teachers to get a fifth year or a Master's Degree to keep their licenses current. Summer school to complete this requirement, the birth of two children and continued teaching were my life. About twelve years into my career, the late 1970s, some of the students of my middle school began wearing "camo" pants shirts, jackets, boots and hats as their garb for the day. When asked about their clothing choices, they replied that their dads or moms had worn them when they were in the Viet Nam War. They were the original outfits of their parents, who died or had saved them upon their return home. For many of these youngsters, the war was not over yet. They were being raised by parents of divorce or widowhood, or even step-parents. This fashion took hold and continues today as a silent, and maybe forgotten, tribute.

Life happens to us all. After twenty years, my husband and I divorced, and I became a single mom. I had a couple of relationships that ended disastrously, and in the course of this time, I discovered massage therapy as a new part-time job. I considered it my "very expensive hobby." When I retired from teaching, though, it became full time, and has been an extremely rewarding retirement career. In the last four years, I have decided that after a quarter of a century in this wonderful practice, I wanted something more conducive to real retirement. I wanted to tell stories, and I also discovered energy healing as an adjunct practice to massage therapy: A perfect marriage to healing the body, mind, and soul. When I was still teaching and doing massage therapy part-time, I began to have the idea of writing about the Viet

Nam Veterans. They had not been getting the celebrations of returning heroes, and after about two decades of being ignored by the government, their own towns and even families, they were making headlines about homelessness, a rise in drug and alcohol abuse that continued from their days in service, the lack of opportunity to be educated, treated for PTSD, and to be productive members of society. This lack of celebration, the Viet Nam Wall of Remembrance notwithstanding, bothered me greatly. Since I have been studying energy healing, I have been moved to tell the story of these veterans, about their sacrifice, their lives, their quiet dignity while living lives in anonymity.

Not long after my sons graduated from high school, they began to look at the military for the next step in their lives. My oldest decided to go into the military, as two uncles and a grandfather had been military men, and it seemed like a good place to begin adulthood. My youngest son studied at a junior college for two years, before joining the military, too. Both children have seen the best of the military life and some of the worst. They have served in the Iraqi War and other theaters in the Middle East. I know that they suffer from PTSD on some levels, though this is never discussed, admitted or treated, as the military considers the admission of needing psychological help to be a weakness, and therefore, said sufferer is not material to be worthy of rank advancement.

I consider this practice of non-treatment of such an important mental issue to be a crime against the citizenry. When the military creates a fighting machine as is its purpose in "creating" a soldier, sailor or pilot, deprogramming should be the first treatment a serviceman or woman receives upon returning home. It should be *mandatory*! Then, physical therapy for any physical wounds, and finally an ongoing medical treatment for any other physical or emotional issue should be part of their future lives. Job training and businesses should be given incentives for getting these men and women back to civilian life as quickly as possible. Their lives should be honored for their choices to serve and protect us all, just as our government officials are given protection and homage for the rest of their lives. Expensive? You bet! Our monies are not always used wisely, but how better to keep us safe if our soldiers are rewarded for their sacrifices by always giving them their due, without having to fight for years to receive it, when their military service is complete. I will present this argument in greater detail at the end of the book. Some will say my words are too repetitive, too pedantic. I want to make sure readers are getting my messages.

The issue of PTSD will be a recurring theme in the course of the stories you will see in this book. Every military serviceman or woman will have experience with this disorder, and in some, it will be a piece of their lives, under the surface, but never addressed, while in others it will be the defining quality of their existence. The stories I present will be the tales of real "everyday" heroes, not celebrities. They all have had the right of information control, and have helped me edit any security issues. In some cases, a pseudonym was used for privacy. For a few hours of their time, I was honored to be present with their memories, good and bad. They may be your neighbors, relatives, co-workers or friends. They helped shape us all, and to them I say: *Finally, A Parade for You*.

Table of Contents

*The spellings of the word "Viet Nam" appear differently throughout this book. The country of Viet Nam is actually a name with two words. The Americanization of the spelling made it one word. One or two veterans wanted the spelling to be one word, and some of the books and articles use that spelling as well. I have tried to be true to each authority's desire.

**Some veterans did not have access to photos taken during their time in Viet Nam. Therefore, recent or "modern" pictures appear instead.

The opinions of others do not necessarily match mine, as will be evident throughout this book. A recurring theme of accessibility for Veterans' assistance is mentioned during many stories and in the essays at the end of the book. It is time for the general public to "carry the flag" for our Viet Nam Veterans, as they did for us, so long ago.

Name: Robert (Bob) Beatty

Branch of Service: US Army

Rank: Specialist 4th Class (Corporal)

Time served: Arrived in Viet Nam: October 1967

Left Viet Nam: September 1968

Honors: recommended for Purple Heart, Silver Star (William O'Brien is an eyewitness to this. See attached letter.) Bob is still waiting.

"I should never have cut off my fingers with that saw!" This statement began the odyssey of Bob Beatty, a soft-spoken man with a twinkle in his eyes who carries the story of his life on his body. Shrapnel in various areas, a right hand that was favored from childhood when a window smashed it(making him left-handed to this day), scars on his fingers and burn marks from Agent Orange tell the story of a person who has jumped into life with both feet and lived to tell the tale.

Bob was born in Vancouver, Washington and raised in Seaside, Oregon. His dad and several siblings had served in the military, and many of the men in his family worked at the local logging company. When he was sixteen, he was working a saw at a Ridge Mill in Warrenton, Oregon and for just a second, he looked away, and the saw kissed the first and little fingers while stealing the tips of the second and third fingers of his right hand. A really exceptional doctor reattached the fingers, but it took two years to recover fully. When high school senior tests were administered, his teachers gave Bob his tests orally, since he was writing impaired, or so they thought. When a teacher noticed he was writing with his left hand, he asked, "Why didn't you tell me you were left-handed?"

His reply: "You didn't ask!" To this day, Bob is left-handed, and his right hand remains nerve-damaged from the window crunch as well as the saw.

The Viet Nam draft came up, and boys were called to register in Portland's induction center. Bob did not have a doctor's letter telling of his injuries, and that the use of his right hand was compromised (The doctor said he wouldn't need it...). His draft board doctor took a look at his hand, and said, "You look good to me!"

That very day he was inducted into the Army; he called home and said, "I'll see ya' when I see ya'." PTSD was already a part of Bob's life, but it was about to get more pronounced.

Bob did very well in basic training which took place in Fort Lewis, Washington. He excelled in a bivouac training exercise with a buddy named Dennis Boyle, whom he had known at home, and they were part of a group 'capture' game. Dennis' and Bob's families were hunters and fishermen, so they knew survival secrets pretty well. They were the only two of their group who had not been captured, so they put a tent under a tree with hanging branches to keep out of the rain. When the other team arrived, surrounding the rest of their team, Bob and Dennis went unnoticed and were able to capture the opposing group, freeing their captured teammates who were joined in a circle, AND getting drenched by the rain! Bob and Dennis earned the right to ride back to camp! The rest had to march back. Because of his atrophied right hand, his Drill Instructor (DI) looked the other way with a wink, wink! when physical tests were required, and the recorder checked the charts as a "pass." Bob did well with artillery, math testing, fire direction control, and was even "awarded" KP duty for the last three weeks of Advanced Individual Training (AIT) as part of the only team to pass artillery volleys training on the first try! What a deal!! Fort Benning, Georgia saw him being kidded about going to paratrooper school, but he was assigned to mortar platoons. He received his orders to go to Viet Nam, via Hawaii from San Francisco, then to the Philippines and Viet Nam. This excursion was supposed to calm everyone; however, Hawaii never happened, and they continued on their way, arriving in Tan Son Nhut, Viet Nam, in the dark, with explosions and firelight blossoming all around the area. Excited and terrified, each man was assigned to his station and was loaded into a Deuce and a Half (two and a half-ton truck). Bob reported to Tan Son Nhut, the airbase out of Saigon. Never having been much of a churchgoer, or particularly religious, Bob decided to visit the small chapel there. It was empty, but Bob was inspired to say a prayer and ask God for protection. He was afraid, and would rather have died, than be wounded and maimed. A colonel from Seaside, Oregon wanted to talk with Bob about home so he was held back for a visit, instead of heading out on a transport truck to his base. This was a part of true Divine Intervention. When Bob woke up the next day, his particular transport truck had run over a land mine killing those aboard. Bob had trained with them all. Another piece of the fabric of PTSD...

"In the way that war is," Bob noticed that at first, members of his compound were a little wary, doing their own jobs and keeping to schedules. The bunker to which Bob was assigned was lined with 13 layers of sand bags on the sides, 11 on the ends and on the top with camouflage netting over all. Twelve-foot by twelve-foot creosote poles held the roof with radios, maps, and phone operators, and with only one window. This might seem like a secure site, but with bulldozed flat land which created a protective berm around the entire Base Camp, hiding places for the enemy were located in every tree beyond. Being "on watch" took on an almost paranoid meaning. Life was full of danger, and the bugs, crawling things and weather in a climate that boasted seasons of "hot and wet" and '"hot and dry" made life a survival game. Air warnings, artillery around camp and one-half mile away, howitzers run by our allies, the Filipinos and our air units surrounded the camp like horrific beasts.. Bob sometimes worked two radios, and when Special Forces needed help, Bob was able to assist them in several ways. In one instance, his five-foot, six-inch height, at 120-pounds, served him well as a "tunnel rat." The Vietcong would tunnel underground to elude our troops, and the Green Berets would need to have these tunnels exposed so they would not be captured or killed. On one of his underground missions, Bob had a special surprise waiting for him. His torch and gun leading him forward lighted the way for a six-foot cobra to be seen and shot with expedient dispatch! This situational subterfuge was a tactic used by the enemies to alert them about when and where our soldiers were nearby, so they could escape through a camouflaged hole upon hearing the shot they knew would be coming!!

Life was not always terror replacing abject fear. Ever resourceful, Bob had a little help from home from time to time. His mom would send canned venison to him, and he knew the officers' mess had a cold freezer with little oversight regarding inventory contents. Steak was the go-to treat of choice, and Bob and the men on duty with him would prepare a feast-for-the-famished of wild game, beef steak, veggies and sundries for the young men so far from home. Most of the time, Filipinos who cooked their food for them told the men, "Don't ask; just eat." Once, Bob's mom even won a "Hi, Mom" contest drawing held by the Communications Workers of America, and their ham radio operators, who thought it would be great if soldiers could talk to Mom for a few minutes via ham radio. The mayor of Astoria, Oregon, Harry Steinbock, drew the four names and Bob's mom was the first one picked on January 4, 1968. The only man in his unit to get the privilege, Bob was flown in the Commander's Huey to Saigon for the call. There, he made the call from a ham radio pre-arranged and set up just for this event in a Saigon hotel! {Author's Note: Read news article at the end of the chapter.} Seeing Bob Hope, and Raquel Welch, who at the time was Miss World, at a USO show in Cu Chi, and meeting John Wayne when he was doing research for the movie, *The Green Berets,* were other highlights of a very dangerous life. For just a few moments, being afraid was pushed into a dark corner.

"Tet," or the Vietnamese Lunar New Year, was the occasion for the Tet Offensive. Vietnamese locals had been hired to make sandbags, and at one point Bob noticed them lying on sandbags, spying through the bunker's solitary window to stare at the maps that were tacked to the wall. They were able to see gun placements and troops' routes, learning limit parameters. Commanders were immediately notified. When Bob explained why he was shutting windows and alerting everyone, he shouted, "Mark my words, we're going to get hit tonight!"

Sure enough, that night enemy mortarsortars were fired at the bunker bracketing both sides, back and front, to zero in for heavier mortars, and then the bunker tower guard was killed by an enemy sniper. Hidden Vietnamese were seen in the trees one minute, then vanished the next. Koreans, Vietnamese, and Filipinos looked similar, and many were in the military police. Although not politically correct for today, blacks and whites were more trusted, but it was difficult to tell racial differences in the heat of battles. Bob had climbed the tower where the guard was killed, and located the enemy mortars that were bracketing other positions. Then, Bob called out the enemy locations and gave the order to fire an 8-inch Howitzer, with a range of 1000 meters and the only weapon in camp that was not out of commission. That stopped some mortar fire. Our soldiers, in different locations, stopped the main forces coming out of Laos and Cambodia, killing thousands of Vietcong (VC)and North Vietnamese Army (NVA) soldiers. Their mission was to overrun Saigon.

Bob was injured with shrapnel from rockets and mortar fire, so he was medevaced to a hospital in Cu Chi, part of the 25th Infantry Division main hospital. During his exams, doctors discovered Bob had kidney stones. They were going to do surgery by sending him to Ukoda, Japan, when Bob passed them a few days before his transport was to occur. He was sent right back into the action. Earlier, he had asked to have his deployment extended from 12 to 17 months, so that when his time was up, he would have less than 90 days to go in his enlistment with the military. As painful as passing those kidney stones was, if Bob had had the surgery he would have been hospitalized for several days, and another deployment to Viet Nam might have occurred.

Reports came in with results about the placements of troops and where they were at different times. A high ranking officer, General Westmoreland (called "Westy" by soldiers when he wasn't around), coordinated operations. He wanted names and other pertinent information, like checking first to get clearance for moving ahead and was flying in his chopper into their air space. He had Robert Kennedy with him!!! Westy's chopper pilot radioed for clearance to land and wanted artillery check fired (halted) for their approach. Bob would not give that information. He told the pilot, "You can go over, under or around, but they're not stopping firing." After the VIPs had arrived, they accused Bob's unit of shooting into Cambodia, even knowing that firing was occurring. This was untrue, and Bob refused to hand over any information. He was told he would be charged with insubordination, and waited for a while, but nothing ever came of it. Bob's Date of Separation (DROS) arrived. A Bird Colonel knew Bob had taken pictures during this campaign, and took them from him,. He informed Bob that with those documents in his possession, and talking about what he had seen or done during his time in Viet Nam, would have been grounds for imprisoning him in Leavenworth for life!

Back home, Bob began civilian life. It took a few years, but Carol, a pretty 19-year-old who worked at the Job Corps in Astoria, Oregon met Bob at a party when he was 25. Life happens fast, and in three weeks, Bob proposed! Carol said, "Yes," and within a few more weeks they were married. The doctor who had mended Bob's hand when he was a teenager said it would never last more than three months! He was wrong. The Beattys were blessed with three daughters: Christine Ann, who has given them their only grandchild:Ashley Rose; Sarah Beth who passed away at age 37 of cancer; and Jennifer (Jenn) Rebecca. These women are the light of Bob and Carol's life.

During the course of Bob's working years, he held many jobs. First, he worked at 3 Boys Market. Then he worked at Crown-Zellerbach as a parts chaser for the shop, a rigging maker, dump truck driver, as well as road grader operator, and water tanker driver. During this time, the company had a forest fire started by a chain saw. A stranded logging crew could not get out, so Bob quickly rigged up the hose to the water tank he was driving, and raced through the fire to the stranded men, chained the hose to the top of the tank, turned it on so it manually "rained," and got the men to safety. Later in Central Oregon, Bob went to college studying criminal justice. Carol earned her BA general degree and studied communications and multi-cultural anthropology. She worked for a time as a case manager at the Central Oregon Council on Aging (COCOA). She's even gone to Mexico and slept under the stars. Next time, while Bob did not have to do it, they both went, but slept inside and let the youngsters contemplate the wonders of the nighttime skies. Work took the family from Seaside to Warm Springs and Culver. In Warm Springs, Bob was able to live a dream he had always had of being a police officer. He was known to be a no-nonsense officer who earned the nickname of "Boss Hogg." When an opening came at the Jefferson County sheriff's office, Bob applied and got a position as a deputy. Life was with its usual challenges of the police officer's role in a community when a bloody tragedy struck. A very fine couple, Pete and Janet Reed took in a foster child, gave him a good home life of security and religious faith, were murdered in their home by the troubled teen. This event re-triggered Bob's PTSD. Some of his spirit left him, and as a result, he was forced into Corrections by the Sheriff. He finally resigned his commission.

This couple lives their lives loving God, their family, and their country. They are happy in their retirement, but want young people today to think about what it means to be a part of the military life. "If you join the military, you won't be the same person when you leave that you were when you arrived.

War changes you. Many {don't} understand, but when you have seen combat then leave the military, you will then know this truth." The Beattys are lucky in that they are together in a long marriage, with good friends and close family. They have suffered the loss of their daughter, loss of possible career advancements, and loss of Bob's health with the effects of shrapnel and Agent Orange, as well as prostate cancer and diabetes, leaving their imprints in his physical self. Their great sense of humor and sense of kindness toward their fellow humans just about erases a lingering sadness. They are people I could call neighbor, and I am grateful for their service to our country.

In a Post Script to this story, I have added two documents written on Bob's behalf dealing with his military service struggle, to gain the honors and awards he so richly deserves. I cannot reiterate enough the importance of getting these awards earned with honor, blood, sweat and sacrifice. When events are denied, hidden, countermanded and covered with lies by those in charge, it is very difficult if not impossible, for our heroes to receive their awards. Again, shame on the country {ie. DOD} for this atrocity! Too many other Viet Nam Veterans also face this struggle.

About five years ago, through the Internet, Bob contacted William O'Brien, who had been his Commanding Officer (Second Lieutenant) in Viet Nam. Bob was supposed to be awarded the Purple Heart and Silver Star. He has been waiting for these awards for decades. He explains that during the Tet Offensive, Bob's commanding officer, Cecil Whittenger, had been at his huch (bunker) when it was attacked…NOT at the perimeter where he should have been. (No official witnessing occurred.) This made O'Brien angry. He hand-delivered a letter to the Department of the Army, which in turn replied, "Do you have any eyewitnesses?" During the attack on {Bob's} bunker, O'Brien had gone out the back door and saw Bob get hit with shrapnel and then climb the tower where the guard had been killed. When Bob got back to the tower, the enemy was sitting on top of defensive concentrations. He got on the radio to signal operations, as mentioned earlier. O'Brien saw that Bob was wounded and bleeding and called the medevac. At the hospital, another mortar attack occurred. Bob was mobile, as he was outside. Another patient was walking into danger - Bob tried to stop him from picking up a shell, and it exploded… more PTSD. Again, no documentation and no witnesses. Apparently, veterans who wish to receive their awards and medals, must complete documentation of proof consisting of several pages of inquiry, which require names of officers who give orders, witnesses, places, events leading up to and including the circumstances of said events. When those in charge bury (hide) said documents, it is difficult, if not impossible, for a veteran to come forth with these records. It is my own understanding that it is the DOD's responsibility to provide these documents if requested by the soldiers who are trying to get their awards. One of the problems Bob has had with even completing the said forms is that they are so poorly copied from the offices where they are located, that it is virtually impossible to read the application forms, much less complete them. Bob and Carol are not giving up, though many others would have long ago called it quits.

In another Post Script to this heroic story, Bob has been awarded the Quilt of Honor through his duty to our country. Each quilt is designed and made for a particular veteran in mind. With specific protocols for design, size, colors and how the seams and edges are finished, the quilts are truly works of art. Bob was to be presented with his own quilt in his home, sometime in the spring of 2016, by national committee members, who for the Central Oregon area, are from Eugene, Oregon. Bob, like many of his kind, richly deserves this honor of thanks from a grateful nation. However, at this November 2016 writing, Bob is still waiting for the presentation of his quilt.

Another situation has developed in Bob's health. He has been diagnosed with trans-global amnesia, which means that his short-term memory is sketchy at best. He has trouble remembering directions for travel, so driving more than short distances is not recommended. His other health matters are prohibiting him from being able to drive or sit for the three-and-a-half hours required to get to the VA Medical Center in Portland, Oregon. His world consists of family, helping others in his church and neighborhood, and being a part of the Bend Band of Brothers when his health allows, which can change on a day-to-day basis, and is requiring more and more medical care. He finally has 100% service-related disability awarded by the VA just for prostate cancer alone, with other diagnoses related to the disability, but that, too, took much too long to occur. If Bob should die before Carol, the VA compensation for her would be only $1100.00 per month, with permanent residence in their home, using 15-year mortgage contracts. {Author's Note: It is a shame that getting help in obtaining Bob's awards is such a difficult task. The stress of this time-consuming effort is also taxing Bob's family's energy, energy that could be better served in knowing that he received a well-deserved thanks from a grateful nation, before it becomes too late.}

Winners of free "Hi-Mom" phone calls announced

Winners of the "H i - M om" program, sponsored by Local 9202, Communications Workers of America, have been announced by Seth Gray, president. The four Clatsop county families who won free phone calls to talk to sons or daughters in the service anywhere in the world are Mr. and Mrs. Charles Lindsey, Warrenton; Mrs. Robert C. Beatty, Warrenton; Mrs. Peter Koppinger, Seaside, and Armas Johnson, Hammond.

Mayor Harry Steinbock, Astoria, made the drawing Monday. Those present were President Gray, Mrs. Esther Englund, chairman of the program, and Geraldine Letzinger, co-chairman.

The free calls can be made anytime from now through January, as some servicemen are in remote areas and not easily contacted. This is the 11th annual "Hi-Mom" program.

1. News article announces Bob's mom as winner of one of the "Hi, Mom" prizes.

16

To Whom It may concern:

This is being written in support of my claim for correction of my military records.

During the TET OFFENCIVE on January 30 and 31, 1968. I was attached to HHB 2/32 Artillery Tay Ninh Base Camp located in Tay Ninh province, South Vietnam. We were an 8 inch and 175 mm Battalion, (2) 8 in and (2) 175 mm guns.

I worked in the operations bunker and it was known as Artillery Control. We controlled all Artillery in the entire province. Not only 2/32 Artillery Battery's, but other artillery and Mortor units as well.

I was approaching the operations bunker for my assigned shift in the late afternoon of January 30th. As I neared the bunker, I observed that there were several young Vietnamese women laying on top of the sand bags that were protecting the bunker. The military used Vietnamese civilians to fill the sandbags that were used as re-enforcement's around all of our buildings. The bamboo shutter's on the only windows in the bunker were opened to allow for ventilation. These civilians were laying there looking in and directly across from these windows were our situation maps. On these maps were plotted all of the Artillery and Mortor Battery's and their firing radiuses, as well as troop placements.

The sight of these civilians and what they were doing and knowing what was laid out in front of them made me angry and concerned about what might happen. As I entered the operations bunker I went directly to the shutter's and closed them. This drew the ire of all inside. I immediately went back out, but they were already gone. After being chastised for my actions, I explained my observations and what I felt was going to happen. I told 2nd Lt. William O'Brien (Who was the duty Officer) that it was my belief that our installation would be hit (attacked) that night. We indeed were attacked! As were our gun battery's in Dau Tieng (A Btry) and Cu Chi (C Btry) B Btry was at Base Camp with us.

I was operating two radio's that shift. One was for our gun batteries as well as 1/27 Arty, a 155 mm Self Propelled battery and a separate radio for the 5th Special Forces. One on top of Nui Ba Dein and one at Katum near the Cambodian Border.

We had a fourty foot high observation tower at the west end of our bunker with an armed guard posted there at night. We also had a sandbag barrier in front of both the west and east doorways. When the attack I had feared started the first mortar, an 81mm, hit, it took out one of our generators. We had four of them and they were by the road on our south side. I immediately turned to Lt. Obrien and exclaimed "Their bracketing us". The second mortar hit at the east end of our bunker which was our intelligence section. The third was on our north side and that hit the officers section. While this was all happening, I was trying to contact the tower guard on the field phone, but got no answer. We needed to know where those mortors were coming from. I felt that the bigger ones were coming. No one was doing anything about this so I left my position and went out the west door to climb the tower when I went around the sandbag barrier I was hit by shrapnel from the fourth bracketing mortar causing injuries to my head right arm and right leg. I continued to the tower and climbed to the top where I found a dead tower guard. I focused on the mortar flashes because other positions were also being bracketed, and located them. I knew that the mortor's were coming from an area near one of our defensive concentrations which I had

actually plotted that day and had sent to our battery. I climbed back down out of the tower and rushed to my radios and called our (B) Battery and gave them the fire for effect order. Unknown to me the enemy had breached their position and put three of their guns out of commission. The one remaining gun, an (8in) was able to fire the mission and the mortors stopped. The attackers were repelled and the base secured.

LL. O'Brien wanted me to be med-evac'd out, but I wanted to remain on duty until the attack was over. Later when the attack was over I was flown out to the 25th evac hospital in Cu Chi where I was treated for my injuries. About a week later I returned to my unit and my position. I lerned from Lt. O'Brien that he had put me in for a purple heart and the MOH for my actions. He said that he felt that if not for my quick actions we would have all been killed or injured. Lt. O'Brien also told me that Maj. Whittenger, our Headquarters Battery Commander told him that we were a support unit and that no one would be receiving any awards or citations.

In 2010 I made contact with Mr. O'Brien on the internet. He and his wife came to my home in Bend Oregon and he hand delivered me the attached letter recommending the Purple Heart and the Silver Star.

In our conversation he told me that he still felt that I deserved the MOH, but that maybe I could get the Silver Star.

The above is true to the best of my recollection.

Respectfully

S/P 4 Robert Louis Beatty

2. Letter from Commanding Officer

To Whom it May Concern: 20 August 2010

 I am writing this letter of my own accord and initiative having recently learned of an injustice which occurred during the Vietnam War which should, and can easily be corrected.

 I was assigned as the Communications Officer and Executive Officer of HHQ Btry of 2/32 Arty based in Tay Ninh 1967-68.

 On the night of 22 May 1968, the Btry Commander, Anthony Wingenter, was away on official business and Tay Ninh Base Camp was attacked by elements of the North Vietnamese Army. Due to the Btry Cmdrs absence I was the Acting HHQ Btry CO.

 The ground attack was preceded by a heavy mortar and RPG bombardment. The enemy managed to penetrate the perimeter in two places, the Tay Ninh Base Camp West Gate in the area of the Bn. TOC and the B Btry 2/32 area of responsibility. The 2/32 Bn. TOC was in the vicinity of the West gate and clearly a target of the NVA assault. Robert Beatty, who presently resides in Bend OR., an SP/4 at the time from HHQ Btry 2/32 was assigned to and on duty inside the the TOC when the attack was initiated.

 Realizing that the West Gate guard tower was either unmanned, put out of commission, or was ineffective for some other reason and was incapable of directing counter mortar and rocket fire SP/4 Beatty voluntarily departed the TOC, climbed the 40' tower under heavy small arms fire directed at him by hostile ground forces and began directing counter fire which was dramatically effective and contributed significantly to repelling the attacking force.

 During this singular act of bravery SP/4 Beatty was wounded facially by shrapnel. His wounds although serious did not keep Specialist Beatty from continuing to perform his duties throughout that nigh and the following days until he was eventually admitted to Cu Chi Hospital. Many individuals who suffered wounds they felt were not too serious refrained from seeking immediate medical help due to the overload facing the BN Medical Staff during and immediately following the attack.

 I recall being present at an HHQ Btry staff meeting the day following the attack, held by Major (I believe at this time he was a Major and he had returned to base camp) Wingenter , when he stated that he did not intend to submit any recommendations for medals or commendations based on the previous nights action.

 It is my opinion that Mr. Robert Beatty is entitled to, at a minimum, the Silver Star for his actions and the Purple Heart for his wounds suffered in combat.

I certify that the above is true and correct to the best of my belief and knowledge.

Sincerely

William F. O'Brien III
Maj. USAR Ret

3. Bob's Letter 'To Whom it May Concern'

4. Tower Bunker is left of photo, and is considered 'homes' for new arrivals. The mortar pit is in the center.

Peace On Earth

"PROUD AMERICANS"

5. Bob's Christmas postcard, 1967. Photo is of 175 mm Howitzer. "Long Tom." Location is of "B" Battery, 2/32 Artillery.

6. Bob stands outside a bunker,
cyclone fencing with 'camo' in rear.

7. Bob Hope Show is presented in Cu Chi,
featuring Raquel Welch, "Miss World."

8. Bob kneels near remnants of a 122 mm rocket fired at a bunker, which is covered with hand-applied cement. Surrounded with piled sandbags, this is called a 'dead man.'

Name: Joe Cantrell
Branch of Service: US Navy
Rank: Officer/destroyer, Diving officer/skipper/salvage boat
Time served: 1968 (two tours in Viet Nam)
Honors: Viet Nam Service Medal

I met Joe Cantrell several years ago, when the idea of my book was just a carefully planted seed that had yet to come to fruition. My life took many paths, and several events postponed my dream to write the story about the Viet Nam Veterans. In the year 2015, the dream finally materialized and told me it was time. I wanted to include Joe, as he was one of the first veterans who actually shared some of his history when I was still thinking about possibilities. Here is Joe's story...

In 1945, Joe was born in Colorado Springs, Oklahoma to a Cherokee Native American family. He had two younger brothers, Jay and Jonathon. His parents, Roy Joe and Wanda, were "less than perfect" parents. Very little information was forthcoming, and I suspect the reason was to protect the innocent. At one time, when Joe was 13, his parents made the decision to have a 15-year-old teenager, Enrique (Henry) Pota, stay with them for a while. Henry's family had escaped from Cuba and sent him to a doctor at an Indian hospital for being incorrigible. Joe's parents agreed to host Henry for two weeks; he stayed for four-and-a-half years! Within the first two weeks, Henry broke Joe's nose and took out several of Joe's teeth. From what Joe knows of Henry's future, he became a right-wing racist building developer in Florida. The only balm to Joe's soul was his grandmother, Wanda Martin, who spent her time gardening and patiently educating Joe with her natural wisdom. She had raised four daughters, losing one in childbirth in Oklahoma during the Great Depression. She was the epitome of Christianity, and wore it like a "cloak of goodness."

Joe did two tours in Viet Nam beginning in 1968. The first was as a Naval officer on a destroyer that chased carriers and bombarded the coast with cannon fire. "The first night of my first tour, aboard a vintage destroyer, our Captain, a cold-hearted Russian, insisted on speeding through coastal fishing waters with the lights out at 30 knots." (The ship was supposed to provide fire support.) "I was Junior Officer of the Deck, and we ran over a sampan with a Vietnamese family in it." (An old woman and two kids were killed.)

"The Captain came onto the bridge, and said, "That's okay. Don't worry about it. Next time, back down and suck 'em through the screws; we don't want to leave any witnesses." {Author's Note: PTSD had been part of Joe's early life, and now it was growing during service to his country.}

Joe's second tour saw him being the diving officer/skipper of a salvage boat operating in the Mekong Delta, which took the crew into Cambodia. He tried to photograph scenes, "to escape reality" as part of his experience, but found he could not. He has very few photos from Viet Nam. His head "simply could not be in that space" while being responsible for a 152-foot converted landing craft with a crew of 35 men. As events unfolded, a camera wasn't even on his mind's radar.

During the time Joe was in Cambodia, his hometown sweetheart wife, Brenda, "who had always been sketchy," took to the road traveling cross country with a friend of hers. With the Red Cross tracing her to Berkeley, it was reported that she "came to the door of some guy's house in a shorty nightgown!" Joe and his wife were divorced by mail, and he never saw her again. However, she wasn't through with Joe: about a year later, he received subpoenas from several sheriffs saying he would be arrested if he entered their counties, because his "ex" had used Joe's credit cards to pay for her trip. She neither informed him nor paid him back. Joe paid all the bills from Singapore! He was discharged from the military in Southeast Asia, became a photojournalist until 1986, when he finally moved back to the United States.

Photos! Records of a slice of life whenever and wherever a person lives... Living with urban peasants in Manila, being a part of their lives, Joe had his first ever photo exhibit of the years between 1971 and 1986. He had thought just to make some prints, and let it go, but "the images grabbed {me} by the throat, figuratively speaking, and damn near tore {my} figurative head off."

Beer and wild times also helped bring people back to life for him. While working overseas, Joe met Nancy Ch'ng, a personal friend and co-worker of the sage, Thich Nhat Hahn. He met her at the airport, and showed her around town. He could have married her sister, but in 1971, he was too "screwed up!" The influence of Thich Nhat Hahn was to become a greater influence later in Joe's life, as he began to live the relatively quiet life of a semi-retired father.

Joe also worked as a freelance photographer for the _New York Times_, and stayed in Southeast Asia through the Ferdinand Marcos debacle. Marcos had declared Martial Law, and Joe made the call to NBC, sharing a picture with the news people that showed Marcos flying out in a formation of three US helicopters. The assassination of Aquino of the Philippines, similar to a US senator, was a direct threat to Marcos, and Marcos was going to be hit next. Security was at its tightest. Now, Joe had his photographic work on the cover of *Newsweek*, as well. A Congressman on the House Committee for Asian and Pacific Affairs tried to keep each killing just that: affairs of other countries; but, it wasn't to be. In the end, Imelda Marcos was elected President of the Philippines.

Another life-altering event was the single parenting of his daughter from 1992 to 2013. An important back story tells how his child's name came to be. In one of his 2007 letters to me, Joe wrote: "I just found out an hour ago, that my best friend in my Navy Diving Unit, Dan Johnstone, may well have died as a result of exposure to Agent Orange." Dan had once saved Joe's life. While waiting for orders to leave the Navy, Joe uncovered a Chinese smuggling ring which produced heroin so pure, 92% pure, that if someone used it uncut as it was, it would kill that person. The Chinese shipped it from Manila to Olongapo, in Subic Bay, Philippines, where Americans all along the coastline would buy it and resell it in the States, for a fortune. Somehow the mayor and police chief were involved, but Joe could not prove anything to substantiate his fears. Joe discovered a teddy bear that was stuffed full of the deadly substance, and reported his findings to Naval Intelligence, which resulted in a major drug bust. Someone discovered that Joe had been the snitch, and a hit was put out on him. He went to two different restaurants, where he was told to get away and hide as men were gunning for him. "Invited" to an amusement park where he would be quickly and quietly 'dispatched,' Joe rushed back to the main gate at the Naval Base. He had some trouble, as he was now in the Reserves, but his friend Dan came to his rescue. He smuggled Joe back onto the Subic Bay Base, gave Joe his spare bed in his Bachelor Officers' Quarters room, and an AK 47 to sleep with until he could sneak out to Singapore for a year. Joe recalls, "I promised him on his deathbed at Bethesda Naval Hospital that I would name my kid after him if I ever had one"… Joe's daughter, Danielle, is now 28, as of this writing. Their lives have not been without family strife, however…

In 1986, Joe and his wife, Patti, moved to Portland, Oregon from the Philippines, and two years later, in 1988, Danielle was born. Patti's father was a Filipino, but he had cancer, and died four days after Danielle's birth. Patti's mother, a brash blonde who was now a widow, decided she should travel the world, helping her children with their problems. She brought her son and his boyfriend, who had left a wife and children back in the Philippines, and moved them into Joe and Patti's home in Portland. They stayed for a year. Then, "Mom" decided to move to California, and proceeded to set Patti up with a new boyfriend. Mom had a plan: she would have Joe thrown in jail as she accused him of molesting Danielle. Mom was crazy, and the courts agreed, giving custody of Danielle to Joe. Bigoted feminist psychologists were convinced he was "psycho." However, Patti was off the charts with diagnosed borderline narcissistic disorder. Joe got custody, with punitive alimony. When President Bill Clinton took office, Hilary put in place the law of "punitive alimony" in case deadbeat dads moved. (Meanwhile, at the first deposition for divorce, Patti was already wearing a new engagement ring!) The courts agreed that Joe was not guilty. The Judge's final comments reamed Patti and her Mom up one side and down the other for all the nonsense and stress that Joe had suffered on their behalf. All court officials were women, except Patti's lawyer, who was infamous for defending a strip club's men's tour to Thailand, for "the boys."

Danielle has now moved to Los Angeles where she works for Sony as a Regional Sales Supervisor. When her supervisor was promoted, she took his place, against the advice of the leadership of "good ol' boys," who first thought women should not hold such positions of responsibility and prestige. In her first quarter alone, she beat everyone on the West Coast, winning a $10,000.00 television and many other goodies and expensive toys. Joe is very proud of her in her own right, but she had beaten 500 of the best applicants for her first job as PlayStation representative for Sony. When Danielle won this latest promotion, one of the most conservative of Japanese Vice-Presidents was even more impressed when she addressed him in fluent Japanese, apologizing for her lack of skill. This Japanese business leader told her she had nothing for which to apologize. Father and daughter enjoy a close relationship even though they live in different states, and are devotees of Thich Nhat Hahn, a profound irony in itself: Life can be lived in joy and peace, even when one is surrounded by chaos. Joe says, "I highly recommend his writings about the war, and everything else."

Until his daughter was raised, Joe's photographic passion took a back seat until a couple of years ago. He had three exhibits, and opened another exhibit in the Portland Center for the Performing Arts from May 7 to June 1, 2015. The images for this show were exciting, because they were an Existential Gate, a passthrough, if you will, to other worlds. One of the prints of the Milky Way points to a tiny smidge with a label that says, "You are here." Another print of a rock displays something growing on another planet. The point is that the human perspective is still with us when {it} is swimming around us, and is as potentially as crude as our physical size. An electron microscope can fill a screen with a grain of pollen from a single flower. {Author's Note: I saw one of the prints that showed the veins of wings on a fruit fly embedded in a piece of amber about the size of a 50-cent piece. It was and is truly amazing.} Other recurring patterns are around us, if we look from our capillaries to veins in leaves to the bone marrow of dinosaurs, which can look like something the dog brought in from the yard last week; all this can be a wonder: This creature really did walk the earth. Each of these shows has no resemblance to each other, but it has been a bit of a "brain popper" for Joe. "We think of infinity as unbelievably huge, but it goes backward, too, to the unimaginably sub-microscopic."

Today, Joe has been part of a geological dig in Oregon. He was approached by the chief curators of the La Brea Tar Pits, and the Natural History for the US Park Service to photograph the findings of the most spectacular dig in Woodburn, Oregon. In 2007, 2007-2008 high school seniors found a skull, and for their senior projects assembled the pieces. One senior girl put the skull together. Using a 3D scanner and a 3D printer and fragments of a femur with bone marrow inside, a few pieces of plastic can assemble the whole thing. The skull in the classroom is a plastic replica: 9 feet tall, 15 feet long, with a weight of 3500 pounds… what is it? One scientist in charge thinks there are tracks that could be a mammoth, a short-faced bear, or a dinosaur in some of the granular sandstone. The tracks last about one hour, then fold in on themselves. Joe takes stacked focused photos, as they uncover, then these photos are put into a computer, and the size and weight of the animal can be determined. "We can figure out how the planet changes as it is happening now {in real time}. It's astonishing… so much fun!"

In a recent conversational update with Joe, I learned of another fascinating project in which he will participate during the weeks of November 8th through the 19th, 2016. I told Joe that I could call him and get an update on another project about every six months, each one as "mind-popping" as the last, to borrow a phrase from Joe. This time, Joe will be on the Umatilla Indian Reservation, near Pendleton, Oregon at the Crow's Shadow Institute as an Artist-in-Residence. He will be working with Frank Janzen, a world-famous lithographer. They will design tapestries in photographs, and then stone, to create lithographs, using fractals, groups of mathematical patterns that are replicated throughout nature, from something as small as a slice of bone marrow to whole galaxies. They will be dispelling the stereotype that Indian "art" only comes from the "John Wayne" idea of the Noble Savage portraits in nature. They will use any medium to disprove the standard opinion of fine art. One of the ways they will make this art form happen is to use a diptych technique: For instance, take a stone, shave a tiny slice (1/4 of an inch thick, or smaller) of it, show the pattern of one side of the slice, then turn it over and see the pattern on the other side: Voila'! Three different perspectives of the same thing! Photographs and lithographs make these things permanent, for us to enjoy. We, as a species, lose so much of our environment and the beautiful "awe" of life's patterns all around us when we remain unobservant and asleep, even though we claim to be part of it. We *are* here, are we not?

For inspiration, Joe calls upon the muse of the Cherokee Chief, Sequoia. This man was the only person who ever invented a written language by himself. He devised 88 symbols, which represented the entirety of the sounds in the Cherokee language. If one could memorize all these symbols and their matching sounds, he could read and write a new language in as little as three days. This was quite a feat in the 1800s! It would be quite a feat today! The ideas for creativity are endless and rich for the awakened mind and spirit, and Joe is part of those opportunities waiting to be discovered.

Joe is also a volunteer for a food bank, the Waterfront Blues Festival, the Symphony, and the Classical Up Close Series. Leading symphonic musicians give from one to three volunteer concerts a day. He spends less time "trying to keep the dummies happy" and more rewarding times "playing with smart kids."

Joe's story is important as he feels that with all the misinformation and disinformation that surrounded the whole Viet Nam experience, he welcomes the chance to right some of the faulty information. "Many of {the} vets blame the hippies and "peaceniks" for their miserable experiences when they returned home." When Joe was returning home, steaming down the Mekong Delta out of Cambodia, he had the epiphany that if they (the veterans) had had their way, the United States would never have been in this mess. "It was the Establishment that sent us there, kept us there, profited from us being there, and turned its back on us when we came home. They had power; the liberals had little to none." That was when Joe "turned from the former President of the Young Republicans for Goldwater (of Tahlequah, Ok) into a 'lefty'."

Another "myth" as far as Joe is concerned, is the subject of being spit on, and being called baby killer. In Joe's recollections, "not one of us, with the noted exception of a verified nut job, claimed any such experience." {Author's Note: Joe was one of the lucky ones. Several returning veterans did not receive warm welcomes; indeed, they were considered part of the problem with the Viet Nam War.}

"Much later," Joe recalls, "I came to a strong suspicion that Naval Intelligence had set me up, but it all becomes long and convoluted, as if this isn't already. That war just keeps on giving, and the irony of hearing public lamentations that "what happened to us won't happen to Iraq vets," while the abuse gallops on so egregiously and seems over the top, even in this surrealistic horror of an American Vision."

Joe has been the victim of PTSD, like his fellow sailors and soldiers. He has visited hundreds of veterans' groups, mainly through the Portland Veterans Center, and has had hundreds of private counseling sessions. In order to put his military experience into the perspective it deserves in his life, it needed to be just "another experience in a life rich with many."His technique is to visualize "those kernels of horror like a mental thistle," and addressing them: "You have been a pain in the ass, you've caused me and those I love a lot of pain. But, you are, and always will be, a part of me, and I love you, and now we start again." It works for Joe, and he has shared this philosophy with other vets and friends with ugly things in their past, and it almost seems "too easy." The prickles are still there, but once "you have loved the Thing in your heart, it loses most of its power to run, or ruin, your life."

Joe's thought to ease the pain of PTSD: Most of PTSD is just that: A thought pattern that has imbedded itself into the mind, and as such, it is something that is not tangible. It is just energy, and if it is fed, it grows brighter, and if it is starved, it can be dimmed until it no longer burns.

{Author's Note: A final thought from Thich Nhat Hahn: "If you take a life, save a life." I sometimes wonder if that life is one's own.}

I am honored that Joe chose to share his story. His life is a model for rich experiences being molded into photographic art: Little pieces of truth as vivid as yesterday and eternal as tomorrow. I thank you for your service to our country.

Joe's daughter, Danielle

Example of Joe's latest
work in slivers of stone with
photography (See text.)

Example of color effects in
micro-photography

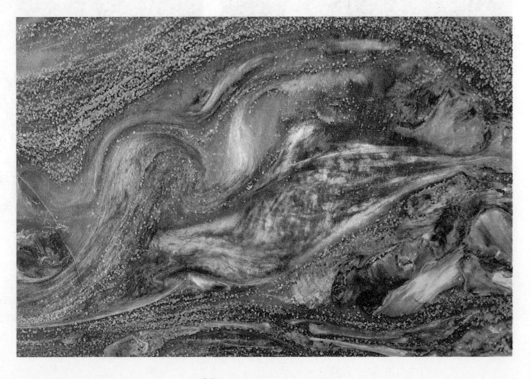

Joe Cantrell, today

Name: Gary Hartt

Branch of Service: US Army Combat Infantry

Rank: Acting Sergeant

Dates of Deployment: 366 days: December 1965-September 1967

Honors: Purple Heart

Combat Infantry Badge (CIB)

Order of the Red Ant*

... Love thy Self as thy neighbor... our hearts are big enough to hold us all...

Gary Hartt was born on August 18, 1944, in Franklin Square, New York. He had two older brothers, Kirk and Ken. His parents, Earle (Buddy) and Gertrude (Trudi), were "wonderful, hard-working blue collar" employees. When Gary was 13, the family moved to Port Jefferson, New York. Both homes were a part of Long Island, but he has not been back since 2012, when he attended his 50th-year high school class reunion. He feels he had a "normal childhood" and looks upon his teenage years as the "best part" of his life. In the eighth grade, he met a girl, Vickie, whose nickname was "Scarlett," as her maiden name was O'Hara. Scarlett would one day become Gary's wife, but that story will happen later. He was fun loving; indeed, his nickname was "Goof!" He still keeps in touch with three of his best buddies, Bob Merkle, Pat Benson and Billy Griffen. Gary graduated from Port Jefferson High School in 1962. A mere four years later, on Christmas Day, Gary would be contemplating how he would tell the parents of one buddy, Bruce Kerndl, how their son was killed. Bruce was killed in action (KIA) in Viet Nam while part of "Operation Attleboro: Phase I." Gary will always remember creative artist and star baseball pitcher Bruce in a bathing suit, driving his Corvette to the New York World's Fair...someone who was "so full of life." While Gary attended St. John's University for three years, it was evident to him after two years that finances were too thin, and even taking 18 hours of classes two days a week, and working full time in construction four days a week, was a perfect storm for overload. By June of 1965, he was "dismissed academically." His new status reclassified him from 2-S to 1-A, just in time to be invited by Uncle Sam to join the US Army.

Gary was drafted and began training on December 7, 1965, at New Jersey's Fort Dix. On December 22 of that year, the Army "in their great wisdom," flew Gary and other east coast draftees in a propeller plane for 10 hours to Fort Lewis, Washington. They arrived at 3:00 AM, then a few hours later were told that Basic Training would not start until January 2, 1966, BUT, if one had an $800.00 paid airline ticket for a first class 3000 mile flight, one could have a Christmas leave. In less than a month, the Army had screwed the draftees! Gary entered the 4th Infantry Division, in which they did eight weeks of basic training, then eight weeks of Advanced Infantry Training (AIT), then eight weeks of Basic Unit Training, and five weeks of Advanced Unit Training. The draftees were given two weeks' leave after Basic Training, and two weeks at the end of Advanced Unit Training. If one was trained to go Viet Nam during this time, then he was able to get a 30-day leave. About this time, Gary and 34 of his comrades became "Absent Without Leave" (AWOL), being gone for 31 days. Gary was singled out as the ring leader by his commander, Ken Both, and wound up with a "special court-martial," which could have earned him six months in the Long Binh Jail and a fine, or worse. Gary's special training as a computer operator was vital, as no one else could do his work as quickly and accurately as he could. Gary was given conditional probation for six months. He had his salary deducted, was fined $80.00 per month and was placed on permanent "kitchen police" or KP duty on the ship. He was reduced in rank to Buck Private E1. Obviously, the military has no sense of humor... or, maybe it does! Thirty-five years later, Gary's former commander and he connected again, and are now part of the same veterans' group of comrades that meets regularly in the spirit of brotherhood and community.

{Author's Note: As part of Gary's application for Veterans' Assistance, he needed to write a history of his experiences in Viet Nam. He wrote in detail the most trigger-producing of his encounters for 366 days, and then wrote a list of those KIA and the causes of death. See the list at the end of Gary's chapter. He has kept this list open as updated information comes to the fore. As he entered Viet Nam and battles for him began, his PTSD began with shock and horror and fear, which were relegated to dark corners of his mind, because survival was uppermost with each next breath and moment. It would be years before he realized that the man he had become, an angry, bitter, sad and guilt-ridden spirit, was suffering from a classic case of PTSD. Though each of Gary's assignments was written in specifics, I will summarize his months in highlights.

Gary's troop ship left from Tacoma, Washington for Viet Nam on September 22, 1966, and arrived off the Viet Nam coast near October 9, 1966. Alpha Company, 2nd Battalion (Mechanized Infantry), 22nd Infantry Regiment was Gary's individual unit. Within a month, on November 4, the first man was KIA, during "Operation Fairfax," beginning the depletion of 175 soldiers. Gary did not know this at the time, but it was also the day his buddy Bruce was killed. Gary's PTSD had begun.

Early on November 11, Gary's platoon left Base Camp Bear Cat, and drove through Saigon to Cu Chi. There, they stopped for re-supply and to refuel the armored personnel carriers (APC's). By nightfall, they were deep in the jungles of the Northern Tay Ninh province in War Zone C on "Operation Attleboro: Phase II." During this time, Gary was relatively safe in his fire direction control (FDC) position, as he had guard duty and radio watch at night. As controller, he had to provide direction for artillery and mortars. Today, calculations are done with computers; back then, these calculations were done on a plotting board to get direction and distance. Then, the controllers used paperback books to convert the information to the number of charges needed and gun angle. On November 19, a firefight resulted in many injuries, with one casualty in their sister company, Charlie Company. Gary assisted with getting the wounded on the choppers for medical evacuation (medevac). November 22 saw another comrade killed: John McCabe. Lonnie Hart lost an arm and a leg in the same skirmish, and Frank Lomento and K. Shepard lost parts of a thumb. What should have been a bright spot in an ugly mess was Thanksgiving holiday. President Johnson insisted that all the troops get a hot turkey dinner. The mortar platoon was the last to eat, as they served their comrades first. Another unlucky twist: A monsoon arrived drenching everything in its wake. By the time Gary was served, his dinner looked like "cold turkey soup," and he tossed it all away. Not only was he disgusted by the whole event, but he was also homesick. To top it off, right before or after the actual holiday, he remembered that about five minutes after he served chow and they had disbanded the chow line in a field near Prek Loc, a short 105 round hit and exploded right where Gary had been standing! This was the first of many times that he cheated death.

On November 28, the unit left Tay Ninh and arrived at the new base camp, Dau Tieng (Tri Tam District of Bing Dough province). Dau Tieng was headquarters for the French Michelin Rubber Company and their massive rubber plantation. During December they alternated with another battalion doing search and clear operations and filling thousands of sandbags to form a berm line and to surround their tents at the Base Camp. Although they were near a supposedly friendly village, many times snipers would fire on the men. Also, punji traps (disguised pits with sharp punji sticks in them to impale those who were unaware) were everywhere, and while the plantation workers avoided them, they failed to tell the soldiers about them. Gary fell into a pit and missed the stakes by inches. He was ready to fire on the workers, but his platoon leader stopped him. No civilians in this "friendly" village were to be attacked! Christmas Day, a really good piece of luck came Gary's way. He was one of four men from his company to fly to Cu Chi to see the Bob Hope Christmas Show. They boarded a Chinook helicopter around 5:00

AM and arrived at 5:30 AM. Front row seats for a show that did not start until 1:00 PM were reserved for the group. Thinking about Bruce and the sad news he would one day need to tell his parents, Gary went to the A/1/27 company area to see Bruce's buddies. They told him that Bruce was one of 12 in his squad in which three were killed, and six were wounded. More PTSD was layering itself into Gary's heart and soul. After visiting for a few hours, the company invited Gary to eat Christmas dinner with them, but he excused himself from the invitation, saying it was their honor, not his. It was Mr. Hope's habit to prefer to eat with those who had been the worst hit by battle. The Wolfhound Company was singled out for that honor, and the Commanding General of the 25th Infantry Division told Bob Hope that this was the group with whom he would have dinner. As Gary turned a corner, Bob Hope materialized with his iconic golf club in hand. Gary mumbled what was supposed to be, "Thank you for coming," and returned to the audience area. His choice seat was gone as around five thousand soldiers had filled the place. Gary, remembering his quiet moment with the great Bob Hope, still enjoyed the show and its pleasant diversion from the "too frequent blood and guts of Viet Nam."

January 5, 1967, saw Gary's battalion start on "Operation Cedarfalls," in the Iron Triangle. It was huge, involving the 1st Infantry Division, the 173rd Abn Brigade, the 11th Armored Cavalry Regiment, the 1st and 2nd Brigades of the 25th Division and 196th Brigade. Gary's battalion was attached to the 196th. Between January 5 and 26, two of Gary's friends were killed: Jerry Rice from Chicago, Illinois and Yvonne Hebert, from Clairemont, Vermont. On January 27, Gary's battalion returned to Dau Tieng Base Camp, and resumed filling sandbags, doing berm guard duty and going on ambush patrols. That night, his first platoon went to an ambush site about 3000 meters northeast of the Base Camp in the Michelin rubber plantation. Attacked by nearly 100 Vietcong, the 16 men whose M-16s kept jamming did not have a chance. Eight of the 16 were wounded, and two days later one died from internal bleeding: David Berkholz. Having served with Gary for eight months, David's appearance and mannerisms had reminded Gary of his friend Bruce.

Between February 1 and 7, 51 of Gary's comrades in the 3rd Platoon, a full contingent, headed out of base camp, to Tay Ninh province and War Zone C where Operation Attleboro had occurred. This time the battle was named "Operation Gadsden." It was supposed to be a preparation for upcoming Operation Junction City. During this time Gary's platoon had 15 KIA's. Seeing only a couple of mortar attacks the first four days, Gary and Terry Humpert left for R&R in Saigon on February 5, returning about February 12. Three hours after they had left the field, Terry's entire squad was wounded or killed. Another fellow draftee and drinking buddy, Ed Schell, was also killed that day. February 6 saw a second firefight with the 3rd Platoon in which eight soldiers remained out of 51 Art Sisco of New Jersey was wounded that day, and because of the jungle terrain it took six hours to evacuate him. With both legs and an arm amputated, because of gangrene, he died a painful death on February 22 in a military hospital in Japan.

With the end of "Operation Gadsden" on February 21, the 22nd saw the beginning of "Operation Junction City," one of the largest operations of the Viet Nam War. It did not officially end until May 15. The first day Gary's group traveled on a French-built jungle road. They were supposed to be a blocking force for the 173rd Airborne which made the only combat parachute jump of the war. Gary's Company Commander did not like the roads as they were full of mines. The Brigade Commander twice ordered Alpha Company's Commanding Officer (CO) to go by road to save time, and twice he was refused. He then replaced the company with Charlie Company and told them to go by road. The result? In less than 100 meters they hit a massive mine. Many were hurt, but no one died that day. With all the mines, their objective was not reached that day; that night they were targets for the Vietcong. (An aside: In January, after "Operation Cedarfalls" ended, a forward observer (FO) had been wounded and the mortar platoon was looking for a volunteer to take his place. Gary rode in the same APC)as the platoon leader, who was, in Gary's words, "a self-centered, egotistical prick." Gary hated him, as did the other draftees, and Gary was afraid if he stayed near the guy he would get a second court martial. He volunteered to be the FO for the 2nd Platoon. He had an agreement with the platoon sergeant that he would do this for three months and then return to the weapons platoon.)Near February 1, Gary was packing a radio and beating the bushes as an FO attached to the second platoon. He alternated with the radio telephone operator (RTO): The guy who carries the radio for the platoon leader, or, if one is a mortar FO, then he carries his own radio. Artillery FO's were officers, and they had a sergeant and RTO with them on ambush patrols. About every third night after beating bushes for 10 or 12 daytime hours, he would get about two hours of sleep. One night, he was patrolling an area near the Cambodian border, when a personal nightmare-come-true struck.

The ambush was set up on ground soaking wet from a recent rainfall. Gary laid his poncho on the ground so his clothes would not get saturated right away. He discovered that he had put the poncho over a snake hole! He assumed the snake was poisonous, as most snakes in Viet Nam were. As he changed positions during the night, the snake kept trying to get further and further out of its hole so it could find food or "whatever snakes do." Gary would not let the snake make more progress, but in doing so, he was forced to stay awake as he did not want the snake to get out of its hole and bite him; he would never make it to medical aid in time because of their position. He could only make hourly negative situation radio reports and let the other guys sleep, as they, too, were exhausted. Heavy rain, evaporated bug spray and ravaging mosquitoes completed the living nightmare for Gary. Daybreak saw him leaving the area with his poncho and not even the thought of a backward glance at his nemesis. Periodically, Gary has suffered nightmares about biting snakes and paralysis born of fear. Another fiber of PTSD insinuated itself into Gary's soul.

Back at Base Camp at Dau Tieng, arriving about 5:00 PM, while drivers and maintenance crews repaired APC's, the combat troops got drunk and left the next morning to do it all over again. This pattern of events usually occurred every 30 days, but one time the soldiers were out for 74 days! On March 15, "Operation Junction City-Phase II" began. On March 19, a red-headed draftee, Russell Root, was killed by a sniper. The acting CO, 1st Lieutenant Tarkenton, on the radio, callously told the battalion leader: "We have one KIA, and he is not going anywhere, so I will develop the situation..." This guy was so cold about the young man's death... how was it possible? Facing a VC squad of what he thought was about 20, the CO ordered everyone out of the wood line to shift about 200 meters. (He was wrong; what they really faced was a camp about the size of a battalion. The CO was simply too new at being in charge.) They re-entered the wood line and advanced about 200 meters when a Claymore went off. A new guy was killed, and Nesbit and another guy were wounded. The CO still didn't withdraw. The CO, 3rd Platoon leader and their RTO's were in front of the 3rd Platoon combat line. (This was a mistake; they should have been behind!) A Chinese Claymore exploded, killing Tarkenton, Lt. Breda, and Barney Joe Kelly, a good guy and friend of Gary's. Another wounded man, Danny Ryan from New York, was someone Gary wanted to reach, but his platoon leader would not let him, as Gary held the radio. Gary was also helping medic Corky Cochran work on another wounded soldier. He told Corky to stay down, but he had to be kneeling to help the guy. A rocket-propelled grenade (RPG) exploded and took off the left side of Corky's head. Other men pulled him to safety, but Gary's ears were ringing from the blast. Now the Battalion CO said to withdraw, and let the artillery and aircraft deal with VC positions. He could go help Danny Ryan, but had to get rid of the radio and rifle. As he was leaving, he was handed four or five more rifles. He decided not to crawl but zigzagged through whizzing bullets so the VC couldn't draw a bead on him. Halfway there his radio antenna became caught on a vine, and he felt hot metal on his neck. Gary was hit in an artery and had two holes in his neck! Blood was pulsating from his wound, and he probably went into shock. Gary was afraid this would happen to Danny. A FNG ("fucking new guy": If the soldier made it through a month without being wounded or killed, he was considered one of the guys.) looked up at him bleeding and scared, his face turned the same shade of green as his fatigues. Gary decided to make the last 50 yards to the wood line. Two men put a compression bandage on Gary's wound and he was immediately evacuated to the battalion aid station. He saw Corky begging for water, and being refused. The medic told Gary that Corky was dying. When a chaplain came over, Gary asked him to give last rites to his fallen comrades. Then a miracle happened: An APC pulled up, and Gary saw his buddy, Danny Ryan. Gary's emotions were elated and plummeting at the same time; they were in turmoil. He was angry at the CO and would remain that way for 35 years. Five people had been needlessly killed because he would not back out and let others soften the VC positions. Gary has softened his heart over time, as he has come to realize that this was his commander's first tour; naivete' at its potentially deadliest. Gary and Danny were medevaced to the 45th Surgical Hospital in Tay Ninh and sent to the 36th Evacuation Hospital in Vung Tau. Word filtered back to them regarding the tragedies of the next two weeks.

On March 21, near 6:00 AM, nearly 2500 VC soldiers of the 272nd VC Regiment commenced firing on Fire Support Base Gold. Alpha and Bravo Companies of the 3rd Battalion of the 22nd Infantry Regiment, their sister Battalion, guarded the perimeter of the 2nd Battalion of the 77th Artillery Regiment. Several human wave assaults followed in the ensuing four-hour battle. Nearly three hours later at 9:00, the second of the 12th Infantry Regiment and the second Battalion of the 22nd Infantry Regiment (mechanized), 2nd Battalion of the 34th Armored Regiment (tanks) raced to help the FSB Gold 450 defenders on the verge of being annihilated. The units saved the day, and the entire 3rd Brigade troops and supporting units were awarded the Presidential Unit Citation. The defenders had 31 KIA's and 151 wounded. The VC had 650 KIA's and another 200 to 300 probably killed from air strikes and artillery. It was known as the "Battle of Soui Tre." That night on ambush patrol, Gary lost another good friend, Edward Amato, from New York, from supposedly friendly fire. Their draft numbers had been one digit apart, Gary's number ending in 63, and Amato's ending in 64.

On March 22, a platoon APC hit a mine, and the driver, Alan Andrews, from New York, was killed instantly, as was Chuck Fletcher, from Michigan. "Skip" Charles Haber, from New Jersey, took 20 minutes to die. On March 23, Chuck McNair, another platoon APC driver, lost his right eye, and several others suffered shrapnel wounds when the APC was hit by RPG blasts. By April 1, Gary's company was down to 37, from 150.

Gary was on the mend and anxious to get back to his unit. Enduring a scary ride on a Canadian Otter built in 1936, he was the last one off after surviving several narrow and short remote runways, and skimming treetops during take-offs and landings. When he arrived at Base Camp, he was "white as a ghost." Once again, he felt as if he had cheated death. His inventory of nightmares has added another in which his plane crashes, and he is alone with a dead pilot. The VC are coming to the wreckage, and he is running away from them, not knowing which way to go. When he awakes, the VC are just about to capture and kill him...

Gary rejoined the 2nd Platoon as FO and continued to beat the bushes on "Operation Junction City-Phase III," which ended near April 29. They headed toward the Iron Triangle for "Operation Manhattan" in the Boi Loi woods. Becoming ill with dysentery with fever and chills and not being able to sleep for four days, Gary became really pissed off" at his Platoon Sergeant for not providing Gary with a temporary replacement. Weakened, he just wanted to die. When the fever finally diminished, he was bitter about not getting sick leave, but has only scattered memories that the jungle was really "thick and nasty." It was monsoon season, and he was just-showered wet all the time, seeming to be on ambush patrol every other night.

Operation Ahina, in May, started northwest of Base Camp and wended its way south and southwest to the Iron Triangle and Boi Loi woods. At this time, Gary took over as FO for another guy who was ill. They were on a search and destroy march in the Boi Loi woods, when they saw two VC digging a fox hole. The platoon leader shot one, but the other one, a female, got away. Gary almost shot a dog handler as he raced to claim a German Mauser rifle as a souvenir from the dead VC. Gary got a sick feeling, and for a moment, he wanted to cut off the leg of the man, then cook and eat it. He was horrified at his depraved thought and has not revealed this moment until this time. The only way he can come to terms with this is to refer to the story, *The Lord of the Flies*, a tale of English school boys who get shipwrecked on a Pacific Ocean island and gradually resort to cannibalism. He still has nightmares about the "damn leg."

The reader will probably be having various unfortunate thoughts about Gary's state of mind about now; however, there is a back story with which most, if not all, "boots on the ground" veterans will identify. When Gary was beginning his Fort Lewis field training in 1966, the trainees were given 1942 C-Rations for their meals. {Author's Note: Now, I am not a food expert, but there couldn't be much of a nutritional meal in those packages, to say nothing about the deterioration of the metal containing those meals. To add insult to injury, later in-field training for Viet Nam provided 1944 C-Rations! When combat troops arrived in Viet Nam, the in-field C-Rations were 20-plus years old. Now, beans and ham as a main dish can at times be truly tasty, given proper seasoning and cooking. If it is 20-plus years old, it should be thrown out as the "Sell by" date is waaaay past due. Included in this survival kit were things like chocolate that had turned white, like the type that shows up after sitting in one's car forgotten from last summer's vacation, and the standard four cigarettes that, while they have a certain aromatic attraction for the smoker who indulges, were probably stale a few months after the seal was put on the C-Ration containers. While on a virtual starvation diet, many hundreds, if not thousandss of our troops were expected to be alert, quickly make life and death decisions, and forge ahead into unknown territory with unknown villains, ranging from humans, to animals, to vegetation, and even the air they breathed. Respect for their selfless efforts and courage in a thankless war is most certainly overdue, I say.}

About an hour after the VC was killed, Gary spotted four possible VC about 1000 to 1500 meters south of their location in a rice paddy. The image was faint even through Field glasses, so he called for confirmation. The next thing he knew was that the Forward Air Controller (FAC) was calling for coordinates and distance. He still was unsure of his sighting, but he watched two F-4 phantom jets drop Napalm and their bomb load... soon Napalm was spreading, and he saw arms flailing, and two of the figures go down in flames. "When I saw the destruction of human life caused by me, I was ashamed and when I was asked to tell what I saw, I lied and told themit looked like it was four black tree stumps." Everyone accepted this and moved on. To this day Gary doesn't know whether it was four peasants or four VC. When he is asked if he personally killed anyone in Viet Nam, he answers, "I don't know." He has never wanted to admit it, denial being another factor in PTSD.

After Operation Ahina, Gary's unit headed for northern Tay Ninh province, in War Zone C. This operation became known as "Operation Diamond Head" and lasted from May 1967 until after Gary's tour ended on September 22, 1967. The battalion operated on its own during this period, and sometimes companies would get separated and pull road security duty. On May 17, Bravo Company had a firefight and lost seven men on their way to northern Tay Ninh Province. Gary was able to get a second five-day R&R to the Philippines. To fill quotas of R&R leaves, some men received two or even three leaves: A welcome respite! During June and July, sweeps were still being done, and road security was routine. Gary remembers that some impatient civilians paid the ultimate price when they would not wait for engineers to sweep the roads for mines. A Lambretta with three Vietnamese civilians was blown up, and days later an overloaded bus with about 60 civilians exploded; both times, Gary's men had to gather body parts and dig mass graves for the victims. Because it was Vietcong/North Vietnamese (VC/NVA) territory, it wasn't newsworthy, but Gary carries this sadness today. On July 14, they moved closer to Dau Tieng, and Gary thought they would get a break, but on the 15th, they were set up along the Dau

Tieng/Tay Ninh road and an ambush patrol had some minor contacts. Gary noticed a light in the distance. As he spoke, "all hell broke loose and about 50 rounds of 82mm mortar landed just outside our perimeter, except for a few that gave several guys concussions." This was not an actual attack; it was done to keep them pinned in position, and the VC went after the first platoon. They were attacked by seven rounds of rocket-propelled grenades (RPGs) that hit the 14 track (weapons squad),, and three guys were killed instantly. The 1st Platoon was hit by a human wave attack, from the 101st NVA Regiment. Gary's men could not go to their aid, as they were preparing for attack. The 3rd Platoon was the only one not under attack, so they went about 5,000 meters to rescue the 1st Platoon, taking about 45 minutes to arrive. Gary's mortar platoon provided illumination rounds for the 1st Platoon when they lost radio contact. The remaining two 1st Platoon tracks retreated to the other side of the road in a rice paddy, hoping for gunship support. The 3rd Platoon lead APC was attacked by RPGs and became inoperable. With the added firepower of the 3rd Platoon, the NVA started withdrawing. Nearly 50 men had been wounded. Fifty-one men were in the platoon.

By the end of August, Gary was close to battle fatigue, but was back in the weapons platoon with another "Gung Ho" lieutenant. Most of the men had been wounded, killed or rotated to a rear unit; however, this CO kept volunteering his men for "Mickey Mouse" stuff. John Carl, Gary's FDC squad leader was burying his M16 ammo that had become mildewed in the gun's magazines. The platoon leader threatened him with an Article 15 (a black mark on his record, with a write-up of the incident and possible fine) if he did not dig up the ammo and polish it. This was, in Gary's words, "a ridiculous request," as mildewed ammo could easily misfire. Gary, with three weeks left in his tour, confronted the lieutenant and challenged him to go into the woods for a knife fight. His men thought he was crazy, but the lieutenant backed off. The next day, when he had calmed down, Gary received approval to be transferred to a gun track and away from the lieutenant.

In late July, August and early September Gary's battalion was conducting search and destroy missions in War Zone C, about a four-hour walk from the Cambodian border. They had about 600 men to the three VC divisions, about 30,000 strong, and were wondering how they would be aided should a firefight start. Fortunately, the VC were gearing up for the Tet Offensive. It was decided to start securing roads for the upcoming South Vietnamese September 2 elections. Gary's battalion was in the sector from the Black Virgin Mountains, north to Soui Da. The MACV Military Army Command Viet Nam (MACV), to quote Gary, "the jerks on Westmoreland's staff that gave us a lot of stupid orders." Leaders decided that if they patrolled at night, the VC could not lay mines. Soon they knew their plan was hijacked, as they were attacked at night on all sides of the roads and the tracks. Once again, Gary's knife-fighting commander had volunteered a mortar gun track full of explosives to do nighttime patrol. The 1st Platoon APC had taken direct hits, and ammo was cooking... all the wounded were removed and then the gas tank blew. Gary knew of six wounded, but the rest he does not remember. September 2 was finally over. September 4, Labor Day, was worse. Around 10:00 AM two VC were spotted in a rice field next to the Black Virgin. The 2nd Platoon in their APC's gave chase, but when they got to the base of the mountain, they knew they had been caught in a trap. Snipers were everywhere. Lt. Mike De Camp, 2nd Platoon Leader, was the first killed. Next, Al Alvarado, Gary's second replacement, was killed. Seven men were killed that day, and nearly 40 were wounded. Gary was behind the 2nd and 3rd Platoons who were pinned down for about five hours. He helped evacuate the wounded and did ammunition re-supply. He was horrified at having to load some of his severely wounded friends into the choppers. After much artillery and AirFire, the VC retreated to their caves. On September 5, Charlie Company tried to charge the hillside and three more men were wounded within five minutes. The battalion CO wisely decided to withdraw, and the entire battalion went back to base camp. On September 6 they arrived in Dau Tieng. The remaining men of those who had taken the ship to Viet Nam stayed in Base Camp for processing to stateside. Gary and Tyrus O'Rourke were the last to leave country on September 22, 1967, but while they waited for their departure, they pulled nightly guard duty and daytime KP duty... the military truly did get every last ounce of their time and strength. Tyrus and Gary had been very good friends, but while Gary attended college, Tyrus was a victim of his severe PTSD and had trouble holding jobs. (During one in-field attack, he had survived by hiding under a dead VC. He was permanently emotionally scarred from this experience.) He became an alcoholic who was institutionalized several times for his illness. He died in 1995.

Gary arrived in the United States from Viet Nam, and was discharged in Oakland, California where he took a flight to New York City, arriving home late Friday night, on September 22, 1967. The following Monday, he enrolled in St. John's University and tried not to look back. It is at this point that our government should have stepped in and provided deprogramming protocols for Gary and others like him, so they could have been given some processing and healing for all the horrors they experienced. He buried himself in his studies, and vowed that no one would ever again have life or death authority over him. He learned really fast not to mention that he was a Viet Nam Veteran to new people. He started dating again and fell in love. Gary re-met Scarlett near October of 1967, when a carload of girls went to the St. Albans Naval Hospital in Queens County, in New York City, to provide some Christmas cheer for a day with recovering Viet Nam Vets. It was evident then that Gary had survivor's guilt, but he did not talk about it. He married his Scarlett, now a nurse, who had worked for a year in a VA hospital. It was the smartest move he ever made. Gary finished his undergraduate degree in September 1969, and started working towards his Master's Degree in Business Administration (MBA) degree. He worked for a large accounting firm, but was laid off when work slowed down. Now, the biggest irony of all: the firm was obligated to hire returning veterans, most of whom had worked in Army Finance stateside. The glut in veterans caused his layoff. He accelerated his studies and earned his MBA degree in 1971, and finally passed tests to become a CPA. He earned a job with Warner Communications in NYC as a tax accountant in their cable television division. A power struggle with the cable division chief financial officer and the parent company tax department brought Gary a transfer to the parent company tax department. The tax director requested Gary's resume, saw that he was a Viet Nam Vet and made some negative comments. Gary kept calm, but realized he was being set up for termination sometime in the future. Fortunately for Gary, a fellow who reviewed his work had left the parent company tax department, and told Gary of an opening with another company for which he worked, and recommended Gary. Job number three for Gary was at Instrument Systems Corp on Long Island. The company was not financially strong, and barely broke even. In addition, in the early 1970s the US economy was hit with the first Arab oil crisis. Gary's termination was inevitable.

Gary and Scarlett decided to move to Oregon in the summer of 1975. Scarlett worked as a nurse, but Gary could not find work for nine months. Then, while he worked as a tax auditor for Children's Services Division, he was unhappy and wanted something that would put his tax skills to good use. He worked for United Grocers for two years, and had another job with Homestake Mining Company for two more years in San Francisco. During the 1980s he had two more jobs. By the 1990s he became unemployable and gave up looking for work.

Even fatherhood was a challenge for Gary. When Scarlett was pregnant with their first child, Gary felt he was not ready, and had a hard time adjusting to his new role. Scarlett supported the family while Gary was out of work, and has worked full time since the 1990s. Recently, they both sat down and had an honest discussion about Gary's work history and job attitude. The general perception of the Viet Nam Vets was that they were, as a group, portrayed as volatile, angry and generally crazy, a perception enhanced by the media. Throughout his working life, Gary was aware of the subtle discrimination about his being a Viet Nam Vet. It usually took the form of a casual mention of his having served in Viet Nam by the interviewer for jobs for which he was applying. A moment of silence was followed by the person explaining how he had served in the National Guard or had had a high draft number. It was the turn-off moment of the interview. What was unspoken was the, "Why should I hire this guy who was dumb enough to get drafted and then go to Viet Nam in an infantry unit?" question that could not be denied. There was no way to hide the two years of his life in the Army on his resume when he was in college. Gary and his wife feel his biggest problem was in dealing with authority figures. No matter who the "boss" was, if Gary did not agree with management, he just could not go with the flow. Anger was his go-to response to any disagreement; he was living his decision to never be told what to do again.

Prior VietNam, Gary was an easy-going person. Post-Viet Nam, horrible nightmares and excessive drinking alternately kept him awake and allowed him to sleep dreamlessly. Around 1984, his oldest daughter ran away from home. This finally alerted him to the negative example he had shown her by his hard drinking and constant criticism of her minor failings. He tried to set a better example for his two younger children. Over the years, his nightmares gradually diminished. He did not watch coverage of the first Gulf War, but in 2003, he was hooked by events in the Iraqi War and could not pull himself away from the news coverage: nightmares began to return. On July 2, 2004, he hauled about three tons of hay and went to bed exhausted about midnight. He woke at 3:00 AM, scared and trembling. He was having a Viet Nam flashback, but could not really recall what it was about. He could not go back to sleep.

Today, Gary suffers from his Agent Orange exposure, with a host of medical problems, including diabetes and its accompanying neuropathy, as well as the PTSD. Gary gets depressed and often wonders why he is still alive. A counselor told him he has survivor's guilt. After he was wounded, his replacement was killed. Later, his replacement as 2nd Platoon FO was killed along with another friend with whom Gary served for four months. He also has recurring flashbacks about when the young medic Cochran died. This memory Gary cannot block, as he was so close to him and did not receive a scratch, just a concussion.

Gary's only close friend is his wife, Scarlett. She credits her background in psychology with help in understanding and living with Gary's "distressed behavior." Without that advantage, she is positive that their relationship would have failed, as is the story of so many veterans. When people try to get close, Gary backs off or sends "stay away" signals. Since 2001, he has become involved with an Army reunion group of his combat buddies and their wives in which he has renewed old friendships. He finally took out an old suitcase that contained letters from family and friends and a diary that he had not viewed in 35 years. He is able to cry healing tears openly. He knows he and his comrades are all "screwed up," in their own way, but with their shared experiences, he wants to stay in touch with them. He says, "They seem to be the only ones that understand me." Scarlett comments that no one reached out to the vets, who are now graying and dying from Agent Orange exposure, but who reach out to each other, and when greeting a fellow Viet Nam Vet for the first time, say, "Welcome Home!" {Author's Note: In a bit of military black humor, Gary and three other men formed The Order of the Red Ant, a spoof of the many awards and honors unevenly placed on military officers just for showing up to do their time, while the grunts, or draftees, who gave their time and sometimes their lives for the war cause, were many times forgotten or completely dismissed when it came time for awards to be bestowed. One of these men, Lynn Dalpez, designed the medal. The history and certificate appear at the end of Gary's story. It became an honor, like a military Oscar Award, voted on and given by one's peers for actions beyond the call of duty. In this same spirit, Gary wrote about his friend, Corky Cochran, who should have been awarded the Silver Star. His story was one of many defining moments in Gary's life.}

This man's journey was hard to relive and heroic for its telling. I am honored to know Gary and Scarlett, as they are kind, generous people who open their hearts to others. The Viet Nam War changed Gary's life forever, but the loyalty and love Scarlett showed Gary throughout his career, though it was difficult for many years, has paid off in the endurance of their life together.

Gary also shared a letter to his children, in which he asks for their forgiveness. He did not know that he buried his entire Viet Nam experience, and in doing so, caused suffering for his children and their mother, as well as himself. In part, he says, "While these Viet Nam memories will always be with me, having you three kids, Jessica, Daphne and Brett, and your mother in my life has given me many joys a lot of my fellow surviving vets never had the opportunity to enjoy. I love you all... With the help of my counselor, Travis, I was able to identify some of my negative behavior traits and manage them... I am extremely proud of the adults you have become and the choices you have made. I hope I am able to be around for a long time to see more of your adult lives."

Even with all the trials of his PTSD and the hard lessons of his life finally coming to the fore, it is my wish for Gary Hartt to finally realize the honor and bravery he showed for his fellow man, and that the man in his mirror deserves his forgiveness, even as he asks others to do so for him, and that he has given to others. To Scarlett, who has fought the war on the family home front, and to Gary, thank you for your service to our country.

Gary Hartl MARCH 19,1967 At Tay Ninh-45th Surg Hosp.

This picture was taken by a hospital orderly shortly after my initial triage. The timing was about 2 hours after I had been shot. After Danny Hoar put a compression bandage on the 2 holes in my neck, I was rushed to the Battalion field aid station and later placed on dustoff chopper for short ride to Tay Ninh. The bullet had nicked my main artery and blood was spurting out of 2 holes. , I had lost around half my blood supply when this picture was taken. Danny Hoar or Al Davis had managed to give me my letter writing kit with some personal effects like my camera. At Tay Ninh my camera dropped out of the bag so I asked the orderly to take this picture. I experienced a wide range of emotions that day and it looks I am sort of smiling. They had just removed my blood soaked shirt and if you look closely at my pants, you see a lot more of the blood spatters. I had an 8 X 10 enlargement made when I got home and took it with me to the VA and got a 10% Disability, only because my claim was early in the War's timeframe. About a an hour after this picture, I was on the operating table because they were looking for bullet fragments, but again I lucked out because it was a soft tissue wound and the bullet, I am sure exited from the second hole intact. The next day I was in Vung Tau at the 36thEvacuation Hosp. with Danny Ryan and Otto Pretzner.I returned to A/2/22 around March 29th. Danny Ryan went stateside and Otto later returned also to A/2/22.

A/2/22 KIA LIST 1966-1967(AS OF 2/2/2012)-ALSO DSV LIST(DIED SINCE VIETNAM)
NOTE-LIST PREPARED BY GARY HARTT (I would appreciate corrections, additions etc.)

COMRADE'S NAME	KIA DATE	OPERATION
EUGENE NELSON(8)	AUG/SEP1966	SUICIDE-TACOMA JAIL
LARRY A. RICE	11-4-66	FAIRFAX(RUNG ZAT SPECIAL ZONE)
JOHN F. MC CABE	11/22/66	ATTLEBORO(TAY NINH)
JESSE RICE(R)(1)	01/16/67	CEDARFALLS(IRON TRIANGLE)
YVON A. HEBERT(2)	01/17/67	CEDARFALLS
DAVID BERKHOLZ(3)	01/31/67	3000 METERS NORTH OF DAU TIENG BASE CAMP
EDWARD E. SCHELL	02/6/67	OPERATION GADSDEN
ARTHUR C. SISCO(4)	02/27/67	OPERATION GADSDEN
RUSSELL L ROOT	03/19/67	JUNCTION CITY(PRELUDE TO SOU TREI)
BARNEY JOE KELLY	03/19/67	JUNCTION CITY
2ND LT DENNIS J BREDA	03/19/67	JUNCTION CITY
CO JAMES C. TARKENTON	*3/19/67*	*JUNCTION CITY*
BRUCE A. CORCORAN(5)	3/19/67	JUNCTION CITY
EDWARD M AMATO	03/21/67	JUNCTION CITY(NIGHT AMBUSH PATROL)
ALAN W ANDREWS	03/22/67	JUNCTION CITY(APC HIT MINE)
CHARLES H HABER(R)	03/22/67	JUNCTION CITY " "
CHARLES E FLETCHER	03/22/67	JUNCTION CITY " "
ERIK WICKENBERG (7)	07/6/67	INFUSED INTO 5/60 MECH(9TH INF DIV)
GEORGE A HOLLADAY(R)	07/15/67	ROAD SECURITY(NIGHT VC ATTACK-7RPG RDS TO APC)
JOHN P. COLLOPY(R)	07/15/67	ROAD SECURITY " "
TERRY D. ALSUP(R)	07/15/67	ROAD SECURITY " "
LT. MICHAEL D. DE CAMP	9/04/67	BLACK VIRGIN MTN MASSACRE
EARL R. COBB(R)	9/04/67	BLACK VIRGIN MTN MASSACRE
ALFRED F. ALVARADO(R)	9/04/67	BLACK VIRGIN MTN MASSACRE
CLARENCE E. DRAKES(R)	9/04/67	BLACK VIRGIN MTN MASSACRE
WILLIAM E HARGROVE(R)	9/05/67(6)	BLACK VIRGIN MTN MASSACRE
FRED K. KAMA(R)	9/06/67(6)	BLACK VIRGIN MTN MASSACRE
CLAYTON A. MARTIN(R)	10/16/67(6)	BLACK VIRGIN MTN MASSACRE
EDWARD L. CLEMMEN(R)	12/18/67	2ND PLATOON FROM MARCH 67

NOTES(#)
========

(1) JESSE RICE REPLACEMENT IN 2ND PLATOON & DIED WHEN HIS GRENADES CAUGHT VINE.
(2) HEBERT WAS AN ALPHA CO. ORIGINAL,WHO WAS HHQ RECON PLT.WHEN APC HIT BOMB ON DIKE.
(3) DAVID DIED OF WOUNDS OF 1/29/67 FROM NIGHT AMBUSH PATROL.
(4) ART DIED OF WOUNDS OF 2/6/67 FROM SAME BATTLE AS ED SCHELL.
(5) "CORKY" WAS MEDIC WITH 2ND PLT.
(6) DIED OF WOUNDS OF 9/4/67 FROM FAULTY ATTACK ON BLACK VIRGIN MTN.
(7)ERIK DID BASIC WITH CHARLIE CO &WAS TRSFRD TO ALPHA IN AUG 1966(EST)
(8)EUGENE WAS AN ORPHAN AND A LONELY MIXED UP KID, MENTALLY UNFIT FOR THE ARMY. CLARENCE SIMPSON'S MOTHER WROTE TO HIM AS HE HAD NO ONE TO WRITE TO. PER CJ, HE WAS CONSTANTLY SCREWING UP AND IN TROUBLE. DEPRESSION SET IN AND HE HUNG HIMSELF IN THE TACOMA JAIL. HE BECAME OUR FIRST CASUALTY.

A2/22 KI A LIST

A/2/22 KIA LIST 1966-1967(AS OF 2/2/2012)-ALSO DSV LIST(DIED SINCE VIETNAM)
NOTE-LIST PREPARED BY GARY HARTT (I would appreciate corrections, additions etc.)

DSV(DIED SINCE VIETNAM)-EXACT DATES NOT KNOWN AS OF NOW

COMRADE'S NAME	DSV DATE(EST)	CAUSE OF DEATH IF KNOWN
CHARLES N GIVEN (CHUCK)	10/17/1969	INDUS. AUTO ACCIDENT(Per his 86 yr. old mother)
GERALD"PIXIE"PICARD %	11/4/1984	SUICIDE
CHARLES MCNAIR	1985(EST)	HEART PROBLEMS (after heart transplant-per Rodger Kloack)
LARRY J DICKERSON %	12/3/1993	LUNG CANCER (Per his son Larry)
TYRUS O ROURKE %	1995(EST)	ALCHOLISM(TY battle FATIGUE in Vietnam & later problems
ROBERT NORTHCOTT	1996(EST)	DIED OF HEART ATTACK(Per Lou Gross)
ROBERT NESBIT *	1998(EST)	DIED OF CANCER (Per Terry Humpert)
TOP SGT VICTOR R ARRISOLA	10/06/97	OVEREATING?
SCOTTY WILFONG	7-11-1998	CAUSE NOT KNOWN
WESLEY W WILSON *	1999(EST)	DIED OF CANCER (Per Thomas Haan)
RONALD E NITCHMAN *	1999(EST)	DIED OF CANCER (Per John Coffey)
LARRY G. TRAVIS(R) *	04/16/1999	Per Triple deuce newsletter
LOWELL GARLAND*	1999	CANCER per wife
GEORGE CORWIN	12-26-1999	MOTORCYCLE ACCIDENT
ROBERT DOWNEY %	07/12/2000	ALCHOLISM
RONALD LEE	11/3/2000	NO CAUSE OF DEATH IN OBIT.
GEORGE C. MCFATE	04/5/2001	" " " "
ROBERT PLOUFF *	06/07/2002	LIVER & DIABETES
GARY PARKER *	07/09/2004	LIVER FAILURE & DIABETES
JEFFREY SNELENBERGER*	09/16/2004	LIVER CANCER
ANDREW LEACH*	02/5/2005	MELANOMA CANCER
ALFRED KERSHNER*	01/12/2006	PNEUMONIA
LT. VICTOR MASSAGLIA*	05/31/2006	LUNG CANCER
LEWIS CORDOVA	08-09-2006	CAUSE NOT KNOWN
GARY WADDINGTON*	03/21/2007	DIABETES/HEART ATTACK
JOE CATAPANO *	11/22/2007	CANCER
TIMOTHY LA WARE*	01/08/2008	CANCER
RONALD MILLER*	05-15-2008	DIABETES
DOYLE HASTINGS*	JUNE/2008	CANCER
DENNIS ALEXANDER*	05/18/2009	DIABETES & HEART PROBLEMS
JOHN M BECK	07-13-2009	CAUSE NOT KNOWN
MICHAEL P MORRIS	08/24/2009	AUTO ACCIDENT
THOMAS E LYONS*	09/12/2009	CANCER
IVAL LAWHON*	10/03/2009	DIABETES & PARKNSON
RICHARD HOLTE*	10/30/2009	DIABETES
ERNEST HENRY	05-25-2010	CAUSE NOT KNOWN (DUBABE)
DARRELL LAUSCH*	12/26/2010	HEART ATTACK
JACK CONRAD*	10/21/2011	ACUTE LEUKEMIA

NOTES ON DSV= % PTSD RELATED, *AGENT ORANGE related illness was highly probable cause of death in at least 22 of 38 total.
NOTE IN FUTURE, I PLAN TO ADD KIA REPLACEMENTS FOR REST OF 1967, SINCE MANY WERE OUR GOOD FRIENDS.

Respectfully submitted by Gary Hartt 503-632-6955

A2/22 KIA LIST, continued

CITATION FOR ORDER OF THE RED ANT

ALPHA COMPANY, 2ND BATTALION (MECHANIZED), 22ND INFANTRY REGMT.
3RD BRIGADE, 4TH & 25TH INFANTRY DIVISION- DAU TIENG, VIETNAM
OCTOBER 1966 TO END OF VIETNAM DEPLOYMENT OF THE SOLDIERS OF THE TRIPLE DEUCE

OCTOBER 6, 2006

HISTORICAL BACKGROUND OF THE ORDER OF THE RED ANT

In early 2003, a bunch of Vietnam Triple Deuce vets were exchanging emails over a couple of months. There was discussion and chatter about the hardships endured by the fellow grunts especially the swarming and biting giant red jungle ants and other insects we encountered. At around the same time there was another email discussion regarding the gross inequities of the awarding of medals for bravery under combat conditions during the Vietnam War. Grunts would describe heroic actions by fellow draftees and other low rank soldiers that went unrecognized. At the same time, most officers who were in Vietnam Infantry company for as short as 2 weeks, received Bronze Stars, for merely being there, regardless of their leadership quality or results. Moving up the food chain it got worse, Senior ranking officers of Major and higher received Silver Stars for merely completing their 3-6 month assignments in combat units. Awards were issued to the high ranking officers in 25th Div HQ including the Division Band members. Many never left the Cu Chi base camp except for R & R. Thus most grunts are of the opinion that 90% of the medals received by senior officers and REMF senior NCOS were phony and undeserved. Thus all medals received by officers become questionable including those received by the truly worthy 10% and it degrades the medals earned by the grunts.

ORDER OF THE RED ANT IS RESERVED FOR THE TRULY WORTHY

Thus the birth of the "ORDER OF THE RED ANT" (ORA), whose criteria of 100 bites would exclude all senior officers riding in helicopters in their pressed fatigues and returning nightly to base camp for a hot meal, hot shower and cold drinks. In addition, because the award committee is made up of real grunts, only real officers respected by their men are eligible and awarded the ORA. While it will be issued by a cultural committee of grunts, we thought it appropriate that it be signed by the 2 individuals in senior command ultimately responsible for the hardships we endured. Namely, Robert McNamara and William Westmoreland. A short history of these 2 men and how they influenced the execution of the Vietnam War follows: Pres. John F Kennedy appointed McNamara (a Republican) to the Sec of Defense position in 1961. Many cynical political pundits felt this was a shrewd political move by JFK as at that time the Defense Dept's share of the Federal budget was around 60%. McNamara, when appointed was the successful President of the Ford Motor Corp. and a real numbers man. He and his "whiz kids" ran the Defense Dept. like a Ford assembly line. Thus if you expended so many rounds of M-16 bullets, artillery rounds and aircraft bombs, you should have certain resulting BODY COUNT. (It is the same as labor, materials and time input to build a car right?) Of course there are those unforeseen events and subjectivism that upset the development of reliable and predictable statistics, It is called the human element, but there is a way to deal with that too. Thus you have the "brownnose" General Westmoreland with an eager to please staff of junior officers, that will give the General any numbers he needs to make him look good. These junior officers are anointed "military intelligence specialist". They produce numbers that inflate BODY COUNTS and underestimate enemy VC/NVA troop strength and ignore conflicting CIA statistics. Thus old Westmoreland issues statements in 1967 of how we are "WINNING THE WAR" and the hearts and minds of the people. The grunt soldiers see a different view and hope their tour is over before the reality sets in. TET 1968 happens, the news media becomes cynical, coins a phrase, "CREDABILITY GAP" and it turns the American public against the war. Somehow the Infantry grunts, who suffered from near exhaustion, are pushed harder than soldiers in America's prior wars, and wind up sharing the blame for America's first war loss. The Vietnam soldier was on constant combat operations beating the jungle 12 hours a day, 7 days a week. Then at night, it was ambush patrol, listening post or perimeter guard duty getting 4-5 hours sleep a night for a year. The grunt, dreams of R & R and counts down to his personal DEROS DATE. The brave grunt returns to America just happy to have survived. They return home not to welcoming parades, but to an ungrateful nation. Many were also made to feel unwelcome by the majority of the VFW and American Legion veterans of WWII and Korea...A sign alleged to be on a latrine in Long Bien, Vietnam in 1970 said it all. "THE VIETNAM WAR IS FOUGHT BY THE UNWILLING, LED BY THE INCOMPETENT, FOR AN UNGRATEFUL NATION."

THUS THE "ORDER OF THE RED ANT" IS AN AWARD FOR GRUNTS ONLY, WHETHER DRAFTEES, ENLISTEES OR JUNIOR LEVEL OFFICERS, WHO CAN ONLY RECEIVE THE AWARD FROM THEIR FELLOW COMRADES IN ARMS WHO TRULY RESPECT THEM FOR HUMBLE AND VALIANT SERVICE IN THE VIETNAM BATTLEFIELDS ON BEHALF OF THEIR SACRIFICE TO THE UNITED STATES OF AMERICA. THANK YOU FOR SERVING AND WELCOME HOME.

CITATION FOR THE ORDER OF THE RED ANT

The Order of   *The Red Ant*

THE ALPHA BOAT ORIGINALS OF THE VIETNAM TRIPLE DEUCE HEREBY AWARDS

_____

Your combat brothers of the Triple Deuce and the ungrateful nation of the UNITED STATES OF AMERICA does hereby award under Executive Order 2/22, the above award for Courage, Bravery and Endurance in the face of an overwhelming enemy. Leaches, scorpions and the NVA mosquitoes were mere child's play in comparison to the humongous horde of swarming red ants. The pain and suffering experienced by a sudden attack of a thousand giant red ants on all body parts of the combat soldier, is forever etched in his memory. This award is symbolic of the hardship endured and inflicted upon the grunt by our giant red ant "friends" who greeted us in the jungles of Vietnam and their pesky "love bites". It is hereby acknowledged that the above award recipient did receive in excess of 100 bites during his Vietnam "back to nature walks" and (or) while riding the APCS during "country road rallies".

ROBERT "BODY COUNT" MACNAMERA   WILLIAM "WINNING THE WAR" WESTMORELAND

SECRETARY OF DEFENSE   COMMANDING GENERAL –US ARMY -VIETNAM

Certificate
_____

CORKY'S SILVER STAR

It was over 40 years ago but I cannot get the memory out of mind. It was March 19,1967 and last night I had another FLASHBACK dream or should I say nightmare? I awoke at 3 AM in a cold sweat and shaking. It was the same dream as I have had too many times to remember. Corky, the too young new medic working on a wounded guy in the middle of a firefight. Green tracer rounds are whizzing past his head and mine. I realize with my radio antenna, I am attracting fire I crouch down and yell at Corky to get down and stop kneeling over the wounded guy as you make too good a target. Corky yells back over the noise of the firefight," I can't help this guy if I am prone." A second or 2 later a rifle grenade hits the side of Corky's head and all his skin is gone. I am less than 5 feet away and do not get a scratch other than the concussion noise which made me deaf for several minutes. A couple of other grunts pull Corky and the wounded guy back. Corky is in the battalion aid station, I would later realize. The firefight continues, one of my best buddies, Danny Ryan, is upfront wounded bad and had sent a radio message asking for help. I asked, begged, pleaded several times to Lt. Massaglia to be allowed to go get Danny. But the Lt. said no because of my dam radio I had was too vital to lose communications. Of course he was right but, I was too emotional to care about logic. Finally, what seemed like an hour but was only 5 minutes later, the battalion commander radioes to me to tell the Lt. to pull back and let the artillery and air strikes deal with the entrenched 272nd crack Viet Cong Regiment who were well dug in. After I give the word to the Lt., he allows me to help Danny Ryan but first tells me to go to the rear and get rid of my radio and other excess stuff. All of a sudden I am carrying five m-16 rifles guys gave me to take to the rear. Then I do a stupid thing instead of crawling back, I get up and try and make a quick run for 100 yards as I am worried about taking too long by crawling. A VC starts unloading his AK-47 rifle on me. I hear bullets whizz by my head on both sides of me. I am zigzagging a little so The VC cannot get a good shot but my antenna catches a jungle vine and I am caught on the vine as I stop to free it, the dam VC gets me with his last bullet in his magazine and now I have 2 holes in my neck shooting blood out. The bullet had nicked my main artery and I was losing blood rapidly. I look down and a new guy kissing mother earth looks up at me and I swear his face turned as green as his olive drab fatigues. I realize in a flash if I fall this new guy is too scared to help me. I make the remaining 20 yards to the wood line and some of my buddies in an APC put a tight bandage around my neck to slow the bleeding. I had lost 3 to 4 pints of blood and am feeling woozy. The Armored Personel Carrier(APC) takes me quickly to the Battalion Medical Aid Station.

The battalion medics give me a quick triage and tell me to await medical dustoff. I am standing over a guy I do not recognize. Half his scalp is gone and you could see part of his brains. I ask the medics why they are not caring for him and they tell me he will die in a few minutes. Then I realize the guy dying is CORKY. I thought just a moment about him and my attention is diverted as they bring the lifeless body of Joe Barney Kelly, and I asked the priest to administer the last rites to Kelly. I then stand over Kelly and am also watching Corky die. The rush of adrenalin is now starting to wear off with me. I am loaded on the medivac helicopter and arrive at the 45 Surgical hospital in Tay Ninh in 15 minutes. As I am walking with the aid of An orderly, my camera falls out of my personal bag the guys handed me just before the dustoff chopper took off. I TELL THE ORDERLY TO TAKE MY PICTURE. Why? I do not know but the range of emotions I experienced that day were all over the place fear, sorrow, elation I was alive, guilt, etc. I

have a smile on my face but there was also the thousand yard stare most combat vets have. While for years I did not want to admit it, the Vietnam War changed me forever.

Corky's Silver Star

October 13,2005

Dear Jessica, Daphne, and Brett

Enclosed is the an abbreviated personal history, I wrote in support of my PTSD CLAIM with the VA. (post traumatic stress disorder). I had buried my Vietnam memories as best I could for over 30 years, but now realize it affected me my entire post-Vietnam life and you 3 kids suffered along with your mother from my occasional outbursts and rantings. While these Vietnam memories will always be with me, having you 3 kids and your mother in my life has given me many joys, a lot of my fellow surviving vets never had the opportunity to enjoy. I love you all and think you are entitled to read this history and it is long overdue, that I share it with you.

Since 2001, I have been focusing a lot of attention on my Vietnam experience and meeting with my combat brothers has been very rewarding as they are all now close friends, once again. It has helped quite a bit in dealing with my Vietnam devils and has helped the healing process and lessened the pent up bitterness and resentment baggage I carry. I do not want your pity etc. as there are millions of people that have experienced much more difficult circumstances than I have but I am sharing this so you better understand your father. Around age 18, I learned not to feel sorry for myself as you probably do not have to look real far to find someone worse off than yourself. When you or I feel sorry for ourselves, remind me of that.

With the help I received from my VET counselor, Travis, I was able to identify some of my negative behavioral traits and manage them.

As some things in the history I am not proud of, I would appreciate it that you respect my privacy and only share it with Mike and JJ.

I am extremely proud of the adults you have become and the choices you have made. I hope I am able to be around for a long time to see more of your adult lives.

Love you all

DAD

October 13, 2005 letter

VICTORIA HARTT

6/23/2015

THE VIETNAM EXERIENCE- A WIFE'S PERSPECTIVE

I have known Gary since we both were in 8th grade together in Port Jefferson, NY. His nickname was "Goof" and he was a bit of a clown, always laughing. We met intermittingly during teenage years. In 1967,(around October) we reconnected for a date. A strange first date, a carload of "girls" along with me. We went to the St Albans Naval Hospital in Queens county, NYC to provide some Christmas cheer for a day with the recovering Vietnam vets. It was evident that Gary had survivors guilt. I had been working at the Manhattan VA Hospital as a RN taking care of the casualties of Vietnam, physical and emotional basket cases, always non-verbal about their experiences. Gary was home about 2 days, when he re-enrolled in college. He was adamant that he would have control over his future destiny.

We married in April 1968. Gary never spoke about the War and never admitted to being a Vietnam Vet publicly. When he graduated from college, he said he felt it was a negative to admit that you were a Vietnam combat vet, on job interviews. However he had to explain where he had been for 2 years in his college gap time. At that time Vietnam vets were portrayed as volatile, angry and generally crazy, with this perception enhanced by the media.

During our marriage, Gary has had night sweats, nightmares, insomnia and exhibited signs of anxiety. I bought a book which was about "how to" help your Vietnam vet recover from the war. Unfortunately, it required listening- but there was not any speaking by Gary. When I was pregnant with our first child, he said he was not ready and had a hard time adjusting to fatherhood.
As time went by, he exhibited signs of anger- outbursts with the family and backed his bosses into a corner at work. He felt that the corporate world was "mickey mouse" and that the things that were valued were meaningless. He lost jobs (although he had an advanced degree and was considered talented) because he could not "fit in" or meet the "corporate image".

He had frequent job changes, sent out hundreds of resumes over the years and finally just gave up. I have been the bread winner since around 1991.

Around 2002, he started to re-connect with his fellow combat vets. He now cries openly and remembers vividly many of the firefights he went through. He took out an old suitcase with old letters from family and friends and his Vietnam diary not viewed in 35 years. The War changed his life, it affected all of us in his family. No one reached out to these vets. Now when these graying men(who are dying prematurely from Agent Orange effects) meet a fellow Vietnam vet for the first time their greeting is "WELCOME HOME." My psychology background helped me to understand and live with Gary's distressed behavior. Without that advantage, I am sure our relationship would have failed, as is the story with many Vietnam Vets.

Letter, from Wife's perspective

Name: Lyle Hicks

Branch of Service: US Navy

Rank: Quartermaster Second Class

Dates of Service in Viet Nam:

Began: 1973

Ended: 1975

Awards: Armed Forces Expeditionary Medal

Humanitarian Service Medal

Navy Meritorious Unit Commendation

Various Viet Nam Medals

Lyle Hicks is a man who wears many hats... literally. He glides easily from war hero to family man, from restaurateur to Master of Ceremonies, from buddy to event organizer, with not even the slightest change of breath or manner. His twinkly eyes and calm, humble demeanor invite those who know him to consider him friend, confidante, and community leader of excellence. His companionship with God he describes thusly: "It is no different than a relationship with a dog: You don't have to change to be accepted, which in turn makes you want to be better than you thought you could ever be." This belief is his faith and guiding light in life.

Lyle was born on September 23, 1952, on the old Hospital Hill, part of downtown Bend, Oregon and was raised in Gilchrist, Oregon, a small lumber town south of Bend. He was the third of three boys, with three younger sisters. Lots of siblings meant hand-me-downs, and Lyle remembers getting new pj's for Christmas one year, and the feel of the new clothes was "unbelievable." He was given the nickname of "Pixie" in school, as he was one of the smallest students enrolled... he did grow during his high school years! He was always in great competition with his older brother, Rudy: A '61 Ford was the first car for his brother, so Lyle's first car had to be a '61 Chevy. Rudy had joined the Navy, so Lyle was going to join the Air Force. The Navy won, and a family tradition was honored as their dad had been in the Navy during WWII.

Lyle became a "Quartermaster and checked aboard the USS Durham LKA-114." He was first to make Petty Officer, and, "when the First class left, (Lyle) became the lead petty officer and then Division Officer, as the department had only one commissioned officer, the Navigator, and no chiefs."

Lyle's first Western Pacific (Westpac) deployment occurred in early1973, and the second one started in late 1974. The ship spent Christmas in the Philippines in 1974 and the New Year in Hong Kong. In early 1975, Lyle began training South Vietnamese officers in navigation. A young ensign named Sau became his friend. In March, orders came to go to Subic Bay, Philippines. They were going to pick up Marines and head to Viet Nam. Sau was dropped off in Subic, and Lyle thought that maybe he would never see Sau again. Lyle later learned that Sau graduated from UCLA in the late 1970s. The ship left with the mission being to collect as many refugees as possible and take them to Phuc Quac Island. One day in and their destination was changed from Da Nang to Cam Rahn Bay. The NVA was moving quickly and the extraction point needed to be changed. Lyle had top secret clearance, so he was ordered to chart mine fields in and out of the harbor. With updated news, Lyle learned that the South was not only not giving any resistance, but were killing civilians to get on the last planes out of Da Nang. This angered Lyle, the injustice of it all, and may have been a beginning of the factors that began to lead to his later PTSD.

On April 1, off the coast of Cam Rahn Bay the ship dropped anchor as basic preparations for refugees had been made: makeshift toilets off ship side had been built, and holds had been cleared. Soon a small fishing boat appeared with the first of the refugees. The "battle hardened" Marines were placed on the ladder to the ship to assist those boarding. As more small boats brought more people, the Marines were not very gentle with frightened, confused and now homeless civilians, and a lot of pushing and shoving occurred. The Captain put a stop to the rough treatment and put his own men on the ladder. The way to get order was to use water cannons to line up the boats. They finally had to pull up anchor and get out to sea. All night long everyone worked to help people, "taking... food and blankets, bringing milk to babies, or escorting them to bathrooms." The battle onshore seemed to be some sort of "distant electrical storm."

The next day was like the day before. Some defecting Vietcong came aboard which did not please the Marines, but the ordnance, Russian rifles, was surrendered, so it was bearable. The battle continued; Lyle used the "big eyes," extra-large binoculars, and focused on a small church with a cross on top: one minute there, and the next minute vanished in a cloud. Later, NVA tanks lined up and fired a shell over the bow of one of their ships. That immediately stopped all extractions, even with more boats and more people needing help. Another link in Lyle's PTSD...

The next day Lyle's ship met with the SS Transcolorado near Phan Rang, and all 4500 of the refugees, were transferred to it. Ten thousand more could not be saved. This was probably the core of

Lyle's PTSD, and was the most defining moment of Lyle's life as a sailor in Viet Nam. During this two or three months in 1975, 1.5 million people lost their lives, more than in any other total years of the war. Later, defecting Vietcong had taken over the ship, black flagging it, trying to bring it into Saigon. Since they couldn't tie up there, they gave the ship back and went to Phuc Quac. The South Vietnamese government red tape was slow, so some refugees panicked and grabbed boards and tried to float ashore, only to be shot by their own people. This was fortuitous for those left aboard, as days later Phuc Quac was overrun by the Cambodians. The ship headed to Bangkok and later to Guam. Most aboard were given passage to the United States.

Lyle's ship was the first ship in station to leave Saigon. Ship's commands changed, and some final events kept immigrants coming. Choppers manned by South Vietnamese pilots unloaded passengers, then surrendered to the Navy. Lyle's shipmates had one choice: they locked up the pilots and dumped their choppers over the side. This happened on several ships and became a "symbol of the entire event." The Navy sent in their own choppers to finish the evacuation. With the evacuation, Lyle's ship had spent more time than normal on their cruise, and was the first to be sent home. Three months more saw the end of Lyle's military service. To this day, Lyle is sad over the tremendous loss of life, and the futility of war.

Lyle met his lovely wife, Judy, on a blind date just before his first deployment, then married her just before the second deployment. The story in between involves another conversation with God. Lyle and Judy were not really sure they wanted to be friends when they first met. Neither Lyle nor Judy had wanted to go on the blind date, and it was not a positive experience. Lyle decided to try another date with Judy, just in case the first date was not really the end of the relationship. Years later, Judy told her daughter Trinity that that second date sealed it: she decided she was going to spend the rest of her life with Lyle! Soon after they decided that their lives would involve each other, Judy went to Europe with her sister, while Lyle went on his first deployment. Then, after the first deployment, and even though Lyle brought her "home" from Australia, to meet the family, he still was not sure about the proposal of marriage. God nudged him and told him to get on with it. When Lyle asked Judy to marry him, saying, "You want to get married, or what?"

She said, "Yes."

They were married on a Friday in Los Angeles, and by Monday, Lyle was on his way to sea for two weeks, leaving her in another foreign country: the United States. They did get to take a trip before he left for his second deployment. He was off the coast of Saigon on their first anniversary. Judy did not know where Lyle was when she saw a newsreel and discovered he was in Viet Nam. He was happy to get out of the Navy to be able to truly begin his life with Judy. They have lived in San Diego, California, Brisbane, Australia, and back to San Diego, and finally in Bend, since the early 1980s. Blessed with three children, their family is an important part of their lives. Daughter Carrie is a single mom raising grandson, 18-year-old Jayden. One of Lyle's great joys is to go fishing with Jayden. Daughter Trinity is a crew scheduler for the airlines. Their son, Casey, works with Lyle in the family's famous restaurant, Jake's Diner.

The truck stop where Lyle pumped gas, and the family restaurant are really both ends of the same establishment. It is here where Lyle's true purpose has come to fruition, with his trust in God leading the way. When Lyle was new to the Navy, he had other sailors, some who were his superiors, watching him. They encouraged him to "knuckle down" and work hard to earn the notice of his officers. It paid off in advancements that allowed him positions of responsibility that others did not get. When he came to Bend in the early 1980s, Lyle enrolled in Central Oregon Community College in Bend, put on his blue suit and walked the streets of the city looking for work. He found a job pumping fuel at Jake's Truck Stop. He was quickly advanced to do accounting and purchasing. By the beginning of the next year, Lyle had earned the position of Restaurant Manager at Jake's. In 1987, Jake expanded on the truck stop and built a completely new restaurant and called it Jake's Diner. Lyle, as General Manager, opened the new establishment. At the beginning of the '90s, Lyle took on more responsibility as the Truck Stop's Assistant General Manager, so he was responsible for much leadership for both businesses. Toward the end of the 90's, things began to get shaky, both in business and in the world. During this time, much was happening in Lyle's personal life. He did not know what his Guiding Light, God, wanted for him. A lifelong friend, Frank Patka, wanted Lyle to go into business with him. Frank owned and operated a printing business, Printer Resources, which is still open today. Lyle was scheduled to fly to Las Vegas to learn the business. On the day of the scheduled plane flight, **9/11** occurred! With the media shooting live-action photos of people running and screaming in terror, Lyle told Judy that he "had seen this before"…in Viet Nam. This brought back Lyle's memories of his military service. He could not make himself go into the new business field now, needing consistency, something familiar. PTSD once again attacked Lyle with depression. He spent much time enclosed in his office, away from the public. In 2002, Lyle's Pastor saw a difference in him, and referred him to a VA doctor, which got him "into the system." His boss was very understanding about it, but Lyle felt his employment was in jeopardy. Business continued to slow down, and in 2004, Jake's closed. Jake had died in 2001, and the land went up for sale. Lyle was told about the sale, but told not to tell anyone, which put him into greater depression. At times, he could barely get out of bed. With the Truck Stop closing, the depression became critical. He had to get help. Judy called the VA clinic, and with more tests, most of them proving nothing was physically wrong; his doctor said it was just depression. After the crew and staff were informed of the truck stop's closing, God spoke to Lyle, and told him to, "Put on your pants and go to work." Through Lyle's hard work; talking with "money" guys, threatened permanent closure of the premises, sacrificing money, time, energy, and equipment that he did not have, needing and finding a new location, asking for and getting new workers to make the new restaurant ready, getting it all back for a song with promissory notes, and hanging on by his teeth, IT WORKED! TV, radio , newspaper, and in-house poster ads blitzed the public, saying, "We're still open!" With the clock ticking, on Friday, April 15, 2005, Jake's Diner opened again in its present location,! Within a year, all debt was paid in full. The rest of the story is visible every day on the east side of Bend, Oregon at this award winning establishment.

In 2008, the Band of Brothers of Bend started with a single meeting at Jake's. These meetings have been a fixture at the restaurant. Once a week on Monday morning, fellow veterans and their families join each other in camaraderie, songs, pledging allegiance to the flag and in planning activities for the many charities for which the citizens of Central Oregon are grateful. Lyle is at the center of it all, supervising a buffet brunch, visiting with members as if they are family, seemingly effortlessly doing what needs to be done. He has even assisted with the Honor Flight for WWII Veterans, by raising funds with such activities as spaghetti feeds. The first time these men went to Salem for the dedication of the memorial for veterans of WWII, the city of Sisters, west of Bend, shut down businesses and schools for the parade of veterans coming through town. In Salem, the Lottery Winners office hosted them in a staging area for organization, and a lunch after their dedication before they returned to Bend. Another activity spinoff is a trip to the University of Oregon for these veterans to visit the coaches and players of the football team that went to the National Championships in 2015. They were able to spend an hour with the team, and the director of the football team organized pictures with the vets and the teammates. One such photo op shows the football team giving their autographed jerseys to the veterans, and these can be seen on one of the walls at Jake's. The Deschutes County Sheriff's office supplies the bus rides for this annual event. Lyle usually organizes bus rides to Salem, but does not ride on them. His PTSD, his quiet companion, prohibits his bus rides, so he follows the honor members in his car, sometimes taking Judy with him. Lyle's other veteran activities include a once-a-week meeting with veterans who are survivors of PTSD.

The walls of Jake's Diner are lined with testaments to war heroes, meritorious awards from community groups, interviews with celebrities and even children for whom the Band of Brothers has made a difference.

Lyle's defining moment in the Viet Nam War occurred that day that his ship had to leave thousands of refugees in the harbor and in boats. This is the reminder that PTSD gives him. He knows how to tame it and make it just a part of who he is. Though he helped save many, he feels guilt that more could not be helped. His sometimes unceasing care that he has for his fellow veterans and community members is merely his way of helping others by doing what he can to ease their burden in life. He hopes that what he does in some way atones for his personal failure during the war, senseless wherever it happens. Lyle Hicks is a hero for all seasons.

Lyle's story continues. In May of 2015, Lyle was notified that the Daughters of the American Revolution (DAR) had voted him the Veteran Volunteer of the Year. He decided that his speech would honor the three men left behind in the Viet Nam War's last battle.

The war was officially over on May 15, 1975; however, on Koh Tang Island in Cambodia, the USS Mayaquez, a supply ship, was seized by the Cambodians. President Gerald Ford wanted to attempt a rescue. Marines were spread out in the Pacific, and had grabbed Okinawa and the Philippines. The crew on the Mayaquez went up against pirates on Koh Tang! Two hundred to three hundred battle hardened Khmer Rouge warriors were entrenched and ready to attack the Vietcong, which they thought the innocent crew on the Mayaquez was! A firestorm occurred, with three of the first five US choppers being shot down. President Ford sent the Air Force attached to South Cambodia with bunker buster bombs; nuclear bombs the only things more powerful! That got the attention of the Cambodians. They released the crew of the Mayaquez, while flying white flags to the Navy. As the Marines were trying to pull out the Mayaquez' men, the US crew went from defense to offense. The crew of the supply ship said that three men in a pillbox had been left behind. The lading Chief Pilot wanted to go back and get them, but the answer he received was a resounding, "NO!" The SEALS that had been brought in for the rescue erroneously determined that the three men were probably already dead. They were later found by the Khmer Rouge and executed. Of the 41 dead, only three bodies were not brought home. Of these three, one was 24-years-old, and another was just 18; two months before this time had been his birthday. These three men were honored in Lyle's speech on the 40th Anniversary of the day they were left behind: May 15, 1975.

Awards continue…

Lyle was a keynote speaker for the 2015 National Yellow Ribbon Day "Stand Down" in honor of soldiers coming back from Afghanistan. His topic was "Transition from military life to civilian life." In a nutshell, Lyle told the gathered audience that soldiers will always be warriors. To be anything else defeats one's transition into civilian life. It is "ok" that a war doesn't have to be fought now that one is home… it's "ok" that a warrior is different than the everyday civilian, in thought, action, and speech… though warriors do not often ask for help from others, they readily seek the help of other warriors; it's what one does in times of the thick of battle… it's "ok" to ask for help any time… it's "ok" to be who you are.

To do this speech, Lyle asked a member of his PTSD group, a buddy named "Zin" Watford, to stand with him for moral support, to be his Rock. If Lyle thought he would "lose a little bit," all he had to do was look at Zin. His buddy had his 'six.' {Author's Note: In military terms, think about a traditional clock. The service person is in the middle and directions on a mission are given as being at 11:00, or 2:00, and so on. One's six is behind him or her. Those personnel in that position act as support and guard the personnel in front of them.}

In December, 2015, Lyle and Judy were honored as the Grand Marshalls of the Bend Christmas Parade. He agreed to do it when parade organizers agreed that his Band of Brothers mates could march with him. Lyle asked his Band of Brothers comrades if a few of them would go with him and Judy to "protect his perimeter." Not only did they show up, but his BROTHERS marched in front of the car in which he and Judy were riding holding a Band of Brothers banner. Double lines of soldiers with each soldier carrying an American flag with smiles on their faces, and World War eterans travelling in busses behind the procession made an impressive statement. {Author's Note: See photos at the end of Lyle's tale.}

I am honored to be part of this healing time of history for our veterans who need our support. It cannot be stated too many times: If our country creates warriors, then when they come home from serving our country with their sacrifice and sometimes, their lives, then the least we can do is help them assimilate into civilian circumstances with mental, physical and emotional healing. The warrior will always be in these veterans, but they need the rest of the population to use their ordnance of skills and compassion to truly make their homecoming valid. It takes money and lots of time, but some of the cushy money that politicians use for their own benefits could be diverted to this really important part of our population. Lyle and Judy, thank you for your continued service to our country.

Saigon rescue efforts
occur on the USS Durham,
Lyle's ship.

One of hundreds of boats filled with Saigon evacuees who await rescue.

Lyle and Judy participate as the Grand Marshals of Bend, Oregon's 2015 Christmas Parade.

Band of Brothers comrades march with Lyle and Judy in the parade.

Name: Donald Kelly

Branch of Service: US Army

Rank: Sergeant E5

Time served: January 4, 1969 to December 12, 1970

(1 year in Viet Nam: January 15, 1970 to December 8, 1970)

Honors: Viet Nam Service Medal

Viet Nam Commendation

National Defense Service Medal

Expert Rifleman Medal

Good Conduct Medal

Though based in a relatively "safe" area, Don spent his year in Viet Nam as a radio teletype operator, in which "moments of sheer terror interrupted days of boredom!"

Donald (Don) Kelly was born in 1950, in Portland, Oregon but home was in a little town called Sherwood. His dad, Donald, was a truck driver and farmer. His mom, Anna, was a stay-at-home mom to Don, and his big sister, Elizabeth (Liz), who had arrived in 1947. The family didn't farm just a piece of land. It was land that lay next to the Sherwood-Wilsonville Road, officially Route 1. Don's parents had 10 acres of the land, and his Grandma Kelly had 10 acres next to it. Interestingly, she lived within the city limits, and Don's family lived outside of those limits. The land for this extended family was prosperous in orchards of fruits and nuts, and lots of berries that the families sold to the local cannery. Sometime near 1957-58, Don's Grandma Galbreath (his mom's mom) had a massive stroke. She lived approximately five miles from the Kelly properties off Cipole Road; this farm was also known locally as the Onion Flats. Historically, the property had been in the Galbreath family for 150 years. Don's mom, sister Liz and he moved in with her, and Don's uncle helped to care for her. His dad stayed at the family home to "keep an eye" on Grandma Kelly, stopping to eat dinner with Anna, Liz, and Don. Don actually grew up in two homes.

Slowly, over time, most of the land has been sold in lots, and most of the bottom land has become a wildlife refuge. Growing up, Don was the "free labor" on the Onion Flats, and as his mom owned a piece of the property, Don was expected to "work both places." His work included chores that helped keep the farm functioning: Cultivating soil, planting, irrigating, fence building and repair and various other activities requiring repair and maintenance. A dog and several cats also lived on the farm, being both companions, with the dog providing guardianship, and the cats, feline mouse control. These farm duties continued for Don until he was 55. Antique cars and car parts were part of the ambiance of this farm, as well. Among this collection were a '57 Chevy and a 1927 Roadster… a bit of fun for Don.

In 1962, Grandma Galbreath passed. Mom Anna and Dad Donald built a new house on their property next to Grandma Kelly. A couple of years later, she became too ill to live alone. She moved in with Don's family, and mom Anna was once again an in-home caregiver. Don's uncle tried to keep farming the bottom land as the family had been "grandfathered" into it, but the wildlife and river keepers kept making it more difficult. Several lots have been sold to others, and the bottom land sits idle as a wildlife refuge, while the high ground is "rented out." With Don's ever-evolving family dynamics, one of the highlights of weeks' end brought the family together for Sunday dinners. These times provided a welcome respite from the work-a-day world.

One of Don's big interests in school was wood shop. He liked to design furniture and other wood crafted items. Generally, though, school was tough for Don, who found sitting through lectures with no "hands-on" making no sense to him. Don graduated from Sherwood Union High School in 1968. For a while, he worked at the Ford Pre-Delivery Corporation "finding squeaks and rattles" in new Fords before they went to the dealers. He was trying to make enough money to go to community college. Good jobs were hard to find when one was classified 1-A in the Draft Selection regime. Don's life would change greatly in the next year. On a blind date, he met Patricia, and in 1969, they were married near the same time that the US Government also set its sights on Don, and he was drafted into the US Army. When Don was deployed, Patricia, who had graduated from school, worked at the State of Oregon Vocational Rehabilitation Division, in Portland.

Portland, about 20 miles from Sherwood, was the location of Don's induction into the military. From there, he went to Fort Bliss, in El Paso, Texas for basic training. Fort Huachuca, Arizona was the next stop for radio operator school, where Don graduated second in his class. Next stop was Fort Gordon, Georgia for radio teletype school. With 20 days of leave occurring during the holidays, Don spent time with family and friends, and, admittedly, probably did a little too much drinking. Then, he was off to Viet Nam, via a United Airlines flight, with two stops for fuel occurring in Alaska and Japan.

Don was stationed in Phu Bai, a military base eight miles south of Hue. The convoys were sent south to Da Nang which had an ocean port to resupply bases to the north. Don was involved because they did not have all of their communications gear, so he and his comrades were sent to pick up these supplies from Da Nang. Led by the command jeep with a radio, the convoy of gun trucks consisted mainly of five-ton semis, and a few two-and-a-half ton trucks with a gun truck, if they were lucky. They had to spend the night in Da Nang and return to their own Base Camp the next day. Once everything was operational in the Tactical Operations Center, a fancy name for communications bunker, the team had to go to other Fire Bases, to help them get their own communications up and running so they could be part of the "net." One time, Don and his team arrived at the northern-most Fire Base of the highway, which allowed them to look at the de-militarized zone (DMZ). They edged a little closer to it, but when bullets were fired at them, they headed south *really fast!*" He doesn't think they were ever actually in the DMZ, but who could tell… road signs were not plentiful!

One week a month, Don was required to be in a bunker doing base security. The bunker line was a series of bunkers, or shelters, which surrounded the Base and stretched for miles. They were the first line of defense for the Base, so they were heavily armed and, hopefully, wide awake!! A sniper took an opportunity to sneak onto the Base and shot at the Americans. Most of the time, Don was merely "on guard," but not terribly afraid. At that moment, however, "terror" was on everyone's mind. Don was fortunate that none of the men he personally knew were killed.

Several locals worked on the Base where Don was stationed. Various jobs were available for the citizens: Base clubs (local girls were employed at the Enlisted Men's Club (EMC)), mess halls, motor pools and laundry were some of the choices for employment. Filippino bands played and sang what few songs they knew. Don never wants to hear "Don't Step on my Blue Suede Shoes" ever again! The climate was warm and sticky. Bugs were plentiful and huge! Praying mantises were a foot long. During this time, Don only encountered one snake. {HA!!} Over time, Don became aware of what the civilians of Viet Nam endured. A camp was set up for village people looking for protection, but this camp was dismantled in 1975. The Tet Offensive had occurred in 1968, so when Don arrived in Viet Nam, he and his fellow soldiers were "doing clean-up work after the guys who did the 'heavy lifting'".

After Don left Viet Nam, he went right to work as an iron worker in Portland. For him, it was "a wasted year." He worked for Fentron Highway Products as a fitter/welder for 12 years. Don then worked for Siemens for 25 years. This company consisted of several divisions: electrical, medical, phone, automotive, communications and building maintenance (HVAC), which were scattered around the United States. Don worked for the electrical division at the Portland Area Service Center (ASC) as a designer/drafter. The ASC manufactured low voltage electrical products with 200 to 5000 amps. Don's working weeks were 65 hours long. In 1994, the company downsized, and his workload was dropped to

55 hours a week. Then, when it closed for good, Don officially retired. For a while, he was a full-time caregiver for his mother-in-law, but she now resides in a care facility. This situation could continue for a "long while," says Don. Patricia has worked for 30+ years with Total Logistic Resources as an ocean export manager.

Don and Patricia have been married for 46 years. They became parents in 1972 with the arrival of Kari, who works for the Burlington Coat Factory. Then, in 1975, Jennifer (Jenny) arrived. She works in human resources for a non-profit pre-school/day care center. Son Christopher (Chris) arrived in 1978. He is a foreman with the Fred Meyer grocer's warehouse. Chris is married to Brandy, and they have four girls: Kaylee, Ashland, Savannah and Brooklyn.

While these two people, who have known each other most of their lives, have not had much time to travel leisurely, they do take time to visit Reno, Nevada to experience *Hot August Nights*, an annual car show that draws people from across the nation and beyond. Don's passion for antique cars and their unique beauty has not waned over the years. He also finds time to continue his love of woodworking, making beautiful furniture in his spare time. Gardening is another joy for Don. He and sister Liz see each other often, usually on holidays, even keeping mom Anna's respectful tradition of decorating the cemetery for Memorial Day. They also remember and practice another tradition from Mom: Getting together with "kids and grandkids" nearly every Sunday for dinner. Some lessons for others include some tried but true homilies, including, "Don't sweat the small stuff." "Work hard and respect people," and for some politicos to take heed: "Don't start wars if you don't have to… " Finally, "Take time for yourself and your family." Don, Patricia and their family are happy. {Author's Note: I knew Don and his sister, Liz, when we were in public school together. My own brother, Tim, was a classmate and buddy of Don's. Don also recalled that our mother, Ione Mc Neil, was a traveling nurse who checked in on Don's Grandma Galbreath. As with most kids then, and even today, we knew each other as classmates, but did not really know the history and lives of relatives and family dynamics. I am proud to know Don, and that he proudly served his country when it was a difficult thing to do, especially with a new wife. Thank you, to both Don and Patricia, for your service to our country.}

1. Don Kelly, service photo

2. Don, back row, second from the right,
is shown with service buddies.

Name: John Lind

Branch of Service: US Army

Rank: Private First Class E-3

Time Served: September, 1967 to September, 1969

Medals/Honors Awarded: National Defense Service Medal

Vietnam Service Medal and Bronze Star Attachment (Double)

Vietnam Campaign Medal

Combat Infantryman Medal

Purple Heart

Expert Badge and Machine Gun Bar

Sharpshooter Badge and Rifle Bar

...With a song in his heart and drumbeats in his hands...

John Lind was born in 1947, in Seattle, Washington to Karl and Martha Lind, older by a year and 22 days than brother David. An Army Medic in World War II, as part of the 4th Infantry, Karl participated in the Battle of the Bulge and Argonne Forest. Karl ran the *Enumclaw Courier Herald*,, the newspaper in downtown Enumclaw, Washington. Cousins lived in nearby Bellevue, Bothell, Mercer Island and Seattle, Washington. The family lived a farming lifestyle with a horse, chickens and 4H memberships for the kids. A next-door neighbor trained horses for Roy Rogers, a small claim to fame, once removed. In 1962, John's dad took a job offer in Portland, Oregon and the family moved. When John was in middle school, his dad, a guitarist, thought it would be a good idea for John to join sports or play an instrument. John tried the accordion, but did not take to it at all, *and* it smelled old and musty. Next, he thought the trumpet sounded great. John has some success with it, but after he started, he tried out for baseball… well, he lost a front tooth… not too good for a trumpet player. It seems that as there was no catcher's mask for catchers to wear, and a batter swinging his bat hit John's face, breaking his tooth, the trumpet was out. Then came the drums, and the rest is history in so many ways! Karl saw possibilities in John, and paid for five years' worth of professional lessons. As a freshman, and through high school at Portland's Centennial High, John reveled in participating in marching and pep bands. He attended Mount Hood Community College for two years, studying business administration, and working with his dad. Drummer John became known as the "human metronome" for his experience with band music, and the classes he took in college would prepare him for so many leadership experiences in his future. Meanwhile, Uncle Sam had other ideas, and John was drafted in September of 1967. His passion for music never faltered, but it was put on the back burner of his heart while he served his country.

John was drafted and went to Fort Lewis, Washington for boot camp. Then he went to Fort Polk, Louisiana for more training for II Training: 11 Bravo, which is 11B20, code for Infantry. He learned to use the M16 rifle, M79 grenade launcher, and the M60 machine gun. Six months into his deployment in Vietnam, John was wounded on March 31st, 1968, during a firefight. Evacuated by helicopter, he spent the next six months in hospitals in Vietnam and Okinawa. John's injuries involved his buttocks and left leg, and seemed to take forever to heal. The mortar bits that hit him contained components that made flesh difficult to heal, and for 25 years the metal remained in his leg and buttocks, slowly growing bacteria. Recently sent to the hospital for leg swelling, the VA doctors took out much scarring, but venous stasis scarring remained due to nicking veins when they removed the metal. Clearly, there was an element of PTSD in John's life, simply by being wounded in the line of duty. It has become a part of his history, and it is a springboard for his assistance to others today. A quiet piece of John's personal life is that he was married from 1981 to 1991. He has no children. He makes his whole world his family, as the reader will soon see.

After leaving the service, John became a full-time student at Mount Hood Community College in Gresham, Oregon working toward a business administration degree. After his second year, he transferred to Portland State University to continue his quest for a Bachelor's degree. He left before graduation to help his dad full time as one of his employees in his publishing company. Today, John has only 53 credits to graduate, as he never returned to school. He is seriously considering going back to Portland State in the spring of 2016 to finish his degree. He has been notified by Mount Hood Community College that he has enough credits to be awarded an Associate's degree with them; indeed, he now has his Associate's Degree in Humanities. He would do well in these classes, as he has incredible life experiences.

John's serious working life began when the Personal Computer Age was just beginning, and computers were selling for nearly $5,000.00 apiece! In 1994, he sold Macintosh and Apple II computers on the 17th floor of the old Meier and Frank office building in downtown Portland. He graduated to Assistant Manager at Egghead Software in Beaverton, Oregon. He retired in 2008 after working for Wal-Mart as an Electronics Sales Associate.

Working in sales has been only a piece of John's involvement with the public. When he was a child, he became interested in health care when he listened to his dad tell his war stories. He took on an increasingly responsible role in providing health care to his aging parents. His dad died at 88, and his mom died when she was 96. "She was very interested in health topics, and researched a lot of articles on lifestyle, medicines, exercise, wellness and nutrition." John is a lot like her. He has become part of the greater health care community for veterans in Portland, Oregon, and the greater veterans' Community Outreach programs:

1. Beginning on October 1, 1981, through November 8, 2001, John served on the Local Board 5 Selective Service committee.

2. He was asked by his good friend and founding member, Kay Dickerson, to join the Oregon Community Health Information Network (OCHIN) Patient Engagement Panel (PEP) in 2014.

3. Shortly after joining the PEP John, was asked to join the Patient Member part of the Clinic and Patient Engagement (CAPE) Work Group (formerly PEW). This group is a patient-centered (all patients) safety net.

4. John strongly believes in OCHIN'S mission and cannot wait to see the type of projects forthcoming in ADVANCE Phase II.

5. John recently joined the Whole Foods Consumer Advisory Board at their 43rd and NE Sandy Boulevard Hollywood Store in Portland, Oregon helping them with input on making the shopping experience better in all areas of the store.

6. John is currently a member of Portland VA CIVIC (Center to Improve Veterans' Involvement in Care).

John created this list and then proceeded to tell me of several resources for my research, many of which are listed in the Bibliography. This man is a walking encyclopedia of vital community information, and he tells it with compassion and a smile on his face.

Advice from John's dad: "If you learn to serve others, it gives you a great feeling at the end of your day."

John's advice: "Don't regret. Move forward and learn from it. If you can't give back, learn to serve. I do the sound technology at my Central Christian Church."

These legacies are the spine of John Lind's philosophy, but the flesh is in his music. In 1984, John's musical life was once again on the front burner of his life. He had been a part of a band called the One

More Time Around Again Marching Band, and upon seeing a Drum and Bugle show in California, he and his fellow bandmates began tossing ideas around about how to get serious about working together as musicians. "They were thinking, 'Well, hey, we could do more during the summer, and we could get a life'. (Bernstein, page 162.)" Bob Pulido and John tossed more ideas around, and the Get a Life Marching Band was born. Miller Distributing Company gave them a $6,000.00 grant to get started with a band that had only 13 people in it. The band has grown to 150 to 160 members; today, it has 41 members, 39 of whom are musicians in their own right. In the summer of 1991 and 1992, the Tower of Power employed John to sell merchandise for their West Coast tour. He was able to meet AWB and Jeffery Osborne of LTD as well as "hang with Tower of Power backstage. Another thrill was performing Michael Jackson's *Thriller* with his marching band for Quincy Jones at the National Association of Music Merchants Trade Show (NAMM) in 2010 in Anaheim, California." This energetic group has played just about any place they have desired over the last 20 years, including Disneyland, Disney World, *Fiesta Flambeau* (the largest night parade in the country), Mardi Gras, The Tournament of Roses Parade in Portland, Oregon, Chinese New Year's Day in San Francisco/China Town, California (taking First Place/All Adult Division in the parade), and the piece-de-resistance, the 2009 Inaugural parade of President Barack Obama, on January 20th, 2009. Even the January Washington D.C. freezing weather did not deter their enthusiasm (Bernstein, page 162-164).

John's gift to his world family is entertaining them with his and his band's music, be it old school soul or stage shows that make the audience want to stand up and dance. Music is the universal language of the heart.

Thank you, John Lind, for your service to our country. You began serving us with the lessons learned at your father's knee, your mother's great love of the health of all peoples, your sacrifice in service during the Vietnam War and your unwavering happiness you share with us through your music. Encore!!

John Lind is pictured
at the Okinawa Army
Hospital: June, 1968.

John, today, smiles for the
camera: October, 2016.

Name: Gary McMullen

Branch of Service: US Army

Rank: PFC: Private, First Class

Time served: 1965-1968 (in country 21 months, 9 days)

Honors: Rifle Badge

Viet Nam Service Award

Of heroes, and countermeasures, and watching a brother's back, Gary was a true warrior. Of plots and plans, and wishes, too, all of Gary's dreams have come true.

Gary Ray McMullen was born in Redley, California on September 9, 1947. His dad, Ray, was his hero, a fair and honest man; if he gave someone his word or a handshake, it was his bond. He also gave his children his fun-loving side when it was time to play. Ray was a mill worker, working in plywood. Gary's parents divorced when he was a young preschooler. Soon after, Ray married again…a big mistake for the whole family. While his stepmother favored his stepsister in all childrearing matters, his biological sister, Carolyn, was "just a sister," another mouth to feed. Ray came after Carolyn and Gary, when he discovered that his now ex-wife, who had left the area, was going to put Gary and Carolyn up for adoption. Ray won custody easily, as his "ex" did not fight him. Years later, Gary feels that most of his early years were positive; even though his early childhood was traumatic. He and Carolyn felt safe and dearly loved, with no fighting, for the rest of their youthful years. It was discovered after the time of Gary's dad's passing that he had left his estate to all three children; however, the "ex" took it upon herself to have the will changed, leaving the total estate to her daughter. Gary and Carolyn received nothing.

Gary had various pets during this time, all dogs: Butch, Blackie and King. The family, including pets, moved from Oakland, Oregon to North Bend in 1960. Summer work for Gary was newspaper delivery. During his senior year, another classmate, Chris Sutton, noticed him mainly because she was editor of the yearbook.The seeds of romance were planted, but it was many years and trials before they sprouted. Gary and Chris graduated from North Bend High School in 1965. Gary's next big decision was to enlist in the US Army.

Basic training was the usual "drill," and Gary's rank became E-2. He was still an E-2 after 21 months. His assignment was for Germany: Three years. His training at Fort Ord, California authorized him to take a pistol with him. He took his grandfather's .38 with him. The humidity pitted the gun in the box in which the Army had placed it, and somehow, one of the screws, and what made the gun a real beauty, pearl handles, had been lost. When Gary saw the condition of that gift from his Grandfather, the Army never saw it again. He broke it down, put the pieces into a cassette tape recorder, and shipped it back to the states, the only way he was going to get it back home. His grandfather's pistol was not going to be owned by anyone else. Gary never shot it. He *was* authorized to take his own weapon, a .38 short on a .45 frame, the type the Air Force had. Gary cut it down so it would adapt to three .38 bullets. Problem for Gary: There was "no way" he was going to stay in Germany for three years. His words: "Too many gays, and too many inspections." He put in a bid for Viet Nam, and got it! He left Germany after seven months.

Upon arrival in Viet Nam, his first experience, and many later ones with Second Lieutenants was "a joke!" In one instance, Gary's 20-man unit braved a monsoon. Their first tent went down, and the Commander issued another one… then, another one. After the third tent collapsed into pieces, the "leader" simply covered everyone's belongings until the storm was over… in Gary's words: "Idiot!" That procedure should have been done in the first place. Gary feels that it is no wonder "so many of the Second Lieutenants were killed by friendly fire!" This was just one of the Lieutenants under which he served.

Gary had five Second Lieutenants during his deployment to Viet Nam. He had one really good one from Oregon. The others were awful, as they kept putting their men in harm's way. Many, if not most, of these men had been "promoted" to Second Lieutenant and sent to Viet Nam as their duty placement. They had desk jobs until promotion, and had received no combat training or experience in the ways of the enemy. Their job was to give orders, and the men under their command were to follow them, in spite of the possible danger or threat to lives. Unfortunately, common sense took a back seat to many of the mistakes that occurred.

Gary's field training occurred in Petersburg, Virginia. His training was as Mechanic: Gasoline. In Germany, as well as Viet Nam, most engines were diesel: Big difference in mechanical functions. In Viet Nam, Gary drove a five-ton truck with a reefer van, delivering frozen food to destinations, then on some trips, taking dead bodies from Oasis to Pleiku: graves registration. He was still an E-2 after 21 months. One trip Gary remembers well: He was in the Oasis, and this time he took 32 soldiers to graves registration. One soldier he remembered well. He had been killed by a crossbow arrow. "When the guys pulled it out, the wound closed and sealed." The guys at Pleiku could not figure out how he died. Gary had seen the arrow pulled out, remembered the guy's face and told them where to look!!

His job began at 4:30 AM every day, seven days a week. He would pick up the five-ton truck at the motor pool, then, pick up a trailer. He would join a convoy at 6:30, joining the main convoy where other convoys met at 7:00. He drove to wherever his supplies were needed and would be back to base around 8:00 PM. He then pulled about two hours of maintenance duty, fixing flat tires and such. Sometimes, the Commander would call a whole group meeting as well, and that meant another hour or so that Gary and the other drivers were not getting any rest. A shower, then a meal and maybe Gary would be in bed by 10:00 or 11:00 PM. The next morning would come, and Gary and his comrades would be ready for the same agenda as the day before, and the one after that, the only difference being at which fire base!

Another really bad experience with a Second Lieutenant had to do with faulty equipment. The Lieutenant's dad had been a Two Star General, and maybe it was a way to "impress Dad" that this near disaster occurred. Although Gary had experience with gasoline trucks and was now driving diesel trucks, his orders were to drive a gasoline truck for a particular convoy. Gary said it was a piece of junk and he did not want to do it. He was ordered to take the truck, and Gary insisted that it would break down. His commander said it was a "direct order!" Well, the truck broke down on the An-Khe Pass. He was going to be left all alone with only his M14 rifle to assist him if he was attacked. Another driver waited with him and said they would go together if fighting occurred with the VC coming down the hill. A military police jeep came off the pass, and Gary was asked if they had help coming, because, "Vietcong were coming off the hill." A wrecker could be seen coming up from the valley below, and it was indeed on its way to help. Gary was so pissed off at the situation in which the Lieutenant had put him, that he unloaded his M14 clip into that "piece of crap"… the truck and its windows!!

From Gary, "It was a good thing the Lieutenant was not there! I don't think I have ever been that mad!" The guy assisting Gary took off after the convoy. Gary went back with the wrecker and his truck. When they all arrived back at Gary's unit, his blown out windows were in front of the Commander's desk.

Gary was told, "It's out of my hands now. Get ready for the Brigadier General. Spit shine your boots!"

The Brigadier General wanted to know what happened after checking that Gary had a clean record, and when Gary told him, the answer he received was, "You can't be doing this. You must follow orders!"

At this time, Gary said, "That is exactly what I was doing, and he left me just like I had told him he would."

The General's reply was, "I should send you to the stockade." Gary was demoted from Specialist 4 to PFC, and fined $100.00 a month from his paycheck for the rest of his time in the Army.

Gary does not know why rank was so hard to get. He says, "I'll take the blame for whatever the reason."

During one more convoy trip out of Qui Nhon, the usual medic jeep was in front of the line. Two medics would always give a friendly wave at the same place, as if things were fine. This time, the jeep was attacked, and everyone saw the explosion. One soldier died, and one was wounded. The engine was blown away. All the men in the convoy piled up around the jeep. Gary's suggestion was that they "get out of a pile," and make a perimeter around the jeep instead, to protect the area from all possible directions of attack. Where was the Lieutenant??? "La La Land, I guess… ?" (Gary's Note: I am no leader; just using common sense. We had just been hit, for Godsakes!)

In still another instance, Gary was assigned to Firebase Oasis, 4th Infantry Division. Gary drove his reefer van (supplies up/bodies back) to the 4th Infantry, and was called before the Second Lieutenant who ran the food supply out of Firebase Oasis, out of Qui Nhon Unit. The Second Lieutenant told Gary, "You're going to start humping boxes with the other guys."

Gary's reply was, "If you're done with me, I'll go back to my company."

The answer to that was, "You're not listening. You are going to hump boxes with my guys."

Again, Gary's reply: "If you are done with me, I'll go back to my unit in Qui Nhon." The situation became physical: Gary later reported that the Lieutenant hit him in the mouth.

Gary looked at the black Sergeant witnessing this situation, who said, "I didn't see a thing."

Gary replied, "OK," and he was dismissed. He got his weapon and caught a ride back to his unit. The "fun" did not stop there. On orders from the same Lieutenant regarding several incidents, the Lieutenant would build a bunker in the back of a Deuce –and-a-Half truck, and have Gary drive it from the Oasis to Pleiku, with him in the bunker he had built, instructing Gary to stop the truck when "they hit us. I'll get em." Months after returning to his outfit, Gary saw a guy he had known in the Oasis. This guy asked Gary if he was the one who put the two grenades in front of the Lieutenant's tent.

Gary replied, "Thought about it, but it wasn't me." The powers that be shipped the Lieutenant back to the states before his own men killed him… !

Once, at Pleiku the cargo had been unloaded, and to give the men something to do, they were given bunker duty. Most of the soldiers drank, smoked dope and/or went to sleep. Gary did guard duty all night. Three or four weeks later, Gary returned to Pleiku, and discovered that the VC had slit the throats of seven guys in four or five foxholes. The situation was devolving. Soldiers were tired, assigned horrible conditions to do their jobs, and not only were they isolated, but saw no point to the whole situation in this Hell. Gary did his duty, as that was the way he could live with himself. However, he, too, was succumbing to PTSD; he just did not know it yet.

The memory of still another incident: The convoy had stopped, then moved a few feet, then stopped again. Gary moved over to the passenger seat, and everything came at them from the woods and on the ground. The back of the axle on the back of the truck was where Gary hid once he was on the ground: He could not stop his reflex action of of flipping on/off safety of his rifle lying on the ground, as he was just looking everywhere. A PC was shooting the mounted machine gun, and Gary was afraid the soldier firing was going to shoot him; he kept waving to him, trying to get his attention, yelling that he was one of them… the good guys! Just then a rocket burst through the axle, with the tire rim taking most of the impact and continued right through the truck's air lines. Although the truck was an armored Deuce-and-a-Half, in front of Gary, the gunner lay down, and just then the windshield was attacked by the VC. Bullet holes riddled his window!

A similar event occurred when the convoy traveled to Fire Base Bong Son. The group had driven for 18 hours, at 15 mph. This put the convoy on a hill between the Vietnamese and a Korean company. As always, the Americans were in the hole, with the enemy firing from above on the hills. At first, nothing happened. Men were on top of the trucks looking around. Shattering the silence, a first rocket aimed for the Korean company; the second rocket went to the Vietnamese company. The fourth and fifth rockets landed in Bong Son Fire Base. Long streams of light making an 'eeeee' sound were fired from C130 guns and a 105 Howitzer, called "Puff, the Magic Dragon."' Shots were fired from the mountain above the Fire Base. Then things settled down. This time, another Second Lieutenant shouted, "Get on the ground and make a perimeter!" They could see better on high ground, so everyone went up on top of the truck's load, too, with the gasoline and ammo, without firing a shot, a miracle. They drove to downtown Bong Son, and unloaded their materials, and began to return to Qui Nhon, going around a corner, and down a hill. The VC had already gone into the town: A priest in front of a church had been tied to a sign, and had been skinned alive.

This event occurred four days before Gary came back to the states. A thought occurred to him: "Am I a runner or a fighter?" He decided he had been a fighter… Gary discovered later that that experience was part of the Tet Offensive!

One exception of tenderness in the whole mess of deployment occurred when Gary stopped in a village of the Mountain Yards, an indigenous group of hill people rather like the American Indians back home. Gary respected them even more than the Vietnamese citizens. Having driven for 18 hours a day, Gary was alone. He stopped, and the villagers just walked around and did not touch anything that was Gary's. They were "just there." He was allowed to rest, and then he was on his way. He still regrets not giving away at least one box of food, in gratitude. For a while, a whole village had protected him.

The incompetent actions just kept coming. The Second Lieutenant whose dad was a two-star General, needed to feel "important." Gary drove his truck from Monday to Sunday, and always packed his rifle, Mighty Mouse. The Lieutenant ordered all men to turn in their rifles for inspection, as they had not been inspected in three months. Gary did turn his rifle in, but a half hour later he drew it back out. Weeks later he was lying in bed in Qui Nhon when the Base took fire. Others who were drivers and mechanics also had their own weapons, very necessary to convoy success. Gary thought about the other 195 people who had to get their weapons and ammo returned through one door. Amazing…and scary, too. (Gary's question/comment: "You are in a war zone, and I guess you're not in a war zone?!?!")

The end of deployment was drawing near. Gary was state-side oriented. He had two days left incountry, and was in the compound with no weapon. He went to the PX to buy things to take home. A three-quarter ton pickup was headed his way! Looking out back, a fire fight was on! He wondered what was going on between the Americans and the Vietcong! Two days to go and no weapon…the Lieutenant in charge yelled, "What do you think is happening?" The compound was in the middle of a firefight!! The next day it took three dump truckloads of dead bodies to remove and bury the attacking Vietcong.

No interaction occurred between Gary and local civilians, except for times when he bought drinks for children when his vehicle was stopped for deliveries. Gary's impression of situations when he left: "I will never go back!" To this day, Gary will not buy anything made in Viet Nam. He even sent back a hat he was later awarded by Bonneville Power Administration (BPA) in Redmond, Oregon because it had been made in Viet Nam.

Home from Qui Nhon in Camron Bay to Fort Lewis, Washington having been discharged while still wearing his uniform, Gary seemed to be teleported to another universe. He could not get a bus ride, as the Trailways bus drivers were on strike, so he hitchhiked to Portland, Oregon which took days. He was passed by kids zooming their car past him, shouting, "Baby killer!" while others spit on him. Finally, he was home. He went to the nearest restroom in Portland, changed out of his uniform and never looked at those clothes again.

As Gary tried to integrate into civilian society back home in the states, he was pissed off at the American public for its lack of support. Gary trusted no one; friends were few. A couple of months after Gary returned home, he happened to go to the bank where his mom worked in Coos Bay, Oregon. Chris Sutton, Gary's former classmate, worked at the same bank as Gary's mom, Margaret. She introduced them. Chris's former fiance', Terry Allen, was a 1965 graduate classmate of both Gary and Chris. He had been an only child, who felt it was his duty to serve in the military. He was killed in Viet Nam. Gary and Chris went out for lunch, began dating, and the rest is history. Close only to wife Chris, Gary was always trying to figure out the motives of others when they interacted with him. Gary respected no one with authority. PTSD was showing itself in these symptoms, but it was basically ignored by everyone, including the returning veterans.

No rehabilitation was available for returning veterans, many of whom were physically wounded and/or emotionally broken. When Gary did try to get assistance from the VA, his evaluator said at the beginning of the first session that Gary had PTSD. Fifteen minutes later, Gary didn't have it. He turned to the private medical sector and paid privately for help, made complaints back to the VA. Another person came out to evaluate Gary one more time: "Damned if I didn't have PTSD!" The VA now gave him a 50% disability rating. His question is "Why do I have to keep fighting?" His struggle for help from the VA lasted for three years, until the VA finally gave Gary a disability rating. Another on-going issue for Gary was a systemic fungus that Gary thought could have been a possible result of exposure to Agent Orange. This statement to a doctor in Roseburg, Oregon haunted Gary for years, as this fungus "could not possibly be from exposure to Agent Orange," according to every doctor he saw after that. The only name that doctors could give the disease was "jungle rot." Gary had been given a medicine that not only did not cure the condition, but it actually nearly killed him. He had been on vacation out of state, and he became so weak that his family took him to the ER. The doctors there told Gary to see his doctor at home. Nothing really changed, but Chris went online, and discovered that this medication could have the potential for liver problems. Gary stopped taking it immediately! Then, an over-the-counter spray, Tanactin, was recommended by a veteran friend. In three months, the fungus was gone! The biggest irony of all was that not ONE person ever gave him a skin test to see what the infection really was, until 46 years from the time of the original infection!

As the future presents itself, Gary's daughter-in-law presently works for a company that is doing research for a product that melts tumors in breast cancer. Would not that type of research be great for all types of toxic exposure for all veterans, past, present and future, as well as for civilians in the same situation, who have strange types of conditions? Think Flint, Michigan! For the record: Chris watched Gary self-medicate with alcohol for 16 years, until he got help. Just a few years ago, one of Gary's co-workers (one of the few people Gary truly trusted) tried to get help from both the VA and private doctors, as well, for what Gary feels was PTSD. The co-worker shot himself in the head. {Author's Note: Read the sections at the back of this book to get information regarding PTSD, as well as exposure to toxic substances. These issues relate to not only veterans, but their families as well.} Gary's oldest daughter has experienced curious bumps on her skin. Both daughters, now in their 40's, have thyroid issues, as does one granddaughter. His son has bi-polar disorder. These issues might be hereditary, and they might be the result of toxic exposure. One of Gary's oldest friends, a truck driver, has two younger children, who have been chronically ill. During Gary's deployment, one time the convoy in which he was driving traveled through Pleiku Pass. They stopped to drink out of the nearby creek. The water in it had been mixed with Agent Orange, and then sprayed into the surrounding area, with a range of 200 feet! An aside from Gary: In 1969, he visited the Roseburg, Oregon VA, and the place was overwhelmed! "It's no wonder that I did not get the correct help."

Helped by the GI Bill, Gary attended a Washington state trade school for three years. He applied for a position with the BPA and began working there. In 1976, the family moved to Redmond, Oregon as it was the place with the closest substation for Bonneville Power, and to be closer to family on Chris's side. In 1984, Gary was hit by a car and sustained a compound fracture of the right leg, and his right shoulder was shattered. He also sustained a brain contusion. The BPA actually created a job just for him, and he stayed with it for 40 years; Gary feels that this job lent itself to positivity from the administration. Some really good friends he had while working there helped Gary when he needed it the most. Again, with the support of the GI Bill, he and Chris bought a house and had three children: Cindy, Wendy and Jerry. Presently, Gary and Chris have seven grandchildren. The fourth one just graduated from high school; three more to go! At this time, Gary has lost connection with everyone in his childhood family, except his dad, who has since passed away. He has no contact with any family members who were part of his youth. He is the patriarch of a close family of his descendants. He finds joy in fishing, hunting, yard work, working on house projects, and he would still like to travel the world a bit.

Lessons Gary has learned in life are riddled with contradiction. He says he learned to hate, especially people in charge who abuse their power… what about children and grandies… do they bring love to one's heart? He also says he learned not to trust… what about his life with his lady Chris? He trusts his heart to her. He thinks she has been his Guardian Angel, helping Gary through some of his darkest days, working through literally mountains of paperwork over the years and doing battle with endless government bureaucracy and regulations that sometimes seem to change overnight. He says one should always try to see what the other person's motives are, and stay one step ahead… plan B is always a good thing to have, as is a countermeasure, always… but, what are your motives for your Self?

{Author's Note: This introspection is a scary business for our Viet Nam Veterans, as it often is for the general public. A major part of PTSD is guilt, sadness, anger and the inability to look into one's own heart for self-trust, self-love and self-forgiveness. It is imperative that we look into their eyes, to see the hearts of our veterans, all of them, and forgive them, for in forgiving them we forgive ourselves. And for all veterans, especially the Viet Nam Veterans, give yourselves grace, because we, the American civilians, did not see or experience your time in the battlefield.}

Philosophy and advice for others is quite simple for Gary. Support service personnel who are in harm's way. He supports the boys in these latest wars by buying meals for them and giving them his thanks. A little light is in Gary's heart these days, as he feels the public is finally beginning to support the Viet Nam Vets in expressing gratitude and offering financial support when it is needed, {on local levels}. To youngsters who are headed for the military: "It probably won't be what you are expecting, or have expected. When you are in harm's way, from both sides, the enemy's, as well as among your own comrades, it makes you work twice as hard to figure your next move to try and stay alive. You should not think that just because you are smarter, you are superior to the enemy. It does not take a smart man to pull the trigger."

Finally, Gary says, "I kept all of my dreams. I didn't want to be beaten, and I wasn't!"

I am proud to know Gary and his wife, Chris. They are quietly living their lives with home and family, a part of the quilt of pride in having done duty to their country and in creating a peaceful life for themselves. To Gary and all the Viet Nam Veterans it has been my pleasure to meet via phone, Internet, and in person, you were so courageous and selfless in a time of unrest and great change in our nation, doing the right thing was a matter of honor, life-changing though it was. Thank you, again, Gary and Chris, for your service to our country.

Loaded refrigeration units
wait to be driven overland and
taken to Pleiku.

Loaded on a truck bed
is the third truck in
front of Gary's the day
the convoy was hit.

Gary, holding his hat, helps unload the damaged truck back in Qui Nhom Motor Pool. Gary's Sergeant Burges stands on the fender left of him.

Regrouping at the top of Pleiku Pass: Some loads were heavier than others, so it took more time for them to climb the Pass.

Martha Ray is driven from the Oasis Airport to perform for the troops at the Oasis Fire Base out of Pleiku.

Name: Don Minney

Branch of Service: US Navy

Rank: HM3 (E-4) Hospitalman 3rd class

Time served: 3 years

Duty Assignments: Boot Camp: San Diego, California

Hospital Corp School, San Diego, California

Bremerton Naval Hospital: Bremerton, Washington, Ward B, Dirty Surgical

FMF School: Camp Del Mar, Oceanside, California

Viet Nam: 3rd Battalion (BTL), 9th Marines

Honors: National Defense

Viet Nam Service

Republic of Viet Nam Campaign

Navy Commendation with V Device

Combat Action Ribbon

When one knows the real price of war, one appreciates the preciousness of peace. Is it worth it?

Born into a military family, Don Minney joined an older brother, Elton, whom everyone called Butch, on September 8, 1948, at Fort Richardson, Alaska. The young family was complete when youngest brother, Steve, was born. Don's dad, Harold, or Hal as he was known, was stationed at Fort Richardson as a Lieutenant at the time of Don's birth, but during the next twelve years, the family moved to military installations in Georgia, Mississippi, Illinois and Washington. Don's mom, Geraldine, nicknamed Gerry, was the traditional, "dutiful home caretaker." This lifestyle, interesting and fascinating, allowed the family to see various parts of the country, its geography and the differences in people, including the black/white issue in the South. The only drawback, a big one for children, was in making friends, and then in two years, having to leave them and begin again.

The family's life was a good life, with good parents: "typically American." Don refers to the movie, *American Graffitti*, as the idyllic way Americans seemed to live. They took vacations to beaches and cross-country road trips to visit Oregon relatives. When Don's dad retired in 1960, the family moved to Eugene, where both parents had been raised,and even more contact with relatives was possible. Dad Hal went to work for the US Postal Service, and later at the University of Oregon (U of O), where Don himself worked while in college. Things settled down for Don: No more moving. He became involved in school sports: Wrestling and football and social activities. He also experienced Boy Scouts for several years. He loved it with the camping and acquisition of useful skills that were useful later in the jungles of Viet Nam. This family's life was solid, as Hal and Gerry loved each other and their sons. Pets completed the family ties. Both parents worked hard, but never pushed their children to be anything other than good human beings and to "treat others with respect."

When Don was a senior in high school, he figured college wasn't his choice for what should come next, but mill work didn't appeal or seem exciting either. When he graduated in 1966 at age 17, he went to the recruiting office and enlisted in the US Navy, with his parents' approval. With no real career in mind, he considered that being a hospital corpsman would be an "ok deal." He believed in what President Kennedy once said: "Ask not what your country can do for you, but what you can do for your country". It still makes sense to Don.

From boot camp to thirteen months on the surgical ward in Bremerton, Don had "the crazy, youthful thought that {he} needed to do {his} part". He decided to go to Viet Nam. His Marine patients warned him…

He landed in Viet Nam with the Fleet Marine Force in July of 1968. "Holy Shit!" was Don's first reaction. He was not sure he was ready for what would and did happen. He learned early on that "Dirty Surgical" on his later resume' of assignments would mean he would be dealing with amputations, open gut wounds and infections like staph. His first night they were hit with a few rockets. During his year tour, his only contact with Vietnamese civilians was seeing them as his unit traveled through villages on patrol, and viewing third world living conditions… NOT the vacation sight-seeing activities of his youth! It was quite the eye-opener for a small-town boy from Eugene, Oregon.

Don's first duty assignment in Viet Nam was the Icorp Northern Section bordering the Ho Chi Minh Trail, along the border of the De-militarized Zone (DMZ) in Ashua Valley, as a Platoon Corpsman with 2nd Platoon, Mike Company, 3rd Battalion, Ninth Marines, 3rd Marine Division. He was in charge of the health and welfare of his platoon, company, and emergency medical care when needed. During this time, he spent nearly six months in the bush. Corpsmen were rotated out to Aid Stations after six months. Within two weeks of arriving in the Republic of Viet Nam (RVN), Don was in contact with the enemy. "It's hard to relate what combat is like for the first time, other than utter chaos. Afterward, you adjust, you learn to focus on the job at hand, and shit your pants after." With these words, Don had experienced his first encounter with PTSD, although it was simply a time of surviving the next minute, without thought to what was happening to his spirit.

"Humping through the bush was, to say the least, God-Awful." Smokes were easy to come by, as was the following addiction to nicotine, a struggle even today. No one ever had enough water, food, or proper clothing, which kept falling off, or adequate gear which had been salvaged from World War II or Korea (See Gary Hartt's story.} Neither was there safety from the real day-to-day fear of the AK 47s being fired, a unique sound that meant trouble was coming. Then, Don knew it was "game time." Having been engaged with the enemy on several occasions, he knew they believed in their cause as we believed in ours. Though he had respect and admiration for them, he would not have hesitated to protect his Marines and himself; after all, the NVA was trying to kill him. He was never happier than when he was rotated out of his platoon assignment to Alpha Command. This was the leadership of the battalion, still in the bush, but not packing 70 pounds of gear every day, like the "squids" who carried rifles. He still feels guilt at leaving his "boys of 2nd platoon, a tight group," not that he had a choice.

In December of 1968, Don was rotated to the Forward Battalion Aid Station at Vandergrift Combat Base located about five miles from the DMZ. Duty there was a piece of cake compared to the bush: Food, water and decent shelter. Occasionally, they took freight-train-sounding rocket fire, sometimes with serious results; other times, it was just scary. Duties for Don included daily sick call and treating everything from broken jaws and fevers to shrapnel wounds. Don's last three weeks were spent at the 3rd Med BTL in Quang Tri. On December 23, a small bunker was hit. A jeep with doctors and Don moved to the affected area. The 9th Marines stationed there were part of the troop withdrawal and were headed home. Don's duties at 3rd Med involved the surgery ward. Now, he worked on both Marines and civilian casualties… his first glimpse of kids "blown to shit," and even contact with "North Vietnamese Army (NVA) dudes, also shot up." During the attack, Don recalled, "Mud, blood and the smell…one Marine held his buddy's brains in a towel. We lost Wheeler, Pitts, and Rick… " By this time, it was evident to Don that the war was pointless. "There was this moment when I offered a cigarette to this POW, and when he smiled and took it, I had the thought that if the two of us could sit down and share a smoke, what the hell are we fighting for? Politics and power… insane."

The day before Don was to catch the flight out, the 3rd Med was hit by rockets. One hit the ward 50 feet away. Don sooooo wanted to be home. He made the plane in Da Nang, and held his breath until the plane had enough air clearance, then the Cheers!!! He flew to Okinawa to process for the States; by this time, Don was mentally through with "the military machine." His attitude was not the best, but he kept his mouth shut; he wanted to go home. "Talk about being treated as used-up gear---that's what getting discharged in Long Beach felt like, but then, {Don's attitude} wasn't the best."

Most of the men arrived home in hopes of "blending in" once again to the American-at-home landscape. At that time, Eugene wasn't very accepting of the military. It was a difficult time in adjusting; reality was like jet lag, only far more severe: not only from one country to another, but from one lifestyle to another. It had not been more than a few weeks since people were trying to kill the surviving soldiers. They did the best they could to adjust. Don felt betrayed by his country and community… "hard to get over that one." Don, like many of his fellow soldiers, had PTSD and simply seemed to "suck it up," and move on with his life. {Author's Note: This telling of Don's story is one of the first times he has had the opportunity to tell his tale of service to someone who listened. I am honored.}

At home in Eugene, Don attended Lane Community College, and the University of Oregon (U of O).He spent five years as a student, worked and got married. Then, as happens in marriages, when one is recently out of the military, with no recuperative support, he divorced his first wife and quit school. Then, he began working for the Lane County Health Department, in environmental science, thanks to a special teacher's influence. There, he met then married his lovely wife, Pat in 1978. Pat, herself, had gone to graduate school at U of O. Don and Pat were now ready to truly begin their lives. They decided to move to a drier climate, and settled in Bend, Oregon. In those beginning days, Bend was "poverty with a view." Don did various jobs as a firefighter, janitor, house builder and then was handed a counseling job with a residential boys' ranch where he developed a wilderness program. It was a great job, but with poverty wages, so he moved on to a position with the Deschutes County Juvenile Department as a detention worker. It was waaaay different than residential work. He was lucky to have a progressive director, whose philosophy was a restorative approach, rather than a retribution/punitive approach to rehabilitation. In 1982, Don and Pat were blessed with a son, Sam, which was "a hoot." Fatherhood allowed Don to coach his son's soccer team for several years, and allowed involvement again with Boy Scouts. After 19+ years with the County, Don retired as Program Manager of the detention facility.

Don loves his Central Oregon country. It's close to mountains where he can spend his time backpacking or be on rivers and lakes or biking. Don's goals since retirement are to be a good grandparent, have more adventures and "just hang… out doing projects {I} never had time to do when {I} was working."

Don's parting philosophy: "In short, life has been very good to me. My experience in Viet Nam gave me that. I got to come home and walked out of the jungles in one piece. The Marines pushed me beyond what I thought I could do. I'll forever appreciate that---it makes life easier to take on. Compassion works, as does maintaining an optimistic outlook, because I know it could be worse."

Finally, Don says that people need to be involved with America's political system… "just get out and vote with intelligence, because we need to take responsibility for who gets elected." {Author's Note:… Very timely in the 2016 elections when this book was being written… } Don's case in point: "I blame those that voted for Bush for my son's three deployments in Iraq. My personal feeling is if you don't vote, then get out of my country. Too many have died for that right."

It has been my privilege getting to know Don and his wife, Pat. His American lifestyle is peaceful and happy, but Don knows the terrible price too many of our soldiers, sailors and pilots pay for that peace and happiness. Though he was on the front lines of battle in Viet Nam, he was also a caregiver, one of too few able to help those who were wounded and some, who later died as a result of those wounds. In enjoying his retirement, Don also has a life of paying forward with his military and lifetime volunteer work. He and his family deserve this reward. Thank you so much for your service to our country, Don and Pat.

1. Don, and his comrades, move through the thick Vietnamese terrain. Don faces the camera, with rifle in hand. He does not want to stand out. Platoon leaders, radiomen and corpsmen were prime targets.

2. Don, in the rear, with comrades, help a Vietnamese youth.

3. Don (R) poses with "some of my guys."

Name: Samuel Morris

Branch of Service: US Marine Corps

Rank: Colonel, Retired

Time served: 28 years, combined active duty and reserve duty

Honors: Air Medal 4th Award

Viet Nam Service Medal

Viet Nam Campaign Medal

Navy Unit Citation

National Defense Service Medal

Armed Forces Reserve

Cold War

Rifle and Pistol Expert

Naval Aviator wings

Army Aviator wings

Honorable Discharge

Philosophy of a gentle, soft-spoken man with a list of phenomenal accomplishments: "Life has always been a continual learning experience, and it goes on for me to this day." When someone reviews his life of nearly 70 years and recounts the deeds of a life of opportunities taken and challenges conquered, it is with humble pleasure I share Samuel's {Sam's} contribution to society in service to his country.

{Author's Note: With the exception of the name of his wife, Bonnie, Sam has chosen to keep the names of relatives, comrades and friends confidential.}

Samuel Morris made his appearance, the middle of three sons, on January 22, 1947, in Auburn, New York. His dad worked for the US Army as an ammunition inspector. The job required the family to move every two to five years to Army depots in the US and overseas: Auburn, New York for years one and two, Tooele, Utah for five years, then to Yokohama, Japan, Hermiston, Oregon, Pueblo, Colorado and finally, back to Tooele. While moving brought opportunities of learning for the family's children, the continuity of Cub Scouts, Boy Scouts and Explorer Scouting through the years brought stability with the philosophies of focus on God and country, in addition to religion and faith. These hallmarks, along with a cohesive family life, provided Sam with "a strong moral compass and patriotism." His parents were married until they died. Sam graduated from high school in the Tooele Class of 1965. He went to college at Utah State University to earn his Bachelor of Science degree in the College of Engineering.

Sam had a draft deferment through college, but even with a teaching degree, he was not draft exempt, now that Viet Nam was "spooling up." Sam wanted a choice about which branch of service he would enter, so in 1967, he signed up for the Platoon Leaders Class Aviation (PLC-A) United States Marine Corp, while still attending college. He attended Officer Candidate School (OCS) during the summers between his sophomore and junior years of college. As a Corporal, Sam traveled to Quantico, Virginia for this program. Upon college graduation in 1969, Sam was awarded the commission of Second Lieutenant in the United States Marine Corp. That fall, he had a class date to attend Naval flight training in Pensacola, Florida. After flight testing, he was given the option to do inter-service training in the US Army as a helicopter pilot. Helicopters were more fascinating than jets to Sam, so for personal reasons, he chose to do the helicopter training with the Army first, graduating in that skill in Fort Rucker, Alabama. While the Army provided only the tactical instrument course, Naval aviators needed to be fully qualified in instrument flying, so he completed that course upon his return to the Marines.

As busy as Sam was, he managed a holiday in the midst of all this learning. While training at Fort Rucker, he and his college sweetheart, Bonnie, became husband and wife. To avoid all the racial legalities at the time in Alabama, they married in Washington, D.C., where the base chaplain made all the arrangements. Sam flew in on a Friday, Bonnie flew from Denver, his parents flew from Utah, a brother flew from Dover, Delaware where he was serving in the US Air Force, and the bridesmaid flew from Wisconsin. The marriage ceremony occurred on Saturday, April 18, 1970. Everyone returned to their homes on Sunday. Sam's and Bonnie's life together, with hardly a wrinkle in daily life, were back in Fort Rucker on Monday, where Sam continued flight training. Bonnie stayed with Sam while he finished the course.

After Army flight school, Sam spent six months with the tactical CH-46 Helicopter Squadron at New River, North Carolina. On September 22, 1970, he was designated a Naval Aviator and received his golden US Navy Wings. Now he had achieved wings in both the US Army and the US Navy, quite the accomplishments for anyone, but Sam had only begun. While he had wonderful skills, they were about to be put to the test of reality…

At this time, he received orders to go to Viet Nam! His first stop on the journey was at Hickam Air Force Base, in Honolulu, Hawaii for refueling. While there, he met some of his graduating buddies from Fort Rucker who were escorting coffins of fallen classmates! This was Sam's wake-up call. His job "involved risky business with no guarantee of returning." His graduating buddies from Fort Rucker did not receive such a break; they had a direct flight to Viet Nam! Sam's next stop was Okinawa, Japan. Sam and his men were outfitted in tactical clothing, with the usual condition of bulk inventories everywhere: "Too big, too small, and out of stock." The men chose what would somehow fit, and flew to the next and final stop on the American Airlines charter: Da Nang, Viet Nam. Sam's destination was Marble Mountain Marine Corps Air Facility near Da Nang. Sam recalls that they were located near the beach south of the US Army Facility near China Beach, the site of a later TV series with the same name. The show starred actress Dana Delany and featured intrigues about the 95th Evacuation Hospital at the China Beach location. Little did Sam know that he would "star" in the real-life drama of the 95th Evacuation Hospital. He would pull medical evacuation duty (medevac), and his crew's patients would be landed at the 95th Evac Landing Zone (LZ). (Call sign: "Single Parent")

Sam's support teams ran like well-oiled machines. He was a pilot attached to the Marine Medium Helicopter Squadron 263 (HMM-263). "Any helicopter while on other missions could support and fly medevac. While in the field, however, Marble Mountain Marine Corps Air Facility had a standing mission to provide medevac on a 24-hour basis." Sam's squadron's medevac flight composition included two CH-46 helicopters and two AH-1 Huey Cobra gun ship helicopters to provide fire support and cover. While every CH-46 had two 50-caliber machine guns and gunners with the pilot, co-pilot and crew chief, plus medical staff aboard, the Cobras, with two pilots each, were armed to the hilt with rockets and machine guns. All pilots stood by in the medevac bunker ready for any field requests. The other crew members attended the aircraft on the ready pad. "When a radio call fragmentation order came in, the four 4 aircraft commanders would write down all the location and mission data, while the four co-pilots would run to the aircraft and start engines and get the rotors turning. All four aircraft and medical staff would be airborne in a matter of 90 seconds. By the use of radials and distance measuring equipment (DME) off the Da Nang variable omni range tactical-navigation beacon VORTAC, these flying ambulances could fly directly to the grid coordinates given them by the ground troops requesting the call. With a little over two hours of fuel on board, they could reach anywhere in the tactical area of operation, recover the injured, and fly them to China Beach 95th Evac.

During the next three months, Sam flew nearly 100 missions, one a day. The patients varied in their emergency conditions only in the locations where the rescue crews were needed, which changed from day to day. On one mission, they picked up a Marine who had stepped on a land mine. On another somber mission, though it was more routine in that it was not in a hot (not secure: Expect enemy fire on approach or departure) LZ, they arrived at China Beach, picked up six burn victims and flew them to the USS Sanctuary Hospital Ship in Da Nang Harbor. "All the injured lay on litters, heavily bandaged. They did not move, for the entire flight."

Sam's crews provided total support for the 1st Marine Division. Missions included "troop insert and extract to and from the field, resupply of necessities like food, ammo and water to fire support bases and outpost elements in the field, medical evacuation, prisoner transport, parachute drops, search and rescue, VIP transport, training of Republic of Viet Nam troops and reconnaissance, to name a few."

On two occasions, Sam's team received fragmentation orders to support the Republic of Korea (ROC) Marines, our US allies, near Hoi An. These were people "not to cross." Their reputation preceded them in that they were "vicious with prisoners and victorious in battle." Once, they picked up a Vietcong (VC) prisoner that the ROC Marines had captured. His arms were "tied to a pole like a crucifix, to immobilize him." Another time, the team flew to the ROC Marine location but shut down to await orders. It was a slow day, so the crew received permission to use the ROC pistol range. They thought it would be fun to try some of the flare pistol ammo they had been issued. Alas, some of the rounds got stuck in the wooden target frames, and the resulting fire burned down the entire range! Humor found its way into the situation, unlike the grave nature of most missions, everything destroyed was expendable.

The USA had instituted "rules of engagement," no-fire zones, around parts of Marble Mountain Facility. Totally political in nature, these rules were to protect the local farmers, regardless of whether or not they were VC at night. This situation was a daily frustration for Sam's missions: "The no-fire zone included the river that flowed south of us. By day we would fly over the river to... destinations only to see boats coming upstream loaded with rockets near the Cau Hoa Xuan Bridge. We could not engage them, and they knew it." One night, around 1:00 AM, "in came the rockets, like scud missiles, just lobbed into our base with no guidance systems." Whatever was hit was "potluck." Helicopters were housed in revetments/bunkers, while the crews lived in Quonset hut bunkers with sandbags as well. Ironically the only personal weapon issued to the pilots was a snub-nose .38 Smith and Wesson revolver! What a joke!! Sam asks: "Can you believe we were armed with a Saturday Night Special???" Dark humor from the pilots was the saying, "if you were ever in a position to have to use the .38 to defend yourself, you were already in a situation that was terminal, and you were already out-gunned, so use the gun on yourself!"

Every time he flew a mission, Sam was comfortable with the reality that he could be shot down. At age 22, he was rather fearless, and "just took each day as another adventure." He feels there was some Divine intervention in his case. His parents had two sons in Viet Nam at the same time, and his mother prayed daily for their safety. Sam's older brother was stationed at Phu Cat Air Force Base, and by law one of them did not have to be there. {Author's Note: The movie, *Saving Private Ryan,* depicts this situation during World War II. In a real situation during that war, five brothers from the same family, the Sullivans, were killed in action during World War II. After that, a law was passed that exempted siblings from serving together in battle situations.} Sam and his brother discussed the situation and agreed that they would stand by their "commitments to our respective services and to our country." Sam thinks that in all likelihood, there was not a master plan to sort out brothers serving at the same time in differing branches of the military.

Sam was one of the last three CH-46 pilots to be sent to HMM-263. That squadron was rotated out before his full year was completed. He stayed with the Western Pacific Fleet (WESPAC) to complete his tour of duty. He was then assigned to HMM-165 based out of Futenma, Okinawa Marine Corps Air Base. HMM-165 (Code name: The White Knights) was deployed on board the USS Tripoli Landing Pad Helicopter (LPH-10), a helicopter aircraft carrier and troop transport. A battalion landing team was on board, with a composite squadron of CH-46s and CH-53s, the Sea Stallion, heavy lift. Various missions took them in and out of Viet Nam waters. One mission was to search for Russian warships in the Straits of Malacca. Other times they flew in the South China Sea. During all the times he flew overseas, Sam says he "may have been shot at. Fortunately, I was missed!" On these search missions, they had full fuel loads plus two 300-gallon fuel cells inside each aircraft, with a fuel transfer system that gave them about four hours of search time. One mission was finished before it really started. Just after taking off and leaving the flight deck of the USS Tripoli, Sam's co-pilot was flying when they sustained an engine actuator failure, effectively rendering one engine useless. Sam took over the controls, immediately going to emergency throttle on the remaining engine, and started to dump fuel to lighten the load. Besides the normal crew of three: Pilot, co-pilot, and crew chief, spotters were on board. Sam declared the emergency to Pri-Fly, the control tower on the ship, and asked for a clear deck. Spot 7 could not be cleared of a CH-53 in time, so Sam was directed to take spot 4, and do a roll on landing. He made a no hover spot landing to the deck with no incident!   Upon his return to the states, Sam did not experience the negativity so many of his comrades –in-arms experienced, probably because he was not finished with the military. He stayed in the service, gradually integrating to civilian life over time. Sam and his wife, Bonnie, now married more than 46 years, always lived off base, as base housing was not always available. Following his Viet Nam tour, Sam served with the 1st Marine Division at Camp Pendleton as a forward air controller, and later, because of an officer shortage, served as the Battalion S-3 Operations Officer for 3rd Battalion, 1st Marines, and 1st Battalion, 7th Marines, a position not usually given to aviators. After a year with the 1st Marine Division, Sam returned to the 3rd Marine Aircraft Wing at Tustin Helicopter Base, and later, El Toro MCAS in California. While he was in the Reserves, Sam pursued a commercial flying career while maintaining his military flight status. Sam holds a Certified Flight Instructor Instrument (CFII) license in both airplanes and helicopters, and taught for a few years. He flew for Air Spur, a commuter operation out of LAX, and did charter flights, as well, out of Orange County Airport, California. Sam also worked in engineering and management at McDonald Douglas/Boeing for 18 years.

Samuel Morris is a man of many talents and incredible life experiences. Cautioning others with his own brand of "the right stuff," he is a firm believer that "any job worth doing is a job worth doing well." Responsibility for one's own actions is the best policy. Life is a series of choices; if bad choices are made, a price will be paid. To youngsters, especially: "Stay within the law, or bad choices will follow a person the rest of his or her life. Commitment to doing the right thing is important; do not shift blame or look for excuses for things wrongly done." Sam says, finally, "I have been responsible for many lives on many occasions, which I have been glad to have been trusted with that honor."

Sam's career and contributions to the American people, as well as to those citizens of other countries, can leave the reader with a dizzying amazement and gratitude for those gifts. I am honored to tell his story. Thank you, Sam, and to Bonnie as well, for your continued service to our country.

Sam discovered this photo when he searched Google. It refers to a comparison of his own family's situation during the Viet Nam War.

Troop Insert near Hoi An, Viet Nam: One mission took Sam to the De-Militarized Sone of North Viet Nam. He landed at the Citadel in Hue and at Phu Bi.

China Beach LZ – US Army
Medical Facility and USO,
near Da Nang

This photo, an Official USMC photograph, was
taken at the end of Sam's last flight in Viet Nam.

Name: Mark Moseley

Branch of Service: US Navy

Rank: OS-2, (E-5)

Time served: 4 years (Specialty: ASAC (Anti-Submarine Air Controller)

2 WESTPACS: 1974, 1975

1 tour to Alaska: 1976

Honors: Armed Forces Expeditionary (with cluster)

Navy Expeditionary Medal

National Defense

Navy Unit Commendation

Navy Meritorious Unit

Duties: ASROC (roving patrol in port guarded missile system)

Master at Arms (Sheriff)

Corrected Top Secret, Secret Books

Shift Leader Underway (watch)

ASAC Operations, as they had a 'helo' (helicopter) on board

Mark's story reads like a romantic old war-time black and white movie: Boy joins the Navy, meets girl who is a WAVE, they fall in love, he asks her to marry him, war must be fought/enemy must be overcome; homecoming reunites the sweethearts, and they go to school/work, raise a family and enjoy grandchildren in their golden years. Not everything was birds twittering, rainbows shining with violins in the background… this was the Viet Nam War, a time when civilian Americans themselves were conflicted about world politics .

Mark Moseley was the oldest of four children born to Edward S. Moseley (now aged 85) and Ramona F. Moseley (deceased). He arrived in Perry, Iowa, on May 11, 1952. He was joined by another brother, Jeffery (deceased), a sister, Siri (Gomes), and finally, a second brother, Edward III. When Mark was six years old, the young family moved to Hurst, Texas where Mark played baseball from then until he was 19. Dad was an engineer at General Dynamics at Carswell Air Force Base in Fort Worth, and

Mom worked as a manager for a doctor. The family moved often, six times, but the new homes were always in Hurst.

Vacations for Mark occurred after baseball season each summer, from the time Mark was 11 years old to the age of 19. Over the 4th of July, Mark would get to ride a train from Fort Worth to Des Moines, Iowa, to his grandpa's dairy farm. There, he worked until late August, when school was ready to start. Twice, Mark remembers, his dad took him, his brother, Jeff, and a cousin, Stan, to San Diego, to see his designs for the F-111 aircraft that was built there. He graduated from Lawrence D. Bell High School in 1970.

Being the good baseball player that he was, Mark tried out with 1500 other baseball players for a scholarship, received a partial scholarship offer, but turned it down and went to Texas Tech University in Lubbock , Texas. He stayed until his junior year, then left his junior year with his roommate, John Spencer, for some young men's adventures. They purchased a VW bus and drove to Alaska intending to go to Juneau to work on the pipeline. Then the government stepped in with its own agenda: President Nixon vetoed the federal appropriations for the pipeline! In May of 1973, the young men actually did drive to Juneau where they lived in the VW while Mark worked as a surveyor at the Juneau airport. He called home to let the family know how they were doing, and learned ominous news.The draft board was looking for Mark! His student deferment had been dropped! Mark's dad and uncle had been in the Navy, so Mark joined the Navy in Juneau. He left John the VW, and went to Anchorage. He was then sent to San Diego, California for boot camp, which he successfully completed in June 1973. He became a seaman because of his college credits. His A School assignment was in Great Lakes, Illinois to train as a radarman. This was in late August 1973. After his first week, he happened to look outside of his dorm, and saw some WAVES (Women Appointed for Voluntary Emergency Service), the women's branch of the Navy, who were disembarking from a bus. In this group of young women was his future wife, Patricia S. Kronfield.

Every day they had quarters at 8:00 AM. Mark noticed Patricia standing at attention while roll call was checked. Introductions were made, and this led to a Friday pizza, and soon after that, Mark asked her to marry him before he went on his first WES/PAC. He was assigned to the USS Harold E. Holt DE-1074. Mark and Patricia married on December 22, 1973, and they have been happily married ever since.

In January 1974, Mark flew to the Philippines (Clark Air Force Base), then transported to Subic Bay. Mark's ship, the USS HE Holt was completing an Indian Ocean cruise, So for several weeks Mark attended quarters and ate meals, but was restricted to the barracks.

Finally, the Holt came into port, reloaded with supplies, fuel and new recruits. Mark was taken on board and assigned a rack to sleep. Then he was taken to the Combat Information Center (CIC). It contained four to six radar repeaters, scopes that looked at air targets and surface search targets. Mark was initially assigned to a watch group which did not have enough staffing, so they worked port/starboard watches, or worked in CIC, or slept. Mark was given chart updating. They stayed in port for a little more than two weeks, then, they put to sea toward Hong Kong. It was at this time that Mark experienced his first ever typhoon!!

Mark's watch was from 12:00 AM to 6:00 AM, then again in the afternoon 12:00 PM to 4:00 PM. During the midnight watch they practiced their communication jobs between ships. They had cruising orders and various OIT training, so they would be ready if needed. Ports attained included Hong Kong, Subic Bay, Kai Shung (Taipan), and Keelung (Taipai). They returned to Pearl Harbor in late June.

A quick R&R for Mark and Patricia saw them at the Royal Hawaiian Hotel. Life was completely different than present day.They communicated with letters."Honestly," says Mark, "you could be devastated by not receiving mail." Mark's ship returned to the Philippines in early 1975. The war had officially ended. At the end of March to early April, the first call to action was to steam to Viet Nam for the evacuation of Saigon. "We formed a line of ships providing safety, food, water, and other necessities. The Vietnamese refugees "clung to ships, canoes, sampans…." A line of ships formed from there to settlement camps that had been constructed in Subic Bay, Guam, Wake Island, and other places in the area to accommodate the thousands seeking safety. Mark's ship dropped people off throughout these areas.

In early May, they received a call to head to Cambodia, to rescue the SS Mayaquez, a container ship, and its crew. Anchored off Koh Tang Island, the ship's Captain and crew had been kidnapped and taken by the Khmer Rouge. Mark's ship had already arrived at the Mayaquez, and the Holt actually towed the Mayaquez; the Holt's fantail connected to the Mayaquez' bow. The Marines on the ships, the USS HE Holt and the USS Wilson, were in the area looking for the crew of the Mayaquez, as well as bad guys. The USS HE Holt went alongside of the Mayquez and boarded her. The evening before they boarded, 41 Marines had been killed. Three of them were MIA . Mark personally stayed in CIC for 32 hours before he was able to get any sleep. As with everything else, they could only tell time by what they ate in the mess hall. On the way to the island, their 5" 54 cannon lost a 12-volt power supply. Mark's friend, Jack Quitas and another FT assisted in cobbling a 12-volt power supply together from less essential equipment. Mark was assigned a sector of the ocean on the surface search radar, while controlling a P-3 and an F.111. If a boat was detected, a P-3 was to fly over the target and identify it; if it was an F.111, the target was to be eliminated. This mission was successful, but they lost a great number of Marines that day. It was not until much later that Mark learned that the three Marines had been left on the island of Koh Tang. The first time Mark heard about the three MIA's was when the Traveling Viet Nam Wall came to Redmond, Oregon in 2011.

The Holt returned to Subic Bay a week later. On July 7th, the ship cruised into the Indian Ocean. It stopped at Penang, Malaysia. A Shellback Ceremony was celebrated, then the Holt made a north to south crossing of the Equator. The crew landed at Seychelles Island, then on to Mombasa, Kenya. From there, they traveled the coast of Saudi Arabia, and Karachi, Pakistan, then returned to Singapore and back to Subic Bay. Other destinations included Hong Kong, China, Yokosuka, Japan, going back to Subic Bay, then returning to Pearl Harbor in early December. Mid-1976 saw the USS Holt making a three-month tour of Alaska to multiple ports. The situation was fairly peaceful.

Mark left the Navy in mid-1977. Mark and Patricia had become parents to Nathan, who was born in 1976. In 1980, they became parents again, when baby Matthew was born, completing the little family. Mark was sent to Treasure Island, California to be discharged. He was not treated particularly well, even with the Viet Nam War now two years in the past. Patricia went to see Mark's parents in Los Angeles, and Mark went to work for a small pharmaceutical company which made pre-digested liquid protein. Mark doubled the company's output. In 1977, Mark started college again. To finance his education, he became a Teamster and drove a forklift. Later, he moved into management in the facility's engineering department. Completing an Associate's Degree, then a Bachelor's Degree by 1991, Mark was relocated to many plants, for his expertise. After 30 years, Mark retired.

Values for Mark's life:

Mark learned his work ethic on his grandpa's dairy farm. "Cows had to be fed and milked every day 365!" His grandfather worked tirelessly, and Mark cannot remember {Grandpa} ever complaining.

For his Naval service, he says, "It was an honor to serve my country." It was in doing his sworn duty that Mark learned teamwork.

"Every young person should in some way serve their country." No, the military is not for everyone, but young people could "join the Peace Corps," states Mark.

Politically, Mark is a member of the Tea Party, and went to his first meeting in Nashville in 2009.

Mark and Patricia's oldest son, Nathan, is an Intel electrical engineer, with two daughters, ages 10 and 8. Their youngest son, Matthew, is a career Air Force soldier, and his wife, Megan, is retired from the Air Force. They have two sons, ages 16 (adopted) and 8, as of this writing. Mark and Patricia enjoy their four grandkids, and their home, where they work in their annual garden, and can and store its produce. They are happy.

While their lives have had some bumps along the way, these two people, Mark and Patricia, have finished what, for many people, is truly a fairy tale existence. The dragons were slain, they were blessed with children and grandchildren, had satisfactory work to do, and are now reaping the fruits of their labor, literally, and in so many ways of the heart. They could be the neighbor up the street, or the one next door. I would be honored to call them friends. They are part of America's heart, and I thank them both for their service to our country.

Page one of an article
with Mark in photo

'DONT TREAD ON ME' ...back on jackstaffs

With eight ships in its fleet—four men-o'-war and four escort vessels—the original American Navy was ready to do battle in December 1775. The infant Continental fleet was up against the most powerful sea force of the day—the British Royal Navy, 270 warships strong.

"The first beginning of our Navy," John Paul Jones wrote later, "was, as navies rank, so singularly small, that I am of the opinion it has no precedence in history." Nor did the bizarre rattlesnake emblem that flew from the masts of some of these first ships have any precedent in history. The 13 alternating horizontal red and white stripes, the serpent, and the words, "Dont Tread On Me," of the rattlesnake flag, broadcast a clear and unmistakable warning. The flag was adopted as the Continental Navy Jack.

It hasn't been seen aboard a U. S. Navy ship for nearly 200 years. That is, until now. Today, Navy ships around the world are displaying the "Dont Tread On Me" Navy Jack in place of the Union Jack with its 50 stars on a blue field.

The Continental Navy Jack was reinstated for the 200th birthday of the Navy on 13 Oct 1975, and it will continue to be flown through December 1976 as part of the Navy's Bicentennial celebration.

The idea for resurrecting the Navy Jack originated with a Chicago attorney, Frederic O. Floberg, in January of 1975 when he tried out the idea on his two sons, both U. S. Navy officers.

With their enthusiastic response, Floberg mailed his

20

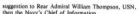

Continuation of article

suggestion to Rear Admiral William Thompson, USN, then the Navy's Chief of Information.

The idea gained acceptance in the Navy's Office of Information, the Navy Bicentennial Coordination Office in Washington and drew the support of Secretary of the Navy J. William Middendorf II, the Department of Defense and other governmental agencies.

Finally, in August, the call went out from the Navy to flag manufacturers in the United States. In order to be effective, the Navy said, the flags had to be sewn, shipped, and on board all U. S. Navy ships in time to be displayed on 13 October, the date the second Continental Congress established the Navy in 1775. A flag company in Virginia Beach, Va., set to work on 20 August to meet the agreed-upon deadline.

In a concession to modern technology, the Navy substituted the more durable nylon for cotton in its anniversary version of the flag. But Navy "salts" decided to retain the unapostrophized "dont" of the original slogan.

The creator of the rattlesnake flag is lost to history, but Benjamin Franklin offered an explanation of its significance.

Franklin wrote that "the rattlesnake is found only in North America; among the ancients, serpents were considered to possess wisdom and vigilance (because snakes have no eyelids to close).

"The rattlesnake does not attack without first giving warning, and the number of rattles increases with age." Hence, the symbol was especially appropriate for the expected growth of the United States.

Snakes on the historical Navy Jacks had 13 rattles, apparently symbolic of the 13 rebellious colonies.

Dont tread on me!

"Perhaps," says one of the flagmakers, "this word to the wise should not be taken lightly—even more so today."

—JOC Joe Sarver

Left: OS3 Mark Moseley (right) and STG1 Thomas Fraser raise a "Don't Tread on Me" flag aboard the frigate USS Harold E. Holt (PF 1074) at Subic Bay, R. P. Below: A seamstress puts the finishing touches on a copy of a Continental Navy Jack, recently revived by the Navy for use in its Bicentennial celebration. Photos by PH1 John R. Sheppard and JOC Joe Sarver.

Marines and their gear are prepared for
the Holt/Mayaquez Affair. May 15, 1975.

AP photos
Freed: Mayaguez towed by U.S.S. Holt

Name: Tom Peterson

Branch of Service: US Navy

Rank: E4 (For each future test, scores were raised to eliminate over-manning in declining need)

Time Served: Three years, eleven months

Honors: Silver Campaign Star (4 separate campaigns)

Letters home: I was privileged to read the letters Tom wrote home to his family during his time in the Navy. His mom kept them all. He wrote 164 letters just to his immediate family, many more to extended family and friends. He was gone 148 weeks. In his letters, he was even counting the days until he could return home! I will let the reader do the math… At the end of Tom's story are a few phrases from some of the letters postmarked from March 1969, through January 1973. Notice that while in combat theaters, postage was free for military personnel, and regular postage was a mere $.06, then it went up to $.08! Tom didn't know it at the time, but he was writing a history of his life, and a piece of the world's history, as well.

Like many others born in the Pacific Northwest in mid-century America, Tom Peterson was born into a family with a rich logging and lumber producing heritage. He arrived on January 26, 1948, in Newport, Washington, the first of four children born to Howard Evan Peterson and Barbara L. (Kerns) Peterson. Brother Dan arrived next, then a sister, Susan, five years later, and then, 18 years later, baby Valerie arrived. Tom's dad, Uncle Norman, and their dad worked together in the woods, as well as nearby logging companies. In 1955, a lumber mill was built on Tom's Grandpa Peterson's farm, and Howard and Norman joined him in a partnership for the business. After five years, they moved the mill to a farmer neighbor's, leasing his land, which was located on Highway 57, 12 miles north of Priest River, Idaho. At that time, Tom's family moved from the town of Priest River, where they had lived for 10 years (from 1950 to 1960) to a mobile home at the mill's location. Five years later, in 1965, the mill sold, and Tom's family once again returned to Grandpa Peterson's farm, picking up the tried and true business of logging. Tom grew up around big equipment, logs, lumber and the men who "did it all." Tom's family ethic was hard work, and Tom began his own training at age 14, working for neighbors and relatives who needed extra hands: Haying, farm chores, hod carrying, building fireplaces, working in the saw mill and a myriad other jobs, most for which he was paid! It was fun and games for him: He enjoyed the experiences, learning about how things were built or produced. While the family lived on the leased parcel until Tom was 12, besides school, there were always chores to do. When the Petersons moved to a parcel of land acquired from his granddad and grandma, it was 12 miles out of town, so there was no time or transportation for sports.The family took only one memorable vacation in 1963, to Disneyland. It was combined with a trip to Tom's dad's sister's home in Newhall, California, about 50 miles north of Disneyland. While it was a "get away" trip for once in a lifetime, many other memories were celebrated at home with the several members of Tom's family, in the form of gatherings during the holidays with dinners and personal occasions. His parents were together for a good marriage that lasted for 62 years before his father died in 2009. Tom's Uncle Norman still lives, and on April 1, 2016, will be 89. Both men were World War II US Navy Veterans themselves, so they were probably highly influential in Tom's decision to later enlist in the US Navy. Granddad Kerns died in April 1967, and then Granddad Peterson died in September 1967. Both of these men had served in the US Army during World War I. Grandma Kerns passed away in 1977, and Grandma Peterson lived to age 104, passing in 2010! Sturdy stock and hard work gave Tom and his own descendants a rich legacy!!

"School wasn't fun, just a mandate," were Tom's words about public school. He was an average "C" student, graduating in May of 1966. When fall came, he began a course at an electronic trade school at North Idaho Junior College, which was, "a lot more fun than high school!," and at which he did decent work… all those years of "learning how things work" at home paid off. Then, Tom turned 20 in the fourth quarter of trade school and discovered… DRINKING! It changed his life, as he experienced what most of his friends had discovered in high school. It was easy for him to "drink to excess," and this behavior continued, during and after his naval experience. While this practice was not in and of itself a condition of PTSD, it may have contributed to the condition as a result.

Tom completed the trade school course in May 1968. He joined the US Navy in September of the same year, on a 120-delay program, going active on March 3, 1969. His trade school training gave him "designated striker" status in boot camp, with pay, and guided him into that field during regular duty. This was perfect, as it was the field he had chosen in high school for his life's career.

Tom's story was "calm participation." He was off the coast many times and earned four campaign stars for participation. He was on ground for eight hours, then flew out to a carrier and caught his ship that night during underway replenishments (unrep). Decommissioning three ships at NAS, Alameda, California, took another eight months of Tom's time. (Tom has discovered a cancerous tumor on his left kidney. He has wondered if it came as a result of toxic exposure, using large quantities of a chemical to clean electric equipment while in this decommissioning period.) After his next ship arrived back in the US, his crew did a nine-month overhaul, then, returned to Viet Nam working the coast. During the course of nearly four years, Tom crossed the Pacific eight times, two by air, and six by ship. Though they were not given "much exposure to bullets flying his way," Tom's men were a great source of support for the air coverage of the ground troops. It was service without much worry about attack, as there was so much power to defend and retaliate. During the course of this nearly four-year duty, Tom missed Christmas at home only one time…40 days before he was finished with his service!

Though Tom's ship never took fire, often it was within reach of land. His first ship went to Da Nang as a first stop in Viet Nam. They anchored away from any pier, dropping food to landing craft. As they approached the harbor, the Captain announced the grouping of two gunboats, to the starboard side. They were shooting at a northern hilltop, and had seen smoke up there. U.S. troops had taken out a "nest" of Vietcong, and the ship's men were to guard the harbor. As they anchored, Tom was called to a work party and assigned to the ship's bow, with a case of concussion grenades and a rifle. He was told to drop a grenade, at random times, to discourage swimmers who might be trying to plant a charge to sink them,and to shoot to kill anything that moved in the water. Keep in mind, Tom was an electronics tech, not a gunner's mate. He was only about a month out of boot camp, and had not expected to have to kill anyone like the Army or the Marines did. Yet, there he was, ordered to do this duty! It brought the war "off the nightly news TV screen," right to his life, in his face! Two years later, another "spooky" experience occurred: At sunrise, they steamed near Hainan Island, closer than 30-mile limits allowed. They kept watch for aircraft, and thankfully did not see any. Though he never had another situation like that first one during his time of service for the next four years, PTSD was on board with Tom as well, though he did not know it.

One time, for one day (eight hours), Tom was "boots on the ground." He was very blessed, considering what could have happened. He worked with a Quartermaster who had been on a riverboat and land, in country, for 14 months. He had some horrible stories to tell. One adventure concerned a missile that came into the bridge, going through another man standing just ahead of him, and exploding just outside the exit hatch, killing another man nearby. The Quartermaster was unhurt, but had a "burned in" memory from that time forward. Tom only saw lots of water and every carrier working the coast of Viet Nam.

Since Tom was actually in country only one day, he did not experience Viet Nam as a culture, per se. He did see Hong Kong five times, Japan four times, Thailand once and Subic Bay, Olongapo City,

Philippines, more times than he recalled, as it was the "home port" while he was overseas. A small bit of trivia regarding Hong Kong: Many people did not want their pictures taken, as they believed that the camera captured their spirit. They would run down the photographers and grab the camera or film, to keep or save their spirit… a most strange and foreign custom/belief, according to Tom. When the men were in the Philippines, they always ate at a restaurant called Susan's, as it was very clean; so much so that the "girls" weren't required to get a monthly "smear" test, as required by the city's mayor during the time between 1969 and early 1973. The culture was all about getting the sailors' and Marines' money. Bars and hotels were all the city had to offer… At morning quarters, the "plan of the day" leadership officers offered this sage advice: "There are 10,000 prostitutes in Po Town. Do your best to stay clean."

Every night was SATURDAY NIGHT! This area was unlike any other places the young sailors gathered. Most other places, like the coastal towns, were hot, humid and smelly, like sewers. Tom's last eight-month cruise only saw him there twice: Once, when a buddy told him he needed a break, and the other was to celebrate his 25th birthday. They were getting out, as in leaving the ship in a few days, to "GET OUT!" Tom left the ship on the 27th or 28th, and flew back that night. He was flown to Travis Air Force Base, from Japan, then from Travis to Seattle, taking a Sandpoint Naval Airbus ride home to separate from active duty. Arriving about a month earlier than expected, he had about four days left, over a four-day weekend. A friend put him up overnight, after Tom caught a taxi to the friend's apartment in Spokane. His friend attended Eastern Washington University, so Tom went with him to a political science class. All Tom could think about was that, "Yesterday, I was in the Navy! Today I am in a class at college. WOW!" The young men arrived at Tom's home around 3:00 PM, first his brother, then his mom greeting him at the door. They were surprised, to say the least! Soon his dad arrived in his uncle's pick-up, his uncle seeing him first. Tom yelled, "I'm out!!! I don't have to go back anymore!!!!!!!!" Checking his DD214, the date read, February 5, 1973. Tom was done with his military commitment and home. He was free to "make choices and forge ahead with life."

As a civilian once more, Tom decided that he needed to take some time for himself. He spent 17 months "partying: goofing off and wasting time. His words. {Author's Note: This is one way PTSD can be managed for many soldiers and sailors: Coming home, doing the chores of home life, picking up the pieces of what one's youth was like: Mowing grass, rototilling a neglected garden spot, planting a new lawn around a bunkhouse built by Tom's dad when he and his brother returned from military duty, cutting firewood for parents and grandparents: Truly getting back to "home," not only in the physical world but in one's spirit.} These chores were really appreciated by Tom's parents: He was exempted from the $50.00 monthly fair rent fee. Of course, there was the drinking, as well. He did a bit with brother, Dan, who had waited for the Draft, then added a year to get a better school and job. He got out of the Army a year before Tom, as the Army was cutting back even more than the Navy. Dan had gone to Germany, and did a full tour there, leaving the service upon his return home.

Tom's partying continued, and the year after he returned from the service, he met and married Pam, in July 1974. When their first child, a daughter named Marcie, was born in late 1974, the partying continued, and the only interruption of their routine meant that now they needed a sitter. To the rescue: Pam's teenage sister Darlene who loved doing "auntie" care for her niece. Tom and Pam drank with friends at a bar they enjoyed. When Tom turned 38, Pam had had enough. They had a second child, a boy named Sean, in 1980, six years after their daughter. Their home was built on land they bought from Pam's folks, who partied too; it was all "very close." The drunk, though, was no longer fun. Even though Tom held a good, steady job, driving a fuel delivery truck for nearly 20 years, it was impossible for Pam to live with him. After completing their house well enough to inhabit in December of 1985, they had been partying a lot less because of the needs of the work on the house. An epiphany was about to occur.

In the spring of 1986, the family attended Easter services at church. It changed their lives. Tom and Pam both committed to a firm belief in Jesus. A day in July 1986, was the last occasion of Tom's drinking. He has been "dry" for over 29 years. Presently, the philosophy for Tom and his family is this: "Now is the time to believe in Him, no matter what stage of life; it's a time for a fresh start, letting Him take the wheel of life." After 41 years, he is still married to the "same gal" he married at age 26. His faith in God gets the credit. This is a tall order for Viet Nam Veterans. According to Tom and several other interviewees, they are a unique group. Those who survive to this point are rare.

They were the ones being average and proper from society's view, before the rebels of the '60s said it was okay to support 'disestablishment.' His Holy Bible teaches Tom's path each day. He thanks God for protecting him from all the "stupid" things he did during his youth and in the Navy. He was usually drunk and not thinking clearly; he drove drunk a lot, only having one accident between his car and a mailbox!

Another perspective of Tom that I admire is his constant connection and involvement with all the people in his life, including not only close relatives, but extended family and friends, as well. His practice of letter writing, mentioned earlier, and his wonderment and awe regarding technology and innovations as our scientists, artists, and inventors strive to make our lives more comfortable, and even

entertaining, have been part of his whole life. Tom is a movie buff, as well. Some of his favorites are war movies, as he wants to see Hollywood's take on a particular time in history. His all-time favorite is *Forrest Gump*. It has the naivete of simple living in a time when history was about to explode, the struggle to hold on to that time, while the old ways crumpled, literally, under our feet, and new revolutions socially, culturally and politically, pushed their way into our lives. It is about parents wanting better lives for their children and sometimes joyfully, but most often fearfully, sending them off to a place they would not see: The future! It is a great metaphor for how people everywhere 'grow up."
 In memory of good times with military buddies and the connections some of them made with Tom over the past several years are summarized in the following:

Tom's first ship brought some close friends: Lucas, Mick Palmer, Ken Davis, all ET's. Maybe an ET: Forest Nickel. Radiomen: CR (Plug) Nichol, Mike Saputo, Jim, Tranthum…

Tom's second ship brought more friends. Robert Stricklin, Mike Wilson, Andy Burns, Jose' Fabella, Eugene Martin, Don Bush, Al (Pooch) Parker, Jim King, Pat Hayes, Baker, Robert Tevault, Bob Orham, Ron Valentine, Larry Reese, Mike Tullos, Clyde Thoren, Chester Black, all ET's…

The men met in Silverdale, Washington, June 28, 2015, for the weekend… Tullos, Fabella, and Burns are gone; Reese wasn't present, but is on Facebook; Hayes is a "Facebook friend," too; Tevault is a Philippines missionary/teacher…

They worked with radarmen and radiomen, too… One is an executive in US Bank -- very busy; Chester Black became Clean Air Director in Nebraska until retirement… contacted a few times…

So many lives, so many paths: It is difficult to keep in touch with comrades from the service days.

"(We) had a common bond, all the time together on the ship, but Navy life is about change, and even if you stayed in, there was always a transfer to somewhere else, either shore, or ship. It was hard leaving all those guys when I left the ship, but I'd looked forward to leaving so much, that trip home was "healing" to losing those guys' friendship as sailors together, in a war effort. All of us wanted out. It was the constant goal, and when each man's time came, we all envied him, but wished him well! My turn was like a dream, or surreal, as it unfolded." Tom remembers that a few of the guys came to Idaho to visit, and exchange stories, some even bringing their wives. One fellow was a schoolmate from trade school, from Bonners Ferry, Idaho. Tom recognized him from Olangapo City, Philippines, "blown away" that they should meet 6,000 miles from home. He was in the Marines. They connected again about three years ago after Tom's buddy was found in Moses Lake, Washington. They have stayed connected since. Another fellow, Bill Dudley, has made a career in music and theater, playing guitar, with an interest in working on sailboats. These visits encouraged talks about everything, often religion… maybe it was the spark of some of those talks that brought Tom to his own spirituality. Our buddies from our youth travel throughout our lives as messengers on our paths, and they are as much a part of us as our own skin.

Thank you, Tom, for taking your time to tell your story. It is of family, home, hard work, honesty, your recognition of a Higher Power guiding our lives and an unflinching duty to our country. Thank you, and Pam, for your service to our country.

:

Tom, on desk
duty, waiting...

Pallets of bombs are moved
from one ship to another.

Tom Peterson

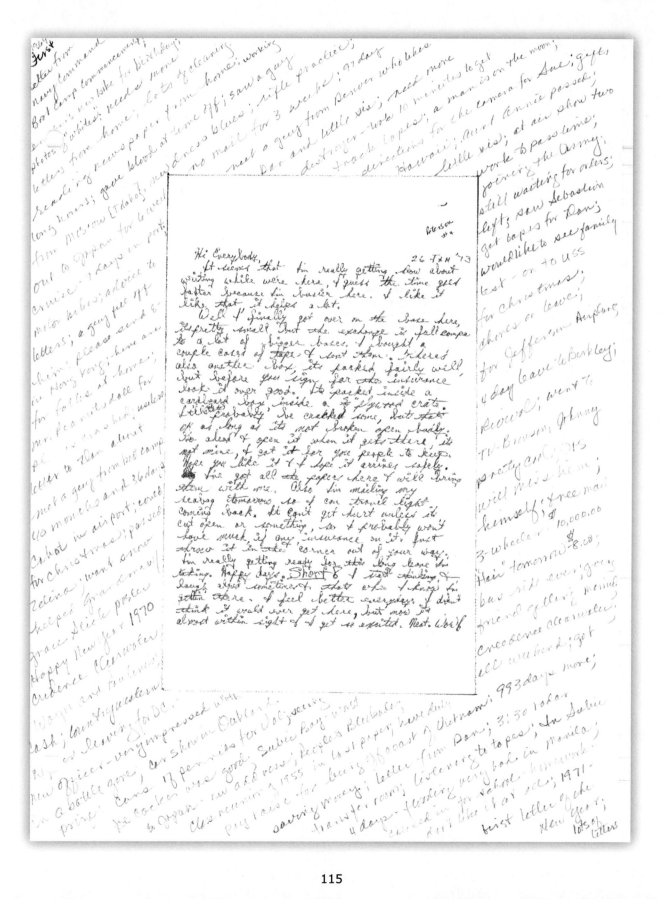

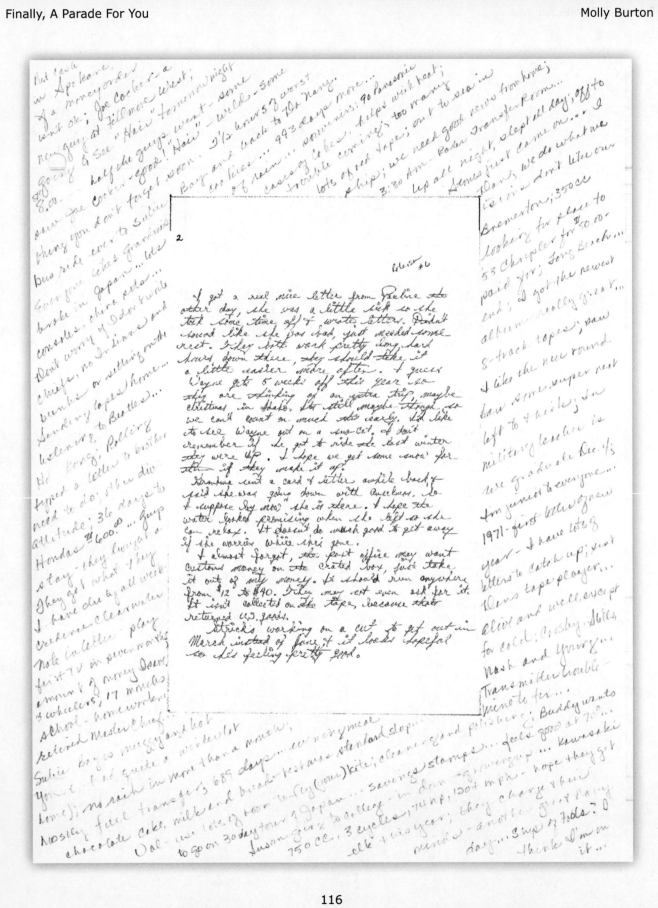

2

Letter #6

I got a real nice letter from Pauline the other day, she was a little sick so she took some time off & wrote letters. Didn't sound like she was bad, just needed some rest. They both work pretty long hard hours down there, they should take it a little easier more often. I guess Wayne gets 5 weeks off this year so they are thinking of an extra trip, maybe christmas in Idaho. Its still maybe though so we can't count on much this early. I'd like to see Wayne out on a sno-cat. I don't remember if he got to ride one last winter they were up. I hope we get some snow for them if they make it up.

Grandma sent a card & letter awhile back & said she was going down with Aunt Lor, so I suppose by now she is alone. I hope the water looked promising when she left so she can relax. It doesn't do much good to get away if she worries while their gone.

I almost forgot, the post office may want Customs money on the crated box, just take it out of my money. It should run anywhere from $12 to $40. They may not even ask for it. It isn't collected on the tape, because their returned U.S. goods.

Struck's working on a cut to get out in March instead of June, & it looks hopeful so he's feeling pretty good.

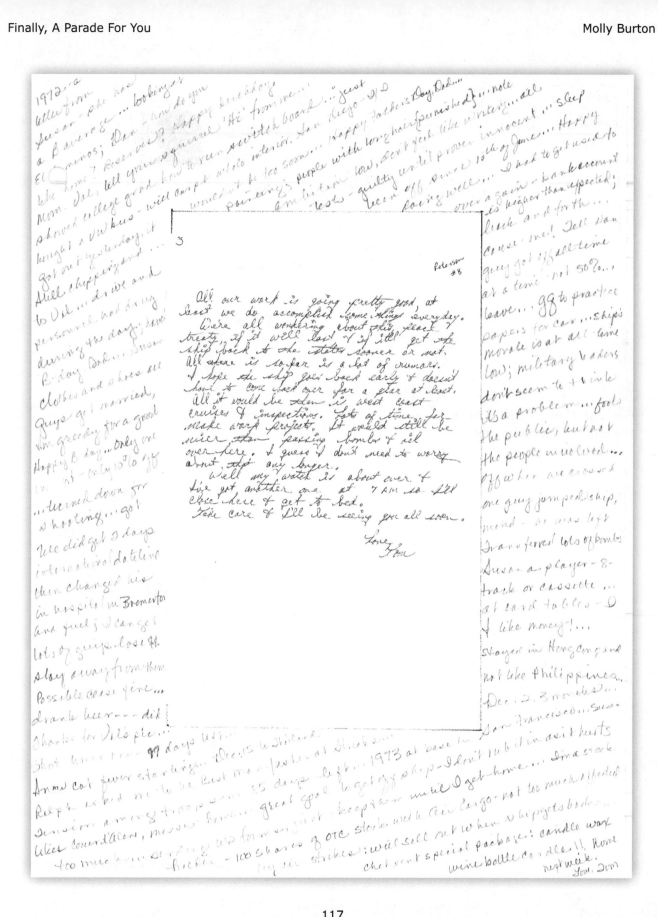

1972...a letter from Susan - she has a B average... looking for El Caminos; Dan - am do you like home; Reservist. Happy birthday Mom. Dale, tell your squirrel 'Hi' from me... shovel college grad. bought a VW bus - will camp to run switch boards... just wouldn't be too soon... Happy Father's Day Dad... piercing's purple with long hair [punished]... note ambition low, don't feel like writing... all cold - guilty until proven innocent... sleep going well... faces well... I had to get used to over again - bank account is higher than expected; back and forth... cause me? Tell Dan guys got off all time at a time... not 50%... guy got off all time leave... GG to practice papers for car... ship's morale is at all time low; military leaders don't seem to think it's a problem... fool the public, but not the people involved... off when we crossed one guy jumped ship, mind... he was left transferred lots of bombs Susan a player - 8-track or cassette... at card tables - I like money!... stayed in Hong Kong and not like Philippines... Dec. 2,3 months... San Francisco... Susan

got out yesterday, it Mall shopping and to Vol... drive and personnel had drug during the day, have B-day Dad... Susan clothes and shoes all Guys get married, I'm greedy for a good Happy B day... only one not - only 10% off ...turned down for shooting... got Wee did get 3 days international dateline then changed his in hospital in Bremerton and fuel; I can get lots of guys lose $$ stay away from them Possible cease fire... drank beer --- did thanks for Vel's pie...

99 days left...
An no cat fever starting... there's a strike...
Ralph asked me to be Best man - [Esther at] Shaka's...
tension among troops... 85 days left... 1973 at base in great good to get off ship - I don't rub it in as it hurts to keep them until I get home... I'm a crook Coeur d'Alene, messes house... hecker - 100 shares of OTC stock with firm longs - not too much affected too much... sending us for several... try in strikes: will sell out when ship gets back... chet sent special package: candle wax wine bottle candles!! Home next week.
Love, Tom

All our work is going pretty good, at least we do accomplish some things everyday.
We're all wondering about this peace treaty, if it will last & if it'll get the ship back to the states sooner or not. All there is so far is a lot of rumors. I hope the ship goes back early & doesn't have to come back over for a year at least. All it would be then is west coast cruises & inspections. Lots of time for make work projects. It would still be nicer than passing bombs & oil over here. I guess I don't need to worry about that any longer.
Well my watch is about over. & I've got another one at 7 AM so I'll close here & get to bed.
Take care & I'll be seeing you all soon.

Love,
Tom

Postage stamps were $.06 at
the start of Tom's service.

Postage increased by $.02 in 1972,
when Tom's enlistment ended.

"Free" postage from a soldier, sailor or pilot meant that
he or she was serving in an active combat zone.

Envelope which
contained the last
letter home from Tom
(Notice the postmark.)

Name: Hugh "HardCase" Rowland
Branch of Service: US Army
Rank: Private, First Class
Time served: November, 1966 to November, 1967
Honors/awards/ citations: DD 214-215

Words from Darlena Rowland: "I am the proud wife of a Viet Nam combat Veteran. His fight was in Viet Nam. My fight is the Viet Nam still in him."

This is the story of a man who fought for a year overseas. He is now a civilian who still serves his country in amazing ways. Hugh Rowland was born on April 8, 1947, in Atascadero, California. His parents were Lawrence Delosier Rowland and Margaret Elinor Rowland. With Hugh's arrival, he joined a half-sister and two half-brothers, Alma, Larry and Harold. The family increased after Hugh's arrival to include Robert, Richard and Peggy. Hugh's dad was the main machinist/mechanic for the Sinton Brothers Cattle Ranch in the hills of Shandon, California. The family lived on this ranch, where they raised their own food and raised horses that they rode on real cattle drives. They made and repaired everything on the ranch themselves. Vacations and traveling were practically a non-issue, as the family had so many responsibilities.

{Author's Note: It is interesting and ironic that the 1940s, 1950s and 1960s were years of transition from an agrarian society in which people lived "off the grid," so to speak, to an urban, mechanized culture in which everything from paid goods and services to devices that do everything for us are the norm. Now, many people are discovering that the old ways of self-sufficiency might not have been so bad after all, and are now chasing the concept of living off the grid as a way to calm high stress and live life more simply and naturally.}

Dad Lawrence was very strict and counted on no one except his boys, Hugh especially. Hugh and Robert were never in school sports nor did they attend social activities like dances, as they had "big responsibilities at a very young age." Mom Margaret worked at Ennis Tag as a bookkeeper in Paso Robles, after Hugh's dad died of cancer when Hugh was 14. It was then that Hugh had to become the "man of the family." Mom, besides her job, also managed to take care of all the kids. Hugh was not always the perfect son/little adult! Sometimes, he and his brothers would have .22 gun fights with the neighbors, competing for squirrels… no one was ever hurt with this harrowing pastime, although great fun, but still really dangerous for boys and squirrels!!!

Holidays were the stuff of cozy, country, heart-warming stories: For Christmas, the kids would watch their dad "hand carve miniature people to put around the train set, make villages out of wood and paint covered wagon murals on the walls." Gifts included "homemade cookies, clothes, and candy." Hugh remembers his first bicycle came from a junk yard. His dad brought it home and refurbished it for him, but…He gave it to his two younger brothers as he had his best friend, his horse Teddy. The kids got the day off on their birthdays, and for Easter, the family raided the hen house for the traditional eggs!

School was tough for Hugh. Though his favorite part of the day was to ride his horse to his one-room school house in the hills, he suffered negative experiences once he arrived at school, like being called stupid, with other kids picking on him, and generally being treated like a dummy, until his dad took him out of school when he was a seventh grader. He had dyslexia, a complex brain anomaly not recognized in the traditional educational world at the time Hugh was in school. Students needed to use visual, auditory and motor skills (writing, visually scanning left-to-right as American text is written and translating oral instructions) to learn reading, writing and math. Students with dyslexia saw words and letters backward, upside down and as jumbles in the pages of a book, and sometimes even when they wrote. When listening to oral instructions, they could hear, but then translated the opposite of what the teacher said to do. Of course, not all students had the same symptoms, or even all the symptoms, but enough of one or more to a greater or lesser degree.

Today, dyslexia, while still present in many students, is discovered in the primary grades, and earlier, when the above learning skills are taught as readiness for higher education in later grades. Dyslexic students are taught with alternative learning methods to assist them in the basics. They will always have this issue in their lives, but with knowledge about how to learn something new, they usually have the skills required to achieve mastery. As new brain research comes to the fore, a lovely by-product of this information is that it is now known that many people with dyslexia tend to be very bright; such was the case with Hugh. He has a very high IQ. He did earn a Graduate Equivalency Diploma/Degree (GED) and learned a vocation, instead of going to a traditional high school. While his dad taught him the important and crucial components of learning and thinking on his feet, he is a self-taught expert on motorcycles… learned by "watching and doing." His expertise also includes wood carving and leather braiding, now parts of his "favorites" hobby list. {Author's Note: The reader will also find in Hugh's self-designed and developed website, included at the back of the book… www.vets-helping-vets.com…

a wonderful, nearly encyclopedic set of references for help for all Veterans and the people who know and love them. Hugh keeps abreast of all issues related to the military, and if he doesn't have information, he knows where to get it. This website has been several decades in the making, and is a labor of love from Hugh to other Veterans. Hugh led a serious, responsibility-driven childhood and one that left little time or chance to develop friendships. He considers himself to be "a loner." He is "real analytical, and people have a hard time getting to know me," to use his words. He likes keeping people on the outside, as few people know the "real" Hugh. That way, he knows "right where they stand, and they don't screw" with him. The ones who do know Hugh describe him as "sensitive." More on this particular aspect of Hugh's personality later…

In 1964, Hugh's brother Larry was wounded when he was shot down in Viet Nam; he later died of those wounds. Hugh joined the US Army to "avenge his {brother's} death." Basic training occurred in Fort Polk, Louisiana. Hugh received Advanced Infantry Training (AIT) at Fort Benning, Georgia which prepared him for Viet Nam. A week or two after Hugh landed in Viet Nam, he received his orders for the unit where he would be stationed. On the way to the unit, he had left his ride, and was walking into the battery area when a grenade went off, killing another man. Hugh was hit in the thigh. The grenade's explosion was friendly fire, but no recognition of this incident was issued. It was a strange way to be welcomed to war! Once he arrived at his unit, one of Hugh's jobs was to provide support for the vehicles' 175-inch and 8-inch Howitzers. Keeping these vehicles fit and ready for combat at a moment's notice was an important part of Hugh's work. He would help stockpile the shells next to the guns, readying the guns for any fire mission. Another one of Hugh's responsibilities was to provide security for the big guns. Many times that would mean walking endless hours of guard duty… no fun! In his spare time, Hugh would do maintenance on the big guns. He earned the nickname 'HardCase' when he was on fire mission duty, helping load the shells that weighed an average of 75 to 135 pounds into big guns. His finger was bleeding from a cut received from this activity, and he was told to go to the Medic tent. He said, "No." He would wait until the fire mission was over.

His Major said, "OK, HardCase, stand there and bleed." Fifteen minutes later, hit by an incoming mortar, the Medic tent disappeared! Again, Hugh cheated death. As "death was always a factor," one did not get too close to anyone: more self-protective defense. Any soldier, including Hugh, could be dead the next day. Each soldier did have his fellow soldiers' backs, but as it often happened, when a fallen soldier went down, someone would yell, "Medic!!" and keep on fighting.

Some of Hugh's first impressions of Viet Nam, when he had time to notice, "notice" being the operative word, were in getting used to how people lived. If a Vietnamese family traveling on the road became hungry, everything stopped. The family would stop their ox cart, sit down in the middle of the road, bring out pots, pans, food, and eat one of their many-times-a-day customary meals. Convoys and other road activity halted until the meal was eaten and cleared away. One time, a seemingly innocent girl walked by and threw a satchel under a convoy truck, which blew up! Another reminder to keep one's gun loaded, always being aware, and at times, shooting anything that moved. Trust of anyone or anything could become a huge issue. {Author's Note: Hugh did not know it, but PTSD was working its way into his soul: difficult early learning years, his dad's passing when Hugh was so young, his brother's death, were all part of his life; things were adding up.} The Army taught Hugh how to fight and kill. He went overboard: No one was going to pick on him again.

Hugh did enjoy the pristine green of the country, among all the death and chaos. He also remembered American music in Viet Nam: The Doors, Iron Butterfly, and other popular groups. He did not know the names of songs, but liked the music. It was played really loudly from a few helicopters to scare the North Vietnamese. He had a record player, and wore his records out by playing them so much. He could not read or write, so there was very little correspondence. He found a "little wimp'" who could read and write for him, and in return, Hugh kept others from picking on him. Others did not like his "faraway look and black eyes." He left the Army a "mean 40-year-old man in a 19-year-old body." He was not proud of that.

{Author's Note: Since the first draft of this story was written, I have learned through further interviews with Hugh and his wife, Darlena, that he needed to be able to spell words to be able to create the plethora of information for his website. He did not recognize letters, but numbers were an easy avenue for Hugh to remember. Different sides of the brain are responsible for these attributes. Darlena put the alphabet in front of Hugh, and then put corresponding numbers to each letter: 1 for A, 2 for B, and so on. It was magic! Hugh could decode letters into numbers, and when they were memorized, he could translate them into meaningful information. If this information had been known to Hugh through his early learning years, his education, indeed, his military experience and his whole life history might have changed! If the military had known this about Hugh, he might have experienced the war as a code breaker, or even a code maker!}

Soldiers leaving Viet Nam, in most cases, were given no deprogramming, counseling or rehabilitation to process the mess they left in Viet Nam. When they lifted off the ground for the last time in Viet Nam, they held their collective breath with fear of being mortared before they left enemy airspace, which was as real as being boots on the ground. Indeed, they still wore muddy boots from recently being in fighting mode. Newer uniform decorations appeared on some soldiers' uniforms. The First Army, Big Red One and helmets that held a black ace-of-spades playing card, indicating "the spade of death" scared the enemy to death. These things were signs that the moral code of these soldiers had taken a left turn into darkness, classic indicators of PTSD. Upon returning to the states, Hugh went to the VA. Doctors there told him he did not have any problems. They summed it up succinctly saying, in Hugh's words, "Go home and have a drink." So much for counseling and a medical check-up, much less, blood work. Today, doctors are telling Hugh that a nerve agent (Agent Orange) is responsible for his neuropathy. He has overactive nerves, and his feet feel like he is walking on a ball of nails. He receives blood work every three months. While this is part of how it should be in treating all veterans, as it is their right, the medical model is limited to what it knows: Treating symptoms, usually with medication of some sort. One of the medications that typically are given to those in constant physical pain is the prescription drug Norco. Hugh was on this drug for 30 years. He suffered kidney stones, flu-like symptoms and no recall of strange behaviors while on this drug. Too often, this medical model of suppressing symptoms without digging for the cause is at the root of physical and emotional illnesses. More about how to deal with the unique issues of veterans, their physical problems resulting from toxic exposure to emotional problems from PTSD, is presented for the reader's perusal at the end of the book.

When Hugh returned from Viet Nam, he was called a "baby killer," and suffered a major mental setback going into survival mode, after being spit upon, having garbage thrown at him and not being respected or liked. He could not get a job because of this attitude. Once, he was called a vagrant for hanging around a bowling alley, even though he had $1,500.00 in his pocket. He was arrested because the officer put his hands on Hugh, and Hugh "lost it." Hugh put the officer in his car and called for backup. The officer had been hurt, and Hugh landed in jail. While Hugh was there, another officer befriended him, and would take him fishing and do other activities with him, mentoring Hugh and keeping him out of trouble; otherwise, Hugh would probably be in prison. He took off his Army fatigues and medals, and buried them, put his past into a book in his head, and put it on a shelf so he could get on with his life, and "not have it in front of my face every day." This thing, called PTSD, has never left Hugh, and some of it surfaces full force even today. "It's really hard to be a nice guy." Although…

Hugh feels he was spared in Viet Nam to help serve his fellow brothers-in-arms. It took a long time to come to this conclusion. He should have died many times. One time he was out on a mission with his shirt unbuttoned, and it was "flying in the wind." When he returned to base, someone asked him if he was all right. His answer was, "Yeah. Why?" Two bullet holes were in his shirt, right where his heart would have been. He asks himself, "Why was I spared? God only knows!!! Today, when people come up to me and thank me for my service, I don't know how to respond. I just graciously say thank you." It is really hard for Hugh not to say, "Yeah, sure… why did it take so ####### long to be appreciated?"

Today, most of Hugh's childhood family is gone; only Alma and Harold are still living. Hugh has been married three times. His first wife was Norma Ann Cole, with whom he had daughter Barbara. They had met at a roller skating rink in Columbus, Georgia. Norma was seven years older than Hugh, but at the time, it seemed to make no difference. She got pregnant, and before he left for Viet Nam, Hugh did not know this. Since he could not read or write, he didn't get any correspondence or read about it in letters or newspapers. It was later that he discovered he had a daughter. Norma had taken another man's name, but never officially divorced Hugh. Hugh put information to dissolve the marriage in the papers for 30 days; that was not good enough for the VA, but was good enough for the divorce courts. When Hugh finally learned that Norma had died, her death certificate was good enough, so he was officially unmarried. He has succeeded in locating Barbara, and has met her. They will never be close, but they acknowledge each other's life in their own existence. Hugh wishes her well. Patricia (Pat) Fisher was Hugh's second wife; he adopted her son Robert, and had two more daughters, Naomi and Shari. Once, when he was married to Pat, he hung her on a coat rack, slammed the door, and left for the day… while she was actually wearing a large coat. He had been pissed at her, and he wanted to get even. Robert came home from school and helped her off the hook… literally!! Hugh remained single for eight years, renting spaces in his house to college women. He actually had to learn how to live with women and their unique personalities, without episodes of his PTSD showing itself. His third wife is Darlena (Dar). Married for 36 years, they have had no children together, but they are grandparents to seven granddaughters, two great granddaughters, and two great, great grandsons. They are the ancestors of a wonderful family legacy. A few years ago, Hugh's granddaughter and her friend traveled to Viet Nam and Laos, as a trip for Grandpa. Though Hugh will never go back, his granddaughter found the people of South Viet Nam friendly. She and her friend, both firefighters, became engaged in Laos. This place in the world now has some measure of good memories in the family dynamic. Hugh and Dar's life together has not been without its trials, however. Although he has never hit a woman, when angered he would take it out on another guy. He has hurt Pat and Dar, and his children with his harsh mouth; he feels really bad, but cannot take it back. He works very hard to make it up to Dar and make a good life for her. He thanks God for his Dar, his angel who keeps him sane, not suicidal, or addicted to anything… she even helps keep him out of prison!! Dar knows his sensitive side, and his big heart, and "puts up with all the other ####, because she knows the real me," says Hugh humbly.

A great sadness resulting from the war haunts Hugh even today. In the years of combat between 1964 and 1975, the world lost 56,000 American lives. According to Prisoner of War/Missing in Action (POW/MIA) records, nearly 1600 Americans are still missing. Although statistics are fluid for all victims, as more information comes to light, even other countries lost too many to the war. Australia, New Zealand, and France lost thousands. For what purpose and to what end? Idaho Congressman, Mike Simpson, helped Hugh through his struggle to get his Purple Heart in thirty days. Hugh had been fighting with the VA to get his Purple Heart with military benefits for many years! One of the major symptoms of PTSD is survivor's guilt. Feeling like what he does is never quite enough, Hugh makes sure that what he does do, counts! Work, Hugh's therapy, and passion with compassion in helping other veterans comprise Hugh's busy life these days. He is a Christian spiritual guide, a Chaplain for the Combat Veterans Motorcycle Association (a group, not a club), Purple Heart Riders, and Patriot Guard Riders. He serves as their road captain. He is also a member of the POW/MIA Motorcycle Association and a Veterans Advocate. (Known as a rogue, he has no office and does not get paid, but he is a Veteran Service Officer.)

Hugh has had simple dreams, but to him, they were big, and at times seemingly impossible. He wanted to come out of Viet Nam alive (he never thought he would come back), and he wanted to find his first wife and daughter. His dreams and so much more have come true. I respect this man, but more importantly, he is following a path to his respect for himself. All of humanity has committed wrongs; it is when people realize no one is perfect, that forgiveness and grace are attainable, even for themselves, that our spirits become one. Hugh, your life is a model for others to follow. Dar, your patience, love, and yes, your own PTSD, and the grace and calm attitude with which you share your life with others, make you a model for those who love veterans enough to see through the wounded hearts they bring home. Thank you, both, for your service to our country.

Cherry Buster,
where Hugh slept

Hugh ran for cover during a mortar attack, while this truck provided some
protection. Though Hugh caught shrapnel in his leg, if the truck had not been
in the correct position, Hugh would not be alive to recount this story.

"Jacob" Rowland: Hugh and Dar's healer

Hugh rides on a Veteran's Burial Mission with Patriot Guard Riders.

Name: Tim (Chuck) Schuller

Branch of Service: US Navy

Rank: 3rd Class Petty Officer/Ship's Serviceman

Time served: September 10, 1972 to September 19, 1975 (2 WES/PACS)

Honors: National Defense Service Medal

Armed Forces Expeditionary Medal

Meritorious Unit Commendation Medal

Navy E Ribbon

Navy Meritorious Citation Ribbon (3)

Viet Nam Service Medal

Republic of Viet Nam Campaign Medal

Humanitarian Service Medal

Republic of Viet Nam Gallantry Cross Medal

Republic of Viet Nam Civil Action Medal

Combat Action Medal

Cold War Medal

{Author's Note: The Viet Nam War was officially over in 1973. The treaty was signed among North and South Viet Nam, and the United States. Reparation promises were made by protestors who grew up to be politicians, but money was never given to do this. However, evacuations still needed to occur. Tim was part of these campaigns: "Operation Frequent Wind," and "Operation Eagle Pull."} Tim Schuller's life's purpose has been to rescue others and help them on their journeys. In living this life, he has rescued himself.

In May 1955, Timmy Lee Collins was born to Kentuckian Charles T. Collins, a man he never met, and Mary Gwendolyn Sammons of Chicago, Illinois. Soon, another son was born to the family: Thomas, born in September 1956. This family split, and Mary met a new man, Robert Winters, who fathered Robert, born in September 1959. Then, Mary finally met Robert John Schuller, Mary's only husband. He adopted Mary's three sons, then they had two of their own: William (Billy), born in December 1969, and John, born in December 1972. That is the odyssey about how Tim Collins became Tim Schuller.

The boys grew up in Chicago, living on the north side, with street names of Wellington, Clark Street, and Lake Shore Drive. Most of Tim's youthful years were spent living at Lake Point Towers. His

Dad, Bob, was a stationary engineer, the head janitor with three shifts of janitors to keep the building clean and repaired when things broke. In exchange, Bob earned a salary, and the family received a rent-free place to live. All the boys attended Ogden School. For high school, some went to Lane Tech, and others attended Lake View High School. No one graduated from high school, nor did they go to college, but most earned their GED's. They grew up with some wellknown sports figures, team owners, and in general, people with lots of money.

Family activities and fun times usually included trips to see family. Arizona was a favorite destination to see Tim's mom's sister Jerry and her husband and two sons. Trips to Miami to see his dad's family were especially fun, as his Grandpa and Grandma were a nice old German couple who made the visits special. Dad's sisters, Lane and Margaret, and brother Frank also lived in Miami, so cousins with whom to play made the trips a lot more entertaining. The Florida sun, Miami air and the ocean… aahh, wonderful.

Family life was happy until sometime after John was born. "Both parents loved us, and there were many happy times," but these parents also drank. Family trouble in the 1960s was just that: Domestic issues. If a kid screwed up, he got the belt. Tim's dad was not a little man: Some said he had arms like Popeye; indeed, Bob Schuller was a Naval Korean War Veteran. Some kids got the belt more than others; Tim is not sure why. He thinks that maybe his dad loved some of the boys more than others. Even wives were beaten; Tim's Mom was not immune to her husband's rage: she was knocked out a few times. Tim recalls: "These memories really turn your stomach."

{Author's Note: It would seem that Dad Bob had some undiagnosed PTSD of his own, although, at that time, men were supposed to deal with their own problems, so counseling was completely out of the question.}

The unhappy home life, combined with the fear of violence, caused all 3 of the oldest brothers to leave the house before the age of 18. Tim, himself, never started his junior year of high school. He was 17 when he joined the Navy in September of 1972. His dad had signed permission for him. "The doors of freedom were open." Even with leaving home, boot camp was not so bad, as Tim remembers: Getting up early, and lots of marching. After boot camp, Tim arrived in San Diego, California, and waited on base about a week for the USS DURHAM LKA 114.

{Author's Note: Sometime before going to Viet Nam, Tim, and three buddies, among them, Bob Gadigan, were in a motor vehicle accident, drinking and driving, a bad combination. The driver crashed the pick-up, and Tim wound up in the hospital for four or five days, with a concussion. To this day, many of his life's activities are non-memories for him. Events will be sketchy with details, so to the reader, use compassion to fill in the gaps for Tim.}

Early one evening, Tim was given his orders to walk to the ship docked at the pier. It was the first time he "smelled" the Navy. Does this seem strange? The pier smelled of harbor waters, garbage waiting for pick-up, running motors, small boat exhaust, and the Naval ships, forever in some stage of being painted. Tim was assigned to the 2nd Division. He was now a Boatswain's Mate, or Deck Ape. He would work outside on the back half of the ship, painting, chipping and sanding. The Durham was like a cargo ship, only with cannons. It had four cargo holes and four levels in each hole. The cargo consisted of small armies with tanks, jeeps, trucks, and eight boats called Mike Boats. Four Mike8's, the larger of the boats could hold tanks. The Mike6's could hold trucks and smaller vehicles. All the boats rested 10 feet above the main deck in their holders, called beds or cradles. They were picked up by cranes, called booms, and put into the water. Then, the crew picked up whatever cargo they had and put that in the boats. Rope nets, as seen on TV, allowed the Marines to go over the side, down these rope nets into the boats... about 40 feet down. They did that in the '70s, and Tim believes that protocol is still done today. The USS Durham also carried about 200 men, maybe more. The troops had a large bunk room; they did not have to sleep in the holes!! This ship transported huge amounts of cargo during the three years Tim was aboard. Destinations included the Philippines, Guam, Okinawa, Taiwan, Hong Kong, and Pusan, Korea, the only place as windy as Chicago.

Fast forwarding to April of 1975... Tim (nicknamed "Chuck" for his time in the military; it did not stick, so Tim remained " Tim" for most of his adult life) had been on the ship for two-and-a-half years and was now 20 years old. They were somewhere in the Western Pacific, and things were not okay in Viet Nam. A rumor said the ship would be going up the river 80 miles to Saigon. The crew was given .50 caliber machine gun practice, something no one forgets! The kids were ready to go... "Let's put the boats in the water, and go get 'em!" LOL... rumors were only half right. They arrived on station off the coast of Viet Nam. They could see other ships in the area. Everyone waited, but they were not sure for what... They waited a day or two, then left and went to Hong Kong. The crew was out on Liberty (fun times on shore) when the shore patrol spread the word: "BACK TO YOUR SHIPS." Tim's ship got under way at night, a little unusual, back to Viet Nam waters. The next morning it started...

The Mike Boats were loaded into the water, helicopters were circling around the area, and the Marines were on board... a new development. They were also carrying weapons; even some of the sailors were armed. Small clouds of smoke puffed onto land where mortar rounds were landing.

Hundreds of small boats were flooding the coastline, heading toward the Durham and other Naval ships. Vietnamese civilians were running for their lives!!

Many boats… Tim recalls this day as a "stream-of-consciousness" memory: "Mike Boats keep the onslaught back as best they can, until everything is ready to take on people. Fire hoses arc used to keep some sort of order in the water… and the boats keep coming. The ship's ladder is put into place along the side of the ship… along the stairway, metal runs form from the main deck to the water… sailors run down the ladder to the water level, one on every other step, three at the bottom platform… the boats come in… panicked Vietnamese eyes… yelling in a language I do not understand… as they get closer, they throw a baby at the sailors… the ocean is not calm, and all the boats are bouncing up and down… a helicopter drops into the ocean… I am four or five steps up the ladder… as the boat get close enough, a sailor grabs a person, man, woman or child, it doesn't matter… the routine: Grab them, lift them out of the boat, and pass them on to the next sailor… those people never touch the ladder steps… up they go, passed from sailor to sailor to the main deck where they get a pat down, and all weapons are thrown over the side… they all have weapons, some even carry grenades! "This nightmare of humanitarianism" goes on all day: Screaming… yelling… fear. The rescued masses do not know what will happen to them, but it is better than staying in Viet Nam… on and on… then, time stops… a girl, maybe five or eight, falls into the ocean between the boat and the Durham. I see her go under water… the boat bounces over where she went in… Sailor Ed Zyer jumps into the ocean next to the ship… he goes under… it seems like a day goes by… screams are coming from the boat, and from the sailors on the ladder… Ed pops up with the girl! She is grabbed up and passed up to the main deck. Ed is not a small guy. I call him "big back Ed." Ed is helped out of the ocean before he is crushed between the boats, ladder and ship. A few pats on Ed's "big back" and he continues his work… now a helicopter lands on the ship's Helo pad . {Author's Note: See Ed Zyer's story.} A Vietnamese pilot lets his family out, and he is asked to fly his copter out to sea and drop it in the water… he refuses, so the copter is pushed over the side of the Durham into the ocean by Marines and sailors… boats are still coming… after those civilians who have come on board are searched, they are taken to one of the cargo holes where they pick out their space…

Tim continues: "We filled that ship… I think over 3,000 were taken aboard the Durham… what about other ships? Did they have 1,000s, too? We were where we were supposed to be: on that ladder, on the main deck, guiding people to their temporary home in the cargo hole… more memories: copters landing on ships, Helos ditched in the ocean, so many boats they could not be counted… more Vietnamese voices screaming and yelling… more helos…

"And, then it was done. Either the ship was full, or the boats could not come back out because the North Vietnamese had overtaken Saigon, or it became too dark… ship's ladder up and away… now it was time to feed all the refugees… reunite families, take them to the stern (fan tail) where we had built portable showers and toilets… night has fallen… lights out with no moonlight tonight… we took people by the hand and walked with them in the darkness… "

{Author's Note: *Newsweek* magazine, May 12, 1975, covers in depth, the political positions of countries involved, as the last days of The Viet Nam War and the rescue of Saigon citizens made their sad imprints of a terrible time in the 20th century.}

Tim made some good friends back then: Terry Pearce, Terry Cannon, Zimmerman, Porter, Scott Duel, Tobianski, Maiava, Bob Gadigan, who lives in Detroit, Michigan, Ed Zyer who lives in Twin Lakes, Wisconsin, Lyle Hicks, in Bend, Oregon and Robert (Bobby) Kelly and his wife, Charlotte, from New Orleans, Louisiana. Tim attended Bobby's wedding to his bride, Charlotte, with whom Tim still stays in touch. {Author's Note: The event of Bobby's and Charlotte's wedding is a non-memory for Tim, as his concussion erased this event.} Bobby, called Popeye by his buddies, died of throat cancer. "REST IN PEACE, Bobby. You were special," is Tim's benediction to a fallen comrade.

At 20 years of age, Tim was no longer in the Navy. He did not have any higher education, but he went to work anyway. His first job was as a security guard at the Water Tower Place shopping mall, where he worked for three years. In 1979, Tim joined the Chicago Fire Department where he retired as a lieutenant after 32 years. His life's work was rescuing people and taking care of them. It seems as if his Viet Nam experiences were his college of higher learning.

In 1984, Tim met the girl of his dreams, Jacqueline, who had a 4-year-old son, Carl. She worked in human resources. They have been married for 25 years, and Carl, who is autistic, is their family. Tim wishes that they had married sooner. He whispers a wish that if he and Jackie had had children together, then maybe they would be part of this already loving nuclear family who would care for each other after their parents were gone…

Tim's dad, Bob, died in 1984, at the age of 55. He was what Tim calls a "hard sleeper." When someone woke him, he jumped! This scared both Dad and the one waking him, therefore, no one really liked doing this activity. One day Bob asked John to wake him at 5:00 for dinner. John heard his dad's last breath and saw him jump for the last time. "Jumped straight to heaven, we hope," says Tim.

Tim's mom, Mary, one of five sisters, was a true gift in Tim's life. She was a good mom, housekeeper and cook. She loved to laugh. She gave up her wish to have a daughter after five boys! The last 10 years of her life took their toll on her. Bob and she had divorced, and Bill and John went to live with their dad. Mary did not have the strength to keep the boys in line, as they were 12 and 15. At this time, their own long road of alcohol and drugs started. As a result, they both died early deaths. Tim recalls that "it took 30 years, but it (drinking) killed her. Too many seizures, too many hospitalizations: Sick, healthy, sick, healthy… " His mom died in 1993 when she was 57. She had another alcohol seizure and had been in the hospital a few days. Tim was at the hospital making arrangements to transfer her to a nursing home. He stopped by his mother's room, but she was sleeping; doctors said she was in "very bad shape." "BUT WE HAD BEEN THROUGH THIS BEFORE." When he arrived home, Jackie told him the hospital had called and told him his mother, Mary Gwendolyn Sammons Schuller, had died.

Tim and Jackie are happy in their retirement years. Both Tim and Tom are close. Tim's advice to youngsters of today is to know that family is the most important thing in life. He tells them to get educated, learn how to invest their money and learn of the dangers of recreational drugs and alcohol; in fact, do not even start down those potentially deadly paths.

Thank you, Tim Schuller, for sharing your story. I am honored to meet you even though we have never seen each other face to face. You have had a most valuable, interesting and challenging life. You have weathered hardships, danger and loss. Your voice and manner of speech show you to be a kind man whom others are pleased to know. You have served our country well, both militarily and professionally, and I thank you, and Jackie, for your service to our country.

Tim Schuller, age 20

People try to escape Phan Rang area.

Vietnamese boat people
come to the USS Durham
to be evacuated.

Refugees from Phan Rang area wait to be taken to safety on the USS Durham during evacuation operations. The Durham loaded over 3,000 refugees and moved them to a safe haven in the south.

Vietnamese family waits on the main deck to be taken to cargo hole on USS Durham.

Name: Ronald (Ron) Smuckal

Branch of Service: US Air Force

Rank: E-4, Sergeant

Time served: December 1, 1965, to September 18, 1969

Honors and awards: Viet Nam Service Medal

This veteran of the Viet Nam War is a fellow who follows his heart in all he does. Ron's war experience did not destroy his sense of good humor; instead, it was a time in his life in which he simply did his duty to his country, then became a civilian who continued that service as a police officer. His philosophy of life heads his business card and reads: "Enjoy the Day." It is a grand philosophy, as one day at a time is all we are ever given.

Walla Walla, Washington was the city of Ron Smuckal's arrival on May 5, 1946. It was only 12 miles from home, as opposed to the next nearest city of Pendleton, Oregon 45 miles away. This was probably a great relief to his mom, Laura, and his dad, Ralph Smuckal. With his arrival, Ron joined a big sister, five years older than he. Both parents have passed away, but they lived in the same place during Ron's youth. Theirs was a home that was quite literally built from the ground up. The property had a small house on it, but the family lived in the new house during its construction. First, Ralph dug a basement where the family lived; it had an outdoor toilet, and running water only for the kitchen. The family phone was the old country type with a horn and a receiver! It had a family plan, in that the whole family used it! Then Ralph built a whole new house on top of the basement. This was going to be a solid residence, since Ralph cut the trees into timber, and built the house with that wood. The term "handmade" took on a rich meaning.

Home was basically a community of extended family. Each family had its own property, but not everyone farmed their land. Farming was the main occupation, a livelihood that nourished the whole community of relatives. Naturally providing a haven for animals, Ron's family farm had all kinds of pets, including a horse, a dog and cats, and though he liked all of them, he favored pigs in high school, for his 4H projects. Even with all the responsibilities of chores and repair and maintenance of equipment, there was still time for participation in 4H and Future Farmers of America (FFA). In fact, if one did not participate in at least three or four clubs, Ron states, "You were not with it." Fruitvale Grade School was a little three-room building with combined grades one through eight: grades 1 and 2 were attended in one room, grades 3, 4, and 5, were housed in another room, and grades 6, 7 and 8 were grouped in the third room. Run like one big family, school recesses found 7th and 8th graders sometimes playing with 1st and 2nd graders. {Author's Note: With such a small school, it is most likely that several sets of siblings and even family cousins attended the school together.} During school plays, like the one for Christmas, everyone had a part. Ron had several friends, and a few cousins, from both grade and high school with whom he still maintains contact even after 55 years. "Flowing with the times," Ron was easy-going and remained close to family. Traditions were kept for holidays like Thanksgiving and Christmas Eve at Auntie Hulda's, Ron's mom's sister, and Christmas Day at the home of his dad's side of the family. Graduation from Umapine High School, near Milton-Freewater, Oregon and then from Blue Mountain Community College in Pendleton prepared Ron for his next step, enlistment in the US Air Force one month ahead of his Draft notice.

Ron's boot camp occurred at Lackland Air Force Base (AFB), in San Antonio, Texas. He attended tech school at Keesler AFB, in Biloxi, Mississippi. He was then transferred to the 636th Aircraft Control and Warning (AC & W) Squadron Radar Site, in Condon, Oregon. His new official title was Ground Radar Surveillance and Height Finder Operator. His next assignment was at Monkey Mountain, at Da Nang Air Force Base in Viet Nam!

Upon arrival, Ron was quite scared at first: "Will I live or die? It scared the 'you-know-what' out of me." There was nothing to do but adapt quickly, as his USAF comrades and he joined forces with the Vietnamese Air Force (VAF) personnel. An astute observer, Ron had his eyes opened since this was the first time he had been to a "third world" country. He saw sampans floating in the harbor, noting that people lived in such poor conditions, but he came to realize that "this was normal for them. They would not be able to handle our way of living." Poverty was rampant, but overall, "people appeared to be happy, and… were basically friendly to us." Ron's experience with Vietnamese food was minimal to non-existent, as he was brought up on meat and potatoes, and rarely ventures from this diet even today. Besides, civilian farm crops like lettuce involved using human waste (night soil) as fertilizer.

Danger lurked everywhere. Even though little kids would climb onto the backs of elephants and stand up on top for two cigarettes as entertainment. One never knew if he was dealing with the enemy. One event that Ron remembers occurred when a youngster grabbed the watch of a South Korean Marine. The Marine grabbed the kid and broke the kid's arm over his knee, drew his weapon and was going to shoot the kid. Another time, Ron saw another kid reach for an Army soldier's watch, and the soldier killed him. Those men on land learned quickly to lob percussion grenades into and across the river even if they just saw a lily pad.

A sad benediction from Ron: "NO ONE WINS IN A WAR. It is a rough environment, and bad things happen to all involved."

Duty schedules consisted of 12-hour shifts, and for Ron, this meant that he would be checking radar screens for incoming and outgoing planes, and plotting their courses. US Army personnel controlled Monkey Mountain, but the runway leading to it was dangerous because those on the ground were exposed to the enemy. These men carried assault rifles to survive and get out alive. When it was time to play/relax/not think about the job, R&R for the men meant that they would sometimes hitchhike to China Beach, getting picked up by those men with a ride. Since it was war, the non-commissioned officers' (NCO) club was available for everyone. Other night scenes included clubs that featured feather strippers, rather like fan dancers, guaranteed to tease as well as entertain. One time, near his leave date, when Ron patronized one of these establishments, some "raunchy" G.I.s grabbed one of the entertainers. She left the stage, and when the Marines caught up to these men, they were banned from entering the Base Club again. On one special occasion, no one had to leave Monkey Mountain Base Camp. A VIP guest arrived for the evening's entertainment: Bob Hope's USO show had arrived. Ron had a really good seat a few feet from the famous comedian; this was a memorable highlight of Ron's tour. On these occasions, when men were tired and nearly always alert to danger, the important work of keeping military personnel safe was pushed to the rear for moments of peace.

One of the most impressive events Ron experienced was an invitation to dinner from a Vietnamese Air Force Sergeant, for a pre-Tet celebration. In Viet Nam, it was customary for the men of the family to eat a meal first, which was served by the wife. Then, whatever was left over was for the women and children to eat. Ron and his comrades asked if the Sergeant's son, a little boy around five or six years of age, could eat with them. Instead of insulting the host, as guests, Ron's group could have their wishes granted. The man's son was given permission to eat with 'the men.' This was a very special occasion all around, as neighbors and passersby could see inside the house that the son of the host was eating with the Americans, a great honor.

Ron left the military with no injuries, even though one time a Napalm bomb exploded in Da Nang. ("No one wanted to break it down… poison!") He "came out fine." Within two weeks of leaving combat military life, he became a full-time college student. He did not have much time to dwell on 'Nam. Once again, he had to adapt to his environment: The "anti-war" people! He did not like this, but had no choice. When he had arrived in Viet Nam, he did not feel that he would come back… but, he did!

Ron became a police officer. He worked for 15 years, before an on-the-job injury ended his career. Ron stated, "I married the best woman alive, and I am happy with my life." Although Ron has a 50% military disability for hearing, and Agent Orange Type II diabetes, with 50% disability, he views these conditions as "inconveniences," and goes on with his life. These conditions do not define him. He keeps in contact with two friends from 'Nam: Ray Saunders from North Carolina, and John Jordon, from Indiana. He also stays in contact with his best friend from tech school, Duane Rowlson, from Michigan. They talk on the phone every day. "Ninety-nine percent of all veterans were not sorry they were there." Would Ron join again? "Yes." Does he regret going to Viet Nam? "No." Ron has many Viet Nam War buddies, and they all feel they have good lives.

A message of camaraderie from Ron goes to all of his military comrades: " Each of our military services has pride in their respective service, but in Viet Nam it didn't matter what branch you were in: We all looked out for each other, and we all wanted to come home alive. A lot of us did {get to come home}, but we lost a lot of good men. They are the ones we owe our gratitude to, and give them the utmost respect. They died fighting for our great country, and gave the ultimate sacrifice for all of us."

Ron has sage advice for future generations. "All men should serve in the regular military. You learn to accept and get along with people of different races and values. You grow up…Life is what you make it to be; you can decide to have a good life or a miserable life." Watch words that Ron has used throughout his life are, "Learn to adapt." Better advice would be hard to find. And, if one looks to each day for enjoyment, then Ron's advice has been heeded, tenfold.

Ron Smuckal, it has been a pleasure getting to know you and hearing of your contribution to our country. When it was time, you stepped up and became a part of a grand group of soldiers, sailors and pilots. You continued to serve our country as part of our brothers and sisters in blue. I am honored to know you. Thank you, and your wife, for your service to our country.

Ron holds prize
"catches of the day."

Enjoying his vacation at
Crater Lake, Oregon, Ron
knows how to relax.

Ron beams approval of the
life of a retiree.

Name: Ed Zyer

Branch of Service: US Navy

Rank: E3 (with 3 stripes)

Time Served: 3 years (September 1972 to September 1975)

Honors: National Defense Service Medal

Armed Forces Expeditionary Medal/bronze star

Viet Nam Service Medal/bronze star

Humanitarian Service Medal/bronze star

Meritorious Unit Citation/bronze star

The Cross of Gallantry/with palm

Viet Nam Civil Action Medal/with palm

Navy E Ribbon/bronze star

Sea-Service Deployment Ribbon/bronze star

Republic of Viet Nam Campaign Medal/bronze star

Navy and Marine Corp Medal for Heroism/ (Highest medal for non-combatants)

"My rescue dog rescued both of us."

He did not know it for 16 years, but Ed Zyer was adopted at 10 months of age. He was born on October 14, 1953. His mom, Janice Nygren, and dad, James Zyer, were the only parents he knew for most of his childhood. Ed grew up on a farm near Markham, Illinois on which one set of grandparents had a goat farm (100 goats), and another set of grandparents had a chicken farm (15,000 chickens). His great grandparents lived in nearby Markham. The road near the family was a busy highway, and Ed's house had three floors in it, with a wrap-around porch. His family lived on the second floor. Markham's grade school, which Ed attended, was German Lutheran for grades K-8, with four boys and four girls as enrolled students.

Ed remembers one Christmas in which 30+ people filled the house. Great smells wafted from the kitchen where the women were cooking, as the men told stories and indulged in smoking and drinking beer. For the Christmas tree, a 20-foot pine was cut down from the back of the property. Other boyhood memories include BB guns, bows and arrows, soaping windows, and bikes. Once, a Cadillac driven by an off-duty policeman ran over Ed when he was crossing the street with his Schwinn Stingray. With 265 feet of skid marks, Ed was thrown 20 feet off the road into a ditch. It took 20 minutes to find him, as he was covered in a mass of grass and gravel. He suffered two broken collar bones, a broken left arm, and a fractured skull with traumatic brain injury. As a result, Ed missed a year of school. To get his coordination back, he studied the accordion for three years!

When Ed left high school, he was considered an "old senior," as he had been out of school for the year of the car accident. He began to keep a secret: He had immediately enrolled in the US Navy but did not tell anyone, except his Uncle Ed. Our Ed had always been a rebellious youngster: "I wanted to do things my way." He did work at his dad's new company, a vulcanizing business that made such things as the huge inner tubes for large trucks and other large equipment, until he was called for active duty. The family had moved to Homewood, Illinois about 20 miles from Ed's boyhood home. As everyone was leaving the farm and its work for other occupations, Ed's Uncle John and Aunt Joann took over the challenges of raising livestock. Though adopted, Ed came from a family of spirited adventurers. His great grandfather was the writer, Earl Stanley Gardner. Ancestors from Bangor, Maine having settled there in 1837, fought in the Civil War from 1861 to 1865. Ed's dad's brother, Ed's Uncle Bob, had served on the USS Alabama during World War II. Ed's mom's little brother, Ed, for whom Ed was named, was a frogman during the Korean War. He also served during the Bay of Pigs skirmish, and in Viet Nam. In 1965, these frogmen, Team 12, became known as the first SEALS. No deferments were granted at this time, for the Viet Nam War was beginning to wind down, but a lot of work still needed to be done. Remember, Ed had told no one except his Uncle Ed that he was going into the Navy. On September 12, 1972, he was called to active duty. Back story: In eighth grade, Ed had four classmates who were girls. One girl stood out from all the others (danger zone!!)! Her name was Carol Krantz, and on the occasion of a gathering with friends and relatives, he gave her a promise ring and said he was going into the Navy. This party was his send off. His mother fainted, and beers were hoisted.

In November, after boot camp, graduation occurred at Great Lakes. Nineteen-year-old Ed went to Chicago and quickly left; it was three degrees! Ten hours later, he reported to San Diego Naval Station. It was a balmy 72 degrees and like an instant sauna, with 80% humidity. His group was met by a "gold guy" in that he had more gold stripes than Mr. T, from the TV show, *The A Team*. They were herded onto a bus that had wired windows with US NAVY printed on the side. At the naval base, they were left at Pier 1, with four ships, two on each side, equipped with bombs, trucks, and jeeps. They had orders for the second ship, the USS Durham LKA 114, painted in huge white letters, seen a quarter mile away. Then they were to report to the 4th Pier. Along the way, they saw cargo, freighters and airplanes. When they reached the 4th Pier, they had to find their ship: The second on the right, the USS Durham. They had to walk three-fourths of a mile to get to it. Upon arriving, like any other person boarding ship, they were piped aboard by the boatswain's mate's whistle.

Ed did not know about the Durham. It was a cargo landing craft assault (LKA). From her main deck to the water was 67 feet, with no cargo or personnel aboard the ship; when it was completely full, it was 45 feet to the water. The length of the ship was 396 feet; the width, 75 feet. It had all sorts of supplies like food and fuel, and lots of people. All nationalities were on board. The craft had four holds, two forward and two aft, 15 to 20 feet high. The newbies observed that one area was the gate for large cranes. Ed's group was taken to the middle berths: Beds were metal bunks with mattresses three to four inches thick, a little pillow and one gray blanket. Bunks were six high with nearby showers. About this time, Ed was rethinking his decision to join up… They toured the mess decks and had lunch. Later, they had dinner and met more people. A movie, coffee with dice, cards and dominos were followed by bed at 3:00 AM, supposedly to sleep. Reveille was at 6:00 AM. The ship seemed to be moving… it was! Anchors have huge chains on them, and tend to be the length of the ship. On the ends of the chains are the anchors themselves, which are about the size of small VW's. Since oceanic waters are deeper than the ships which travel them, when the anchor is released, the ship slows down and drifts in place: Moving but not going anywhere. The Durham carried enough diesel fuel and produced enough steam and electricity to serve the entire city of Los Angeles for 24 hours. Clothing became uniforms with denim bell bottom dungarees and blue shirts with a name on them; Ed's name was on his shirt. To him, it was the "coolest" sort of uniform ever. Then, breakfast, and as the ship was really moving, past bases, and under the San Diego Bridge, seasickness struck. "Vomit over the side," cautioned Chief Jim Wiggins. "Look out forward and aft." Ed threw up for several hours.

Ed's buddies became his friends: Bob Kelly from Louisiana (New Orleans), Tim Schuller from Illinois (Chicago), Bob Gadigan from Michigan and Lyle Hicks from Oregon. They would be living with 300 guys for the next three years, from machinist mates (engineers), to technicians, to "snipes.." {Author's Note: Remember the *Hardy Boys' Mysteries* on *The Mickey Mouse Club* TV show, when novice campers were taken to the woods at night and told to bag a snipe, so they could go back to Base Camp….and there was never a snipe to be seen?} The ship's snipes went up, over and down throughout the ship's turbines, boilers, and huge evaporators with the main propulsion room at water level and the size of a football stadium, and kept the ship running smoothly, often unnoticed, like the elusive birds of the Hardy Boys' stories. They did this for two weeks steady, while learning orientations: HP = turn, LP =

reverse, etc. With 600 pounds of steam, the ship was hot in the summer, warm in the winter.

Great adventures began to happen. Within the first 24 hours, the ship stopped in Acapulco, the place where Ed went, in his words, "from an altar boy to a holy terror!" Acapulco was featured in

The wide World of Sports for many years. It was the playground of such notables as Frank Sinatra, Jocy Bishop, Dean Martin, Sammy Davis, Jr. and Peter Lawford: The Rat Pack. It provided such indulgences as fine cigars, "pot,'" cliff diving viewed from a horse-shoe shaped bar named the Sam Miguel, sailing and chasing women. Leaving this rich paradise, the Durham cruised back to San Diego to pick up supplies and Marines; then it was off to Hawaii. Ed still loved his girlfriend, but he was torn between his loyalty to her and *The Wide World of Ed's Sports!* He visited monuments, volcanoes, and toured the sights. The Durham moved forward on her journey: To Okinawa to pick up more Marines, and to Wake Island, a tiny piece of coral where planes landed, and on to Japan: Okuska and Tokyo naval bases. Eventually, the Durham reached Hong Kong, the Las Vegas of the Far East. Mercedes taxis, open markets, rickshaw races, soccer with a Chinese team, football, exotic foods, beer, basketball with another team were all part of a delicious mix, until a typhoon arrived, bringing winds that blew refuse everywhere. Crew members waited in the "eye of the storm" where the waves were calm, and it was sunny skies, as they could not make it out of Kowloon for another day. The next stop was Korea, where the men played war games with Korean Marines in 40-degree weather, and the engine room on the ship was 85 degrees! More US Marines were picked up and the ship made its way back between Korea and Hawaii. An order called "swim call" was sounded. The ship stopped, and "all hands" were ordered on deck! Anchor was lowered 60 to 70 feet, and a party began right in the middle of the ocean! The movie, *Jaws*, had arrived on screen, but possible attacks did not deter the revelers. Guitars, BBQ and ocean diving in water clear for hundreds of feet down were the activities of the day. Even the bottom of the ship was visible! They were 2500 miles from the nearest land... At 5:30 PM they called it quits. This would be a mini-holiday to remember when the going got tough, and it would eventually get tough.

Next stop was the Philippines, a base for all branches of the military: Marines, Army, Air Force, and Navy. Outside the Navy Base was a village, Olongapo City. It was beginning to be real for Ed, and he paid attention. There was a bar, hotel, doctor's office and...girls in cages. It was a "real Sodom and Gomorrah," and brought more "sinning." Ed was in touch with his girlfriend; he called collect from Okinawa, and a very strict Dad answered. Ed was being paid back. His wayward ways had brought trouble to him, and they made the decision that he and Carol would not see each other again. They would talk when he got home.

Arriving back in San Diego, Ed met men from Maine to Washington, Oregon to Florida and Texas, and even the Philippines, black, white and everything in between. It was a grand time in the '70s, being gone for six months and home for six months. He rented an apartment with three other guys and bought a damaged junker '48 Plymouth for $400.00. It had a steel frame! They lived month to month for several months...the good times were about to be turned upside down...

On May 7, 1973, the Viet Nam War was officially over. In 1973, Operation Homecoming, a 208 Prisoner of War exchange using a TWA prop plane flew out of Hanoi. The Durham was part of the 7th fleet, with ships from Japan and South Korea. These operations continued into 1975.

Ed's journey took him to Hawaii, then to Okinawa to get more Marines, and then back to Hawaii to drop them off. During an R & R in 1974, Ed's girl stopped writing. He told her he was coming home. She did go to a party with him; they got drunk, he walked her home, kissed her goodbye, and that was the last time he saw her. So much for high school romances...

At the end of 1974 and into 1975, the Durham and her crew sailed into the South China Sea. They saw tracers and explosions, but no combat troops were left, except at the Embassy. They went to Okinawa, then during the last two weeks of March and the first two weeks of April, they were ordered to get refugees from Viet Nam. They arrived in Vong Toa, then to Phaung Rahng. It was like China Beach: Four to five thousand displaced homeless souls and more kept coming! Then, the ship went back to Vong Toa. The Durham was the command landing ship transporter. It was the flagship until the carrier the USS Blue Ridge arrived. Refugees were everywhere on the ship, as well as on four Trans-American freighters, which were sent to the Philippines. Bob Kelly used a ladder for people to get on the ship, but droves of humanity kept coming, in anything that would float, even pieces of mortar, bathtubs or floats... hundreds of thousands. Waves churned the water at two-to-four-foot heights. The ship had to do "skyscrapers," coming in sideways, so this human wave would minimize injury to those in the smaller boats. Fire hoses sprayed people and their belongings like out-of-control cattle to keep them in lines, to no avail. Shipmates Tim Schuller, Bob Gadigan, Jim McCallister, and Eli Whitney, along with Ed, were part of the crew assigned to this horror story of trying to keep the sea of humanity at bay… an unimaginable nightmare!

One desperate man yelled, "Take my daughter!"

At that moment, the boat dropped in the waving water, and the 10-to-12-year-old girl was suspended between the boats, one very small and one extremely large: The Durham. The man, who was dressed meticulously in a business suit, shoved a duffel bag full of Vietnamese money, dong (pronounced with a soft/silent 'g'), into Ed's hands, where he threw it onto the ship's deck and, as the father tossed his daughter for Ed to catch, the wave dropped and the girl in her rice-filled pants, was dropped to the water, where she sank like a rock! Ed was commanded to "let her go."

Friend Eli said, "Go get her."

Ed, who loved to swim, dove in past the girl, grabbed her and the 30 pounds of rice she was carrying, by the "butt and both arms." Still under water, Ed could see Eli's hands reaching for them. All this while, the boat and all those around them were in the waving water. Ed could see Eli between the boat and the ladder, and when the wave was high, he pushed as hard as he could to get the girl to Eli. Eli grabbed the girl, and that's when the Durham smashed into the other boat where the girl's father was waiting. Ed swam to an access ladder as the dad's boat floated back, and became stuck, literally, between a rock and a hard place. He went under the access ladder and was safe. He came up to get air, but waited for other little boats to leave before attempting to get back on the Durham. One of the belts on the ladder scratched Ed, leaving a big gash on his arm. When the wave was high again, Eli reached for Ed, as Ed pushed himself up. Others were asking if he was "ok," and he remembers he was taken to sick bay. This moment of rescue was captured in several popular magazines of the time.. The sailor without his shirt in one of the pictures at the end of his story was Ed. To celebrate, a Corpsman gave Ed a medicinal bottle of brandy (the type served on airplanes), and a blanket for a respite; then he was sent back to duty. The Captain called his parents to give them the heroic news about their son. (Aside: Ed's grandmother was the only family member to see any notice of the event. She saw the news on TV and said, "There's Eddy's ship!") The only blight on the action was that Ed was fined because he disobeyed his superior officer, and he was not wearing his shirt! {Author's Note: Really????? A superhuman rescue had just occurred, but the military had to maintain protocol!!} Ed had to go to a Captain's Mast, and was demoted from E4 to E3, and fined $250.00. However, he was awarded the Navy and Marine Corps Medal for Heroism, the highest award medal for non-combatants. It was estimated that several thousand refugees were rescued on the USS Durham that day. Through several ships' logs and helicopter reports, and several trips to the Philippines, Okinawa, and Korea, and the thousands who were turned away, it was estimated that more than 7000 lives were saved. Our men had become heroes. The Operation was called, "Frequent Wind." The heartbreak of this tough job done well was the torture of watching thousands of people swimming frantically toward the Durham as she churned away from the bay. PTSD was now truly part of Ed's life. It haunts him to this day.

Back in San Diego, Ed asked to re-enlist. He was told to "go back to a recruiter." He began a new life as a civilian. He stayed with relatives for a while, bought a sports car and landed a job as a magazine salesman; it was not for him, and he kept his hair short with short sideburns, out of fashion for the big-haired, sideburn-adorned '70s. He lived in hotels and towns in California, working his way through college with a percentage of what he sold.

Then he met a blue-eyed blonde beach bunny, named Peggy Stevenson, somehow related to the former senator, Adlai Stevenson, and traveled to several places with her. He decided to go back to Illinois, and go home. He called his folks, sold his car and bought two bus tickets. He bought a t-shirt that read, "Hang 10" and bib overalls, and presented himself and his girl to his folks in a brim-backwards baseball cap. They got married, went to Steger, Illinois and bought a 3-bedroom, 2-bath house with a basement, and raised two daughters. Ed worked for the railroad for five years until he was laid off. He painted businesses, churches, a water tower, a boatswain's chair, apartments, anything, but really wanted to go to work full-time

Ed had a temper! He wasn't physically abusive to his wife; he was a verbal abuser. He also liked to fight: anything would set him off, and he would get into it with any opponent. PTSD was showing itself, but he did not know it. He and his wife were separated, they started seeing other people and a divorce became the next step. (During this time, he bought a pistol, but did not use it.) He left his wife, kids and Steger, returning to Illinois, and "hot walked" race horses in Balmoral Race Track. He also groomed and washed them and cleaned their stalls. He saved his money for six months while he worked cooling prize-winning horse flesh after their races. He received a call from Peggy during which he said, "Let's get out of here." He had most of the afternoon off, had saved money at $300.00 a week, a lot of cash then, and went to his brother's place in Arlington Heights, in Illinois. They moved into a nice place with mixed tenants. He landscaped, working to buy a new home. This move was not good: Shady people and bad times. Peggy's head had been turned by a black man. One day she went out for cigarettes and never returned. An attorney was called, and a divorce became final. Peggy got custody of the kids.

Then Ed, now 29, met Ann Lauderback: age 22. They dated for a year, then Ann became pregnant, but Ed already had to pay $250.00 per month for child support. He only saw his children on weekends. Ann worked at The Cattle Company, a high-end steak house, on weekends, while they tried to get custody of the two girls. Peggy, Ed's ex, was living in a one-room hotel rental with her black boyfriend, and eating quite well, on what, Ed had no idea. Whenever he saw the girls, they were unkempt, had dirty clothes and needed grooming, like haircuts. He had a lawyer friend in Chicago, whom he asked for help getting custody of the girls, Renee and Savannah, ages four and six, respectively. Peggy was ordered to appear in court for a year and was always a no-show. Finally, behind a locked courtroom door, they started proceedings, unusual in the 1980's, as the mother usually got custody of the children, but it was necessary. The judge gave full custody to Ed, they shook hands, and Ann and Ed were finally able to get married. They had a son, named Sean, and the two girls, a growing family. However, he was a hunter and fisherman, and she was a city girl. It was a case of "your kids, not mine," and vice-versa... One time at dinner with Ann's parents, Ann sat down at the table and stated, "I want a divorce." Ed started punching holes in a door and became more violent. {Author's Note: PTSD with violence and no counseling or emotional help is an ongoing national problem.} He called his sister in Antioch, Illinois on the Wisconsin border and asked her if he could move in with them. He worked as a garbage man and had his child support to help pay expenses. Ed's sister took care of the youngsters for about a year, while he worked.

Ed met still another blonde: Elizabeth Obachowski (Beth), five years younger than Ed. Her own son, also Sean, went to school with his daughter. They moved to Twin Lakes, Wisconsin, lived together for five years and were married for five years. He saw the son he had with his second wife on weekends beginning on Friday night after work. Between his third wife and him, Ed raised all their children: The girls and her son: Sean Michael Zyer, Sean Michael Stech, and their own third son, Zachary. This last child found himself in lots of fights... reasons??? This son was very much like his dad. He had anger issues. Ed took him to a doctor who diagnosed bipolar disorder... like himself?

As the children grew, life changed course, as it will do. When daughter Renee was in her senior high school year, as a gift, Ed searched to find her real mom. He contacted Oprah Winfrey, and Dr. Phil, and for $39.95 the search was on. Mom Peggy had either changed her Social Security number, passed away or was not in the country... no luck in finding her. Dad Ed bought Renee a car for graduation. She met and married a fellow named Jason Snyder. They have a daughter, Traliegh, who at this writing is a senior in high school, with eyes to the future as a child care specialist. Son James is a junior in high school. They live on a 240-acre farm, where Renee is a stay-at-home mom. Jason is a foreman for a construction company. When Savannah was a senior, once again, Ed searched for Mom through Oprah, for $39.95...no luck. After high school, Savannah sewed her own "wild oats" and moved to Florida, shortly realizing she could not live so far from home, especially her dad. Her "wild child" lifestyle wasn't going to help her realize her potential. She settled down and married in 2007. She started working for an online company in Racine, Wisconsin trying to decide what she wanted for a career. She "grew" with the company, and today is the Call Center Manager. Her marriage ended in 2013, but her career flourished; she is loving it, and could not be "more excited." Now, it's baby girls, the four-legged kind, Chihuahuas Maui and Charlotte, along with a wonderful man named Eddie (like Savannah's dad), who was recently honorably discharged from the US Army, and his two children, a boy, Cannon, and a girl, Acely. Son Sean (Maynard) Zyer was a good athlete who won a scholarship for baseball, and earned an Associate's Degree at Western Texas Junior University. He then earned a Bachelor's Degree after five years of college at the University of Colorado. After all this college "work," he decided he needed a vacation, so he started to party a little with his friends, and wound up in Germany for its Oktoberfest. He lives with his mate, Sammy, and two children: Finlee, two, as of this writing, and Reagan, two months. Sean works for a pet food company as a troubleshooter (quality control), and Sammy works as a personal fitness trainer and natural food expert. Ed saw his other son, Zachary, on weekends, then the young man moved to Colorado with his stuff, graduated high school and came home. He works Fridays and Saturdays at a hotel, earning $400.00 and $500.00 in tips alone. He rides to work with a friend to whom he sold his car, and lives with his mom, Beth. Earlier, for a while, he visited Colorado to see his brother but didn't care for the "house rules" imposed by brother Sean. Two of Ed's exes watched as events with all the kids transpired: One lived two blocks away from the family, and the other one block away, in the same town!

The next years brought some of the war back to Ed. He lost a job, became a bouncer in a bar, became friends with the owner and rented a room from him for $300.00 a month. There, he met an old Marine with PTSD, who had been shot in the late 1960's, and who had been disabled for 20 years. His advice to Ed: "You need to talk to somebody." He put Ed in a truck and sent him to Ted Biever, an Illinois Veterans' Service Officer, for an interview. Ted sent him to Dr. Lynn Melenfont. Three years into his counseling at $108.00 a month, he was given a rating of 10% PTSD. Ed had no ribbons or medals, but with the help he was given, officials went through Naval records, and he was finally awarded the National Defense Medal for '72-'73. Ed also joined the VFW. Senator Feingold, from the Department of Defense, came to one of the meetings in 1995. He said he would look into Ed's situation. It took six months, but finally, an envelope arrived stuffed with a sheet of paper awarding Ed with the US Naval and Marine Corps medals for heroism. Since 1975, he had been entitled to these ribbons.

{Author's Note: Today, while most military personnel receive their awards and medals automatically and soon after they are earned, the soldiers, sailors, and airmen of the Viet Nam Era have not been publicly informed that these awards are to be given to them for their services. They must ask, and then the official in charge of these matters must go on a search for the right department to inquire about them, and through rigorous background checks for veracity and any other number of red tape channels, and only then, are the Viet Nam Veterans awarded these medals and ribbons that are rightfully theirs. This is an outrage! While I do not in any way want to discredit or deny the young military personnel of today their own medals and badges of courage, I am angry that our Viet Nam Veterans must beg for theirs, and be further humiliated while some flunky searches for the truth of their claims, often taking years to do so. Many operations during the Viet Nam War were classified, as in, no one was to really know what happened in the fields and forests of the besieged country. Many operations were buried in files that no one could read, or worse, those records were destroyed! }

Ed learned to make copies of everything. In March of 2003 affidavits were sent to Milwaukie, Wisconsin. At the Veterans Disabled Board, Ed was finally awarded 70% PTSD, and because of hearing loss in both ears (he wears hearing aids) he was given another 10%. Also, he is unemployable. Reason: "He doesn't play well with others." He has Agent Orange exposure, because the poison was sprayed from the mountains to the Mekong Delta, and the ships' crews had to take showers with water that had been contaminated. Ed has lesions, like so many others do. Since the US does not re-evaluate, it took 11 years to finally get 100% disability from his time in a war zone.

Ed's life changed greatly in the years after the war. He lashed out at people, had road rage, and while he had work he had to take "pee" tests, and was found "slightly positive" from his partying one night. How does "slightly positive" fit when he'd had no pot or drink at the party? He was sent home and collected unemployment for one month. The Union did get him a new job for a while. He does have money in the bank, and expenses are few. He has seen several doctors for new medicines that come on the market, and goes along with their new ideas about how to help him. {Author's Note: Indeed, during a recent phone call, he seemed to be in better spirits than when I first visited with him last spring.:)} He likes to be alone, with his dog, Polly. He had one service dog, J.R., for 11 years, and when he died, he asked for another one. It was taking several months for this easy request to happen, so when a friend told him she had seen a rescue dog in a kill shelter that she thought he might like, he checked her out. Ed visited the South Suburban Humane Society, and just a few days before she was to be euthanized, man and dog met. She now lives with Ed, a very mannerly lady named Polly. Ed and Polly started her training as a service dog on February 1, 2016. She passed her tests, and now Ed is able to take her with him wherever he goes. Ed might still be waiting for a service-sanctioned service dog!

Ed and Polly have come to some celebrity with their situation. Ed's doctor thought a service dog might help Ed with his PTSD. Since the VA does not seem to recognize PTSD as a real illness/handicap, he gets no disability rating for the necessity/prescription of a service dog. However, as a result of some media coverage, Ed is being asked to speak to various local groups about the help/healing/comfort that service dogs provide. He and Polly are becoming ambassadors for this wonderful way to assist our veterans and others with trauma-induced illness… without drugs!!! {Author's Note: See www.petsmartcharities.org}

{Author's Note: Therapy dogs are trained for assisting someone who needs help for such situations as recovery from an accident, or to brighten someone's day at a care facility. Service dogs are trained for a particular person who is handicapped in some way: Blindness, PTSD victim, hearing impaired, etc. They are like prescription medicine. For Ed, Polly knows when he is getting nervous or upset, and will place herself between Ed and the problem. She checks on him when she senses that he is agitated. She is his constant companion. Ed applied to the VA, who through its usual paperwork, confusion and ignoring Ed's pleas for an approval to have the dog trained, nearly lost the opportunity to have Polly put into a program in which she and Ed would go through her Service Dog training together. He nearly needed his children to come to the correct offices as advocates for their dad, when the approval finally arrived. He and Polly attended ten weeks of in-class training, then 120 hours of public training: Street traffic, restaurants and different business situations as well as social gatherings to certify her. Polly is now a certified Department of Defense working service dog. Again, just one more situation of hard work to get the help our Viet Nam Veterans need; they need it NOW, not after several years of back-burner, bottom-of-the-pile-phlegmatic lassitude on the part of the government.}

Ed hunts deer, has a bass boat, a jeep and goes ice fishing... with the dog! His daughters live close to him and he goes to see his son often. A sad note: Two of his friends recently committed suicide: Charlie Nelson, 63, and Jeremy Lutz, 29, a veteran of Afghanistan's war. Ed has volunteered with firefighters in his town by saving people in disastrous situations and has been awarded several citations from the fire department. On one such occasion of helping someone else, he broke his leg and tore some ligaments. He still has nightmares about these events, those from this year in which two buddies killed themselves, and those from Viet Nam, especially all those thousands of people who could not be saved.

Ed has not spoken to his brothers and sisters in 20 to 25 years. At a family reunion, he talked with his brother, Jim, who informed him that his parents, especially his dad, were upset that he had contacted his birth father. Ed had to look to Ancestry.com to know that he has his first grandson; all the other children had daughters.

In 2003, Ed was invited to his 30-year high school reunion by none other than his old girlfriend,

Carol. Six of the original eight from grade school attended, as well as about a thousand of his high school alumni.

After the usual, "Hi, how ya' doin'?" and promising to get together, it was over. Almost a footnote now, several years after the fact, Ed's first ex, Peggy, was found in Arkansas, living with her husband. She has remarried and has two children, one a son, whom Ed has met. Ed commented that the young man seems nice. Arrangements were made, and after an introduction to Dr. Phil, two weeks later, Savannah was flown to California, went to Grauman's Chinese Theater, saw a movie, was picked up and she saw her mother for the first time in nearly two decades, on the Dr. Phil Show. Ed said his ex "looked like the Liberty Bell with piercings and tattoos."

Another footnote: The last battle in Viet Nam was the USS Mayaquez Incident. Refugees off the island of Cambodia were being shot by Cambodians, who were also shooting at those in helicopters who were trying to help the refugees.. The Marines came in and rescued over 70 Americans, all but three. Then, the Marines were ordered to leave! It was called "Operation Eagle Pull." One of these men left behind has just been brought back home, to Burlington, Wisconsin. Ed has been asked to be part of his honor guard, to pay tribute to the life of a brave man. It is a great honor to Ed to be able to participate.

Ed has mixed feelings about life at this time. "Our generation is now 60 to 75 years old. Veterans from Afghanistan and Iraq owe us a debt of gratitude for our experiences in getting help for PTSD and toxic exposure." He has a little resentment that "we fought for what they get for free." However, he is contented. He likes and enjoys life, and with his few creature comforts and his canine girlfriend.. Would he do it all over again? He would, "and then some!" He's been there, done that, led a colorful life, has children and grandkids… "It's been a great time."

Ed Zyer, it has been a pleasure getting to know you. You have been a man who takes matters into his own hands, deals with it and goes on. You did not wait for others to step in and help; you did the right thing, and others' lives have been richer for it. Know that you are a hero to thousands, who will never meet you, but will keep you in their prayers. I thank you for your service to our country.

THE SECRETARY OF THE NAVY
WASHINGTON, D. C. 20350

The President of the United States takes pleasure in presenting the NAVY AND MARINE CORPS MEDAL to

EDWARD A. ZYER
FIREMAN
UNITED STATES NAVY

for service as set forth in the following

CITATION:

For heroism while serving on board USS DURHAM (LKA-114) at Phan Rang Bay, Republic of Vietnam on 3 April 1975. Upon observing a Vietnamese woman fall into the water and in danger of drowning and being crushed between DURHAM's accommodation ladder platform and the refugee boat alongside, Fireman Zyer, with complete disregard for his own safety and fully aware of the personal dangers involved, unhesitatingly leaped into the dangerous area between the unloading boat and the platform to effect the rescue of the woman. Fireman Zyer's courageous and prompt actions in the face of great personal risk undoubtedly saved the woman from being crushed and drowned; thereby reflecting great credit upon himself and upholding the highest traditions of the United States Naval Service.

For the President,

J. William Middendorf

Secretary of the Navy

THE UNITED STATES OF AMERICA
THIS IS TO CERTIFY THAT
THE PRESIDENT OF THE UNITED STATES OF AMERICA
HAS AWARDED THE

NAVY AND MARINE CORPS MEDAL

TO
FIREMAN EDWARD A. ZYER, UNITED STATES NAVY

FOR
HEROISM

ON 3 APRIL 1975

GIVEN THIS   12TH   DAY OF   NOV   19 75

SECRETARY OF THE NAVY

2. Heroism medal certificate

3. Navy men and Marines on the USS Durham load refugees who came in boats of all sizes to be rescued. Ed is shown, back view, without his shirt.

4. Ed shares affection with his official service dog, Polly, who is his constant companion.

5. Ed and Polly stroll near Ed's favorite fishing pond.

Central Oregon Veterans Ranch
The Story of Alison Perry and Her Evolving Dream to Help Veterans

Because the format of biographies in this book discusses the back story of persons involved, as well as their growth into the people they are today, I feel that it is important that the story of the Central Oregon Veterans Ranch begins with the story of its founder, Alison Perry. Hers is an amazing journey of growing into herself as a mover and shaker, through her childhood, education, work experience and evolution of focus for her life's work. She did not come into this project lightly, but with determination, dedication and great love. I first heard about Ms. Perry in the spring of 2016 when I was still doing research for this book. I met her at the Central Oregon Veterans Ranch, located between Bend and Redmond, Oregon. Her passion and kindness, and a bit of a driven intensity impressed me so much. With the depth and breadth of her dream, it is certain to be a hallmark project for the welcome and care of warriors who need a place to rest and feel safe at the end of their lives.

Alison Perry was raised in what most people would call a middle- to upper-class family. Economically the family was "stable, privileged compared to most of the world," but the scars of physical and emotional abuse were present. Alison was the first child of the family, her brother arriving 13 months later. Their parents divorced when Alison was five. This event precipitated a bond between her brother and her, as they survived the challenges of both "broken" and "blended" families. Both parents remarried within several years following the divorce, each marrying persons with substance abuse and mental health issues. Dad was the basic "Disneyland Dad," and while there were love and passion in the home, the routine with Mom and stepfather was rigid and strict, with the added ingredients of physical and verbal violence, alcohol abuse and other boundary violations and abuses. The stepfather was bipolar and alcoholic. When she was young and unable to stop the abuse, Alison developed a "protector-warrior spirit," presenting an attitude of defiance toward the injustice. With the training ground of those events, Alison has always felt protective of her brother, and this bond contributed to the sense of "kinship" she felt when she began working with veterans. To her, they were family, too.

Alison's education and early work experiences are rich and varied. In 2000, she moved from Georgia to Oregon. At first, she was interested in art therapy, but changed her mind and pursued a Master's Degree in Counselor Education from Portland State University. She began her graduate program exactly one month and one day after **9/11**. Not one of the professors for the program, which included 150 students, mentioned **9/11** at the orientation for the program that evening, or after. Alison was shocked, as she knew that "this would change our nation forever, and that our profession would be impacted significantly in the years to come."

While Alison was in her program, her brother deployed for the invasion of Iraq as an Apache helicopter pilot in February of 2003. Working in the back of a middle school classroom in April of that year, Alison heard radio programming interrupted to announce that the United States had begun the bombing of Bagdad. Tearfully, she knew "the war was real now." Her brother was in Iraq to support ground troops. A fellow teacher joined Alison in tearful emotion, saying her brother, too, had gone to war during the Viet Nam era. Returning from his first deployment, Alison's brother no longer wished to be part of the Apache mission of "death from above." He decided to either fly Medevac or get out and fly as their father had as a 40-year retired Delta pilot. He was granted the Medevac assignment, doing two more tours in Iraq between 2005 and 2011, under the motto, "life from above." The first year of her brother's deployment was scary, and real for her, and she felt isolated in her experience as she dealt with Portland's culture that seemed immune to the personal impact of war.

Graduating in 2004, Alison met her goal of being in private practice, but "felt called to serve in a greater capacity," remembering her and her brother's mutual experiences, and watching the faces of young men and women appear on the screen each night on the Jim Lehrer News Hour, a "roll call" for those who had died in the Middle East. She cold-called the VA Medical Center three times before getting a call back for an informational interview. Rebecca McBee-Wilson called with a work- interview request, as the mental health clinic was flooded with referrals and an 'unofficial' wait list that was increasing daily. Alison met with Rebecca, a licensed clinical social worker, and co-manager of the clinic. She had been with the VA for 30 years and shared that her brother had been a helicopter pilot in Viet Nam: "He was never the same after the war." She hired Alison on the spot for part-time contract work.

This next phase of Alison's journey became the tinder and fuel for her life's mission. Many jobs were the stepping stones for her journey's next act, giving her the tools she would ultimately need in her skill set. She began part-time in the general mental health clinic at the Portland VA, doing intakes, assessments, and one-on-one counseling. Seeing Afghanistan and Iraq Veterans coming in for the first time, she was surprised to see Viet Nam Veterans also coming in for the first time. They would shake nervously, and apologize for tearing up, telling her she was the first person in 40 years to hear their stories. No one else had heard them. She was humbled and honored that they would speak with her. "It was an honor, a sacred gift that I was the first person to receive these experiences."

Within six months, the manager of the PTSD Clinical Team told Rebecca that it was being overwhelmed with requests for family/marriage therapy. Alison's education gave her the qualifications to work with the Team, and thus, she began working under the mentorship and supervision of James (Jim) Sardo, a psychologist serving with the Air National Guard, who had deployed to Iraq. Soon she was an integral part of the Team, part of a mission that bound her to her colleagues in a manner that paralleled the experience of soldiers "being on the front lines." While they were not on a physical battleground, they were entering the battles veterans had raging within themselves, and the fallout that this often caused in their external lives. Experiencing nothing like it before, Alison found the work challenging, meaningful and rewarding. She was fueled with passion and dedication. As an unlicensed counselor, however, she could not get a permanent position. She saw interns being hired for full-time positions, while she remained a contract worker without benefits. This situation precipitated her move to the Bend VA Community-Based Outpatient Clinic (CBOC) in Central Oregon.

Just before leaving Portland, Alison had "**a case that was the spark for the Veterans Ranch**." She received a counseling referral for a 22-year-old Iraq War Veteran. She was shocked at how young he was. While the average age of Vietnam War soldiers was a very young 19, "Operation Enduring Freedom" and "Operation Iraqi Freedom" (OEF/OIF) Veterans tended to be in their early 20's or older when they were deployed. This particular veteran, at age 18, had been coerced into the military by his dysfunctional family and landed in Iraq. After the deployment, this young veteran was sexually assaulted by a fellow service member, and was showing his first symptoms of paranoid-schizophrenia. The system viewed him as a problem child: "high needs" or "complex" client. Alison and a social work colleague took him under their wing, to start building trust and rapport with this traumatized young man. One day they received a call that he was in the psychiatric ward, "lock-down," throwing furniture and threatening staff. Alison's first reaction was anger: "If I'd been through what that kid has been through, I might be acting the same way!" was her thought. "Locked in a fluorescent white-walled lock down unit, with hospital staff poking, prodding, diagnosing and medicating," Alison thought, "Re-traumatizing." Alison spoke to her colleague: "I wish we had a sheep ranch out east, where we could send these guys when they got home from war… a place where they could work on the land, sleep under the stars and be in a community of other veterans… away from this over-stimulating, re-traumatizing urban environment." Such is the stuff of which dreams are made…

In early 2008, Alison transferred to the CBOC where she began working with a significantly older population of veterans, including four combat PTSD therapy groups. Each group contained between 10 and 20 men who were mostly Viet Nam Veterans, with a Korean or WWII Veteran in some groups. The room's wall had a Viet Nam blanket on it depicting helicopters flying over the jungle. Sometimes, Alison wondered if it was "2008 or 1968." She came to know these veterans very well, and she was welcomed into their brotherhood, some of them calling her 'Doc' or 'little sis.' She suddenly had a bunch of big brothers or dads to look out for her.

During the three years at the clinic, Alison began to hear comments from the veterans about death and dying. "When I die, I don't want anyone around, not even my own family. I want to be like the Native Americans and go off in the woods and die alone." "I'm not afraid of death, but I'm afraid of dying." {Author's Note: Alison states here the same facts I have mentioned throughout the stories of the veterans I have interviewed: "With the chronic health issues of Viet Nam Veterans as a result of Agent Orange-related cancers, substance abuse-related illnesses and stress-related medical conditions, death was already approaching many of them in their early to mid-60's." See the Viet Nam Factoids section at the back of the book.} Alison began to realize that she was banging her head against the wall with the traditional clinical, medical model approach in trying to get them to "change," with a system that focused on curing rather than healing. She wondered what death would look like for these veterans, and if she could help facilitate their peaceful dying.

Visions of the sheep ranch returned. Alison began to plan how she could involve "younger returning veterans in creating and facilitating peaceful deaths for their combat veteran elders." She was thinking of "a wilderness ranch, a sacred space where aged or ill veterans could die in peace, a place where younger veterans could find purpose, meaning and community... a hub that would serve generations of veterans."

Alison heard the call of her soul...

At this time, between October 2011, and March 2012, Alison began to plot career steps that would get her closer to actualizing her vision from dream to reality. She pondered Joseph Campbell's question as she considered leaving the VA and taking different jobs: "Are you going to use the system, or let the system use you?" Many roads would be traveled before she reached her destination. She transferred from the COBC to the Vancouver campus of the Portland VA to work as a Contracting Officer Representative (COR), helping set up Emergency Transitional Housing programs between the VA and non-profits in the community. April of 2012 found Alison taking a job through a Department of Labor grant at Central Oregon Community College (COCC) so she could get back to Central Oregon. June of 2012 brought an amazing opportunity for Alison and a group of veterans who traveled to Viet Nam. A mission for "peace and reconciliation" took the group to where Alison's "guys" fought: From Hanoi down to the Mekong Delta, with stops in Plei Ku and the Central Highlands. This opportunity was important to Alison, as she wanted to be able to literally be there and talk to veterans about Viet Nam with a more intimate knowing of their experiences, since she would be caring for them during their dying.

Another significant step occurred for Alison in August of 2013 when she resigned from a position as Executive Director of the veterans' housing non-profit, Central Oregon Veterans Outreach (COVO) to move into more active planning of the Ranch. In October of that year, she formed an Advisory Board of Veterans, family members and hospice and health care workers that started the Rural Veterans Hospice Project. Within a few months, at the beginning of 2014, the name was changed to Central Oregon Veterans Ranch (COVR, as in "take cover/cover me"), and received federal 501c3 tax-exempt status as a non-profit on September 12, 2014. {Author's Note: 11 years and one day from **9/11**… dreams sometimes come true in the most amazing ways. We travel on uncommon roads on the journeys to live our dreams.}

Also in October of 2014, an article in *The Bend Bulletin*, Central Oregon's daily newspaper, featured the Ranch and the Quilt Campaign, which honors veterans, with their name and branch of service. The quilt is personalized with a square for each veteran, and was made stitch by stitch, with love by volunteers who crafted the quilts. The Quilt Campaign and newspaper article aided the new organization in raising $40,000.00 in the last quarter of 2014. Alison met with an investor in December of that year, and formed a partnership in the winter of 2015. The deal for the Ranch closed on the Ranch property on April 20, 2015. Also that year, an active veteran volunteer program was developed on the property, with veterans of all ages and eras (primarily Viet Nam and OEF/OIF Veterans) able to foster purpose and meaning with peer support and access to resources. This year, 2016, the Ranch home remodel is nearing completion, and the organization is preparing to submit its application to the state of Oregon for licensure as an adult foster home (AFH). (Hospice is a legal and medical term, so the Ranch will provide supportive housing and specialized care in the AFH). Also this year, Alison formed a partnership with Deborah Grassman, and her organization, Opus Peace, to develop an informational curriculum and an end-of-life program for veterans in the Ranch home.

On-going and future plans for the Ranch include many avenues. Not only a sanctuary for veterans of all ages, but the Ranch "also would facilitate opportunities for education of the public and health care workers on the unique needs and approaches of healing veterans across the lifespan. As specialized services for the veterans in the home expand, complementary modalities, such as acupuncture, massage, energy work, physical therapy and similar healing techniques might be possible. As part of its unique mission, the Ranch will connect generations of veterans, young to old, in the healing process. Dying veterans will share their stories and wisdom, influencing and altering the trajectory of veterans just beginning their life journey. Eventually, the Ranch would like to offer "working retreats": opportunities for veterans from anywhere in the country to stay in a tiny home, cabin or bunkhouse, volunteering on the property or in the Ranch home with veterans at the end of life. All veteran volunteers and staff at the Ranch will be part of a unique culture that is trained and prepared for coping with the challenges of post-traumatic stress at end of life, understanding the critical element of camaraderie and the value of "having your back" that is developed in military culture."

"COVR has received much public support in grant awards and private donations, and continues to develop partnerships with organizations such as the USDA, the Cascade Center for Community Governance (CCGC), OSU Extension Service and other healthcare providers in the region. COVR has capitalized on Ms. Perry's testimonial to the Senate Agricultural Appropriations Committee in April of 2016, as the USDA and CCGC partnered to secure a Technical Assistance Grant that will aid in the development of COVR's strategic framework and solidification of its business model. The Ranch is actively working with the OSU Extension Service and local farmers to develop economically viable agricultural enterprises. The district Rotary clubs have pulled together to submit a grant for a walk-in greenhouse for the organization, another illustration of the vast community support and integration that the COVR model inspires."

Alison Perry is an inspiration for all whom she meets. Through her own journey of vicarious traumatization, burnout and compassion fatigue (including a period of months waking up from jungle combat nightmares and adrenaline shooting through her body), she finally gained the confidence to pursue her dream, and to articulate and implement the deeper meaning behind the Ranch. "The Sheep Ranch is a symbol: A beacon of community and a haven of peace. It is a sanctuary for healing for those who suffer the soul wounds of war. Veterans are too often "lost" in the wilderness, relegated to the fringes of society by those who do not understand or cannot hold the darkness they carry, much less lead them through it. They need a shepherd… a guide… a community of persons and peers who "bring them back into the fold"; a community that shepherds their souls to peace. The Ranch is that place."

{Author's Note: I am honored to be able to share Alison's story for this book. The Central Oregon Veterans Ranch is a model for other Ranches across the country. They are truly needed for our esteemed warriors who sacrificed their freedom, indeed, many with their lives, to answer the call to arms in the preservation of our American way of life, a privilege millions of the world's population only dream to know. They are made of the "right stuff," and it is only fitting that we honor them for the heroes they are, although they will be the first to say they aren't heroes; they just did their job. Alison is a heroine, herself. Thank you for your continuing service to our country.}

Location and Tours

Central Oregon Veterans Ranch is located between

Bend and Redmond near the intersection of Hwy 97 and 61st Street.

For a tour of the Ranch please call (541) 706-9062.

Central Oregon Veterans Ranch

PO Box 8302, Bend, OR 97708

Or by PayPal on their website:

centraloregonveteransranch.org

Alison and Todd Perry
are both siblings and
each other's friend.

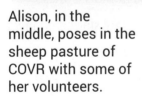

Alison, in the
middle, poses in the
sheep pasture of
COVR with some of
her volunteers.

Alison directs a project
with her volunteers.

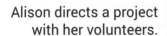

A Widow's Story

An Introduction to Essays on Post Traumatic Stress Disorder (PTSD) and Toxic Exposure (Agent Orange)

It was during an interview with one of the soldier heroes in this book, that I became aware of the difficult battles that spouses, children, and other relatives face not only today, but have fought since their Viet Nam-era warriors came home. Realizing that their returning loved ones would never be emotionally or even physically the same , to the actual reality of dealing with the ensuing symptoms of PTSD, and the forever effects of Agent Orange exposure, this Viet Nam War is still being waged. Recognizing that an unpopular war brought severe consequences as the American public turned its back on the returning veterans and refused to acknowledge their humanity, much less their patriotism, was a bitter pill to swallow for decades. As the veterans have aged the ravages of PTSD, which resulted from no counseling or help from the government , has brought the misery of depression, alcoholism, drug abuse and erupting anger.

Exposure to Agent Orange was a different enemy. It brought cancer, diabetes and skin disorders the medical profession had never before seen. The politics of the time negated any illness or condition as being caused by severe toxicity, such as Agent Orange, when soldiers were "in country." The medical profession followed suit and would not allow any insurance coverage for anomalous situations that were irregular or never-before covered. Many decades later the medical profession began to see these conditions in veterans returning from Iraq, Afghanistan and other Gulf regions. They started connecting the illnesses of Viet Nam Veterans as possibly being related to their overseas experiences. For many veterans and their families, the limited, cautious help has come too little, too late. I will now share the tale of one such widow, whose husband fought in Viet Nam and died at age 63, six years ago. {Author's Note: For the sake of confidentiality, names and specific facts of place have been modified or changed.}

The widow narrates:

My husband was a combat infantryman stationed in Cu Chi, Viet Nam, from March 1967, until March 1968, a draftee. US government records have confirmed that the areas where he operated were all heavily sprayed with Agent Orange. In fact, more than half of all the Agent Orange sprayed on Viet

Nam in the 10 years of US occupation was sprayed in the year he was there, and in three primary areas, one of which being the area he operated from and in.

In 1998, my husband was diagnosed with cancer. Surgery ensued at the VA Medical Center closest to where we were living at the time, though it was quite a drive away. Suffering a very serious infection post-surgery, my husband was hospitalized again to treat that. Removing his own IVs, he walked out of the hospital without being discharged, as he was so dissatisfied and enraged with the quality of(or lack thereof) his care. His post-surgery advice from medical "experts'"had been that he would die in three to five years without chemo and radiation treatments.

For six years, my husband refused treatment the care team had so strongly advised, in spite of continued pressure to comply. We, ourselves, treated his cancer at home with a variety of alternative energy-based methods, and managed to put his cancer into remission twice. Not once did any of his doctors offer encouragement and support, nor ask what he was doing to change the course of the cancer, **or** offer to possibly participate in an alternative form of treatment. They had a singular agenda. One of the methods my husband was using almost daily, required a piece of technology that had been gifted to us by a family member, the cost of which would have been beyond our means. Like all machines, it malfunctioned at one point, and due to the nature of its complexity, had to be sent away to be repaired. It took precious time away from his treatment that allowed his cancer to return. Although he was refusing treatment still recommended by his doctors, he continued going to the VA for tests to keep track of the presence or absence of cancer. These tests were prohibitively expensive, and we could not have afforded them on our private insurance. When he returned for another round of tests during the time the home treatment was unavailable, he found that cancer had returned for the third time. Of course, chemo and radiation were back on the table even more aggressively than before. In spite of all my protests and pleading, I could see that they had worn him down. He refused the chemo, but agreed to the radiation; a flurry of activity began as we prepared him for his "treatment."

Our local hospital provided the radiation treatment under the direction of my husband's doctors from the VA in early 2006. The first serious effects were second-degree burns to his neck and chest. The treatment was done on an out-patient basis, so I was supposed to treat these burns with a bag of first-aid supplies the hospital sent home with him. I felt like I was trying to do the impossible with supplies one would expect for a Boy Scout camping trip, with instructions from a patient who was in too much pain and too angry even to begin to communicate clearly and effectively. A trip back to the hospital so I could get direct help from the cancer treatment nurses did not prove to be any more helpful. The burns eventually did heal, but other complications continued to arise. The radiation had so severely damaged his throat that when he wanted to eat and drink again, it was impossible to do so without aspirating whatever he was trying to take in. Our bodies have a mechanism that usually docs not allow food or liquid to get into our lungs, and for a very good reason! That mechanism in my husband's body no longer functioned. He went back to the VA hospital for a surgical procedure that was intended to repair the damage, but it was unsuccessful. His lungs were so badly scarred that his breathing was seriously compromised, and his thyroid gland was damaged. This was a six-foot tall man who usually weighed in at 170 lbs., and his weight plummeted to 110 lbs.! He was nearly incapable of getting enough food into his body to sustain himself. With the damage to his thyroid, he was not able to maintain his body temperature. He would keep the temperature in his room up to around 85 degrees with space heaters. He managed to live this way for about four years.

Well into this period of trips to the hospital to try to get some kind of help for this myriad of radiation-related complications, I was the one who suggested my husband needed oxygen so he could breathe with some comfort. I was the one who brought to the attention of his supposed caregivers that they had probably damaged his thyroid and needed to test for that, **and** try to prescribe some kinds of meds that could possibly help. They did, and it was never very successful; maybe the damage had become too severe. We were so overwhelmed at this point that it was difficult to figure out what was helping and what was hurting. He was given enough very potent pain medication during this time that could probably kill an elephant. Most of it was brought home and never used. I thought I was living in *The Twilight Zone.* I was having a really difficult time trying to figure out how anyone could consider this situation anything but insane!!

By January of 2010, my husband's physical condition had become so serious that I began to acknowledge the true state of hopelessness that he was experiencing emotionally. I was out of ideas, although I managed to genuinely deny the obvious reality that he was going to die. I'm not sure I could explain to myself, or anyone else to this day, just exactly what I was thinking or feeling in those days. Several months into that year, he awoke with an open wound in his throat that was oozing pus down the front of his chest. He had been at the local VA clinic the day before, and the staff had discovered an infection in the bone in the area of his neck that had been caused by the damage from the radiation. They just sent him home. I don't even remember if he was given antibiotics. Probably…

Nonetheless, the new development that morning made it abundantly clear to me that he needed to be hospitalized, and that would require a several-hour drive to the VA hospital. He was admitted, but the next three weeks remain a blur, even now. When it was decided that the hospital had done all they felt they could do, he was taken by ambulance to a neighboring town to be admitted to a nursing rehab facility. I was home,' three hours away at the time. Instead of getting a call saying that he had arrived at the intended facility, I got a call from the local hospital's critical care unit's doctor saying that my husband had developed severe pneumonia, and was not expected to make it through the night. Although we had agreed years earlier, and had included it in our will that we would not go to extreme measures to keep each other alive, I told the doctor in no uncertain terms to do just that: "Go to extreme measures to keep him alive!" There were now children and grandchildren to be considered and consulted, and I wasn't even close to believing that he was going to die. And, really, does one develop life-threatening pneumonia in a couple of hours, or was he discharged from the VA hospital already well on his way to that condition? No way will I ever know.

 When I arrived at this new hospital, my husband was on life support, a breathing apparatus. I still believed he would get better, and for a short time, even the wonderful staff at that hospital told me it was possible he could regain some quality of life. The staff at this hospital was the one really bright spot in this whole nightmare. They were gentle, and caring and offered me hope. At one point, shortly after I arrived, they sent several non-medical people to make sure I was supported in every way. They wanted to know if I needed a place to stay, or needed a meal or anything else. I so needed someone to give a shit, and I will never forget the depth of appreciation I felt in those moments. The rest of the details I guess, at this point, are incidental. I don't really remember any of it clearly. My fragile patient was shifted back and forth several times from the hospital to the nursing facility, and I came home and returned several times as that unfolded. One morning about a week into this development, I got a call at home, hearing that he had died peacefully sitting in a chair the night before. I wasn't there, and I didn't get to say "goodbye," and I am still really sad about that. We had been married for nearly 40 years. That day, the day he died, I called the VA hospital to talk to the oncologist who had treated my husband for eight years. My husband had really liked this guy. I was able to talk to the doctor's personal nurse. I gave her the news and asked if she would please have him return my call. That never happened. I never got that call.

The widow's story continues:

My husband had filed for compensation from the VA for his Agent Orange exposure and its role in the development of cancer shortly after he was diagnosed. His claim was denied. He did not appeal, as he did not know how the system worked. No one came forward to explain that information to him, and he was too tired and angry to fight the system; it was incapacitating to him. He was, however, during this time, given a partial disability rating for PTSD.

Several years after my husband's death, I again filed a new Agent Orange exposure claim, as it took that long to find someone who was willing to help. It is an extremely complex, overwhelming and time-consuming procedure, sure to thwart even the most determined of souls. The initial claim was denied; the first appeal was denied; the second appeal has been filed, and I have been told that I will probably wait another three years to be given an answer on this appeal. That would be six years of waiting from the date of the first filing of the second attempt, and sixteen plus years from the date of the filing of the first attempt. They may have been waiting for my husband to die, but I am not going anywhere, and neither is my daughter or my grandchildren. Oh, we're in this for the long haul.

{Author's Note: Due to the fact that the VA has continued to deny this veteran's widow the compensation she had a right to receive, she cannot afford the cost of participating in the Medicare program beyond the hospital coverage allowed in Part A of the plan. She needs all moneys from Social Security and a part-time job to meet basic financial needs. I think it is time that the government steps up to help the survivors of the Viet Nam War, **all of them**, including surviving spouses, to ease the senior years of their lives with adequate income to live life with the basics, and that includes proper health care. I **do not in any way** negate or underestimate any of the needs of any of the Viet Nam Veterans, or the needs of war veterans from today's conflicts, as they, too, have earned and should receive their rightful honors and awards. **Many** Viet Nam War heroes have waited decades for their help and honors, and time is running out; indeed, for some, it already has. Dare I say that some of our government officials and Congressional representatives do not want to bother with the messiness of helping our Viet Nam Veterans, and if they wait long enough, our aging brothers, sisters, and spouses will simply die, and voila! Problem solved!}

Words cannot express my gratitude for those who have fought the Viet Nam War from home. They are to be commended for their love, their fortitude and their insistence that right should still win over might. For this heroic widow and her family, I thank you for your continued service to our country.

Toxic Exposure: Agent Orange

Toxic exposure is as old as the first vegetation and animal life on the planet. It protected certain plants and animals from their enemies, and provided protein-eating plants with food from animals, while keeping the balances of the food chain intact within the animal kingdom itself. When man first appeared on the scene, he learned quickly which plants and animals were healthy to ingest, breathe or apply to the skin, and which were not. This knowledge was life-saving, and allowed the human race to thrive. As human populations spread, and either lived peacefully with neighboring clans and tribes, or went to war to claim land and territorial rights for their own, ideas for conquering the enemy began to flourish. For example, poison-tipped arrows, usually obtained from those original poisonous plants and animals, made some of the first weapons, tainting the food and water of not only the animals of the enemies, but also the enemies themselves. As lands became more civilized and unified, government in the form of kings, queens, church leaders and their minions controlled their territories. Suspicious and paranoid rulers often used official "tasters" to taste test the food and drink, to see if the taster became ill or died, before the monarch ate. As the earth became the world's battleground for dominion, power and influence for a nation's standing with its neighbors, weaponry became deadlier: Swords, knives, axes, man-caused fires, floods, avalanches, cannons, assault rifles, hand grenades, bombs dropped from fighter jets, rocket launchers from the ground to the air, the Atom bomb, the Hydrogen bomb and the insidious notion of more poisons. "Toxic Exposure" became a new vocabulary term in the middle of the last century. From mustard gas during World Wars I and II, to atomic radiation, and the experimentation with Agent Orange during the Korean War, to "en masse" exposure during the Viet Nam War, and now sarin gas, other chemicals, and once- eradicated diseases that could destroy whole countries of one's enemies, we humans are slowly, too slowly, beginning to recognize our future: If we continue at this pace, we will become residents of a place in history called the Past.

Is it too late to correct this situation?

For the purposes of this essay, the answer is a "qualified yes." For our Viet Nam Veterans, their families and descendants, toxic exposure is the last enemy of the war, and it will imprison these veterans for many generations.

The widow's tale, regarding one family's experience is, unfortunately, the legacy of the experiences a large proportion of our Viet Nam Veterans and generations of their families have suffered in the last several decades. Since the travesty of this horrific, deliberate poisoning of land, vegetation, animal and human life began, much has been written about what the consequences of this covertly-supported operation, with such overt results, have wrought. Many people have shared what this toxic exposure did to them and their loved ones, while the VA along with the military have stonewalled and repeatedly protested that such claims are unfounded, false, or worse, "all in their heads." It is time that someone who is part of society, and who is on the outside of the circle of veterans who have experienced toxic ex stand up in support of the very people who were promised their government's personal and family care and support if they would volunteer or answer the call of the Draft Board's mandates to join the military to fight the Viet Nam War.

I do not claim to be an expert on the political reasons or the many fronts on which the Viet Nam War was fought. I know what the brave people who told me their stories said to me as their truth, and have heard more stories than are recorded in this book. I do know a few facts about Agent Orange. I do know that it is toxic in the short term, and for many generations to come.

One of the first revelations about toxic exposure, and in most references for the purposes of this book, Agent Orange (AO) and its effects, for me, occurred on November 21, 2015. I attended a Town Hall meeting at the VA Medical Center in Portland, Oregon. John Lind, one of the Vietnam Veterans featured in this book alerted me to this meeting which over 100 people from all over the Pacific Northwest attended. Different panel speakers, including Viet Nam Veterans and their family members, gave background information on the first developments and uses of AO. Some of the literary references given to attendees upon arrival at the meeting are listed at the end of the book. They are able to be obtained by veterans, and their families, of all military branches.

Facts of Reference:

AO was first developed in the early 1940s as a "chemical and biological warfare agent" (Wilcox, pg. 183). In 1946, it began to be used as an herbicide (weed killer) (Wilcox, pg. 183). The United States produced most of it, but its uses were tested and used in other countries as well. Other toxic chemicals were also developed at this time. Each type of chemical was stored in a barrel with a different color band around it to distinguish it from other substances: Blue, green, pink, white and orange, among others (Wilcox, pg. 207). In 1961, it began to be used in Viet Nam as part of the United States' chemical warfare. In 1969, reports came out of Viet Nam that birth defects were being reported in defoliated parts of Viet Nam. In 1970, the Pentagon stopped using AO, as global pressure increased and scientific evidence validated the toxicity for foods that were grown in areas where AO had been sprayed. Dow

Chemical appealed this decision, and the battle for the use of AO versus its terrible damage began (Wilcox, pg. 183-185).

During the Town Hall meeting, more information came to the fore. Not only would the fields and forests lose their plant and animal life, but those people who mixed the batches of these chemicals, the farmers who sprayed it on their fields, the consumers who ate the foods grown in these fields and the soldiers and citizens of the countries where it was sprayed as a defoliant would also lose their lives, but at a much slower rate. Veterans began to complain of 'skin rashes, liver and kidney problems, heart disease, numbness of hands and feet, memory loss and other illnesses," but were accused of "being alcoholics, drug addicts, malingerers, and scam artists'"(Wilcox, pg. xiv). The first "sellout" to big business (Dow) came in the form of an $180,000,000.00 out-of-court settlement for Viet Nam Veterans and their families. The Earth's resources did not belong to people living on the Earth, but to corporations who poison them with cancer-causing chemicals (Wilcox, pg. xv). Then came more health problems… Veterans and their families began to go to doctors and Congressmen to try to get help for strange diseases that had never before occurred in their families. Many veterans had been healthy teenagers or young 20-somethings, who returned from the war and began to age and develop disorders only seen in the very old. One veteran, trying to get answers, contacted Agent Orange International. He had read an article about a Viet Nam Veteran who had a strange form of cancer. He wrote to his Congressman to see if he knew anything about the issue. As the young veteran's wife told his tale on the phone, the aide, or whomever she had reached, wanted to know if Agent Orange was a spy and what did they know about him!?! (Wilcox, pg. 10). If this weren't such a sad commentary, it would be hilarious. Talk about clueless government officials… More records from The Viet Nam Veterans of America (VVA) indicated that on one day of spraying missions, nearly 6,000 Marines were within one-third of a mile from the spray area. Another 10,600 Marines were within nine-tenths of a mile from the spray area. Many more soldiers remain uncounted, but it is verified that more veterans had been exposed than was previously thought (VVA Newsletter, March-April1980) (Wilcox, pg. 10). I personally talked with a Viet Nam Veteran nearly two years ago, who was a victim of AO exposure. He recalled, "I watched it fall from the sky, burn trees on its way down, kill grass in minutes, burn holes in my uniform and burn the skin underneath the fabric, but….it never happened; at least that's what I was told." I believed the man, as I could see the chloracne on his arms. This is a condition that looks like burn scars on the skin, which then scabs over the wounds, flakes off and in a very short time, erupts again. In fact, I saw many of these eruptions on the arms of the men with whom I spoke over the last year and a half. These men were told that no spraying occurred that would hurt them, but during the Freedom of Information Act, not only the chemical companies, but their scientists who had done earlier research and knew of the poisons firsthand, admitted these chemicals were toxic. Added to the injury of diseases was the insult of knowing that 368 pounds of Dioxin (which made 11,000,000gallons of spray) were used to virtually soak the poison into the ground. Low lying airplanes would dowse patterns back and forth over an area much like old-fashioned lawn mowers used to mow pristine patterns on the once-weekly lawn grooming of family homes (Wilcox, pg. 11). Some of the first men to spray this noxious substance were part of "Operation Ranch Hand." They were not always told what they were spraying, but they followed orders and flew hundreds of missions and destroyed millions of acres of foliage. They were some of the first people to be part of studies done on victims of AO exposure: The number and types of missions, how they handled the sprays, the health of them and their children, and when diseases presented themselves (Wilcox, pp. 3-6). At the War's end, "Operation Ranch Hand" had sprayed 1,933,699 pounds of arsenic on the Vietnamese countryside (Wlcox, pg. 63). Finally, another soldier told of his daughters with developmental birth defects, one with a nerve disorder that will eventually leave her deaf, blind and dying an early death, and the other one with half a brain. He remembered that in Viet Nam he and his men would drink water from streams and fill their canteens and helmets with it. They would then put water purifying tablets in it, splash their necks and faces with it and continue their course. Years later, he would learn that using purifying tablets to clean Dioxin-tainted water was "like trying to neutralize a vat of cyanide with an aspirin"(Wilcox, pp. 44-49). When reports came out of Viet Nam that birth defects including "cleft lips, shortened limbs, absence of nose and eyes, malformed ears, club feet, absence of forearm, hydrocephaly (water on the brain) and anencephaly (a condition in which all or major part of the brain is missing) and a variety of heart diseases," the US government, upon hearing about these horrific conditions, dismissed such claims as Communist propaganda. Today, the VA has not changed its response to claims, despite the fact that thousands of Viet Nam Veterans have fathered or given birth to thousands of seriously deformed children (Wilcox, pp.50-58). "There is no medical evidence that exposure to AO has caused birth defects in the children of Viet Nam Veterans" (Wilcox, pg. 51). And yet, mothers are still giving birth to stillborn babies, siblings have little DNA evidence that they are related (Town Hall Meeting, 11/21/15), and a little boy of seven years has webbed toes, sleep disturbances, seizures and learning disabilities (Wilcox, pg. 43).

To be fair, some studies are being done to see if the toxins can be removed from the human body. Kepone, an insecticide like Dioxin, is stored in the fatty tissues of the body. It is also eliminated in the bile fluid, passed into the intestine and then reabsorbed into the body. Kepone and Dioxin might be eliminated from the body by the use of cholestyramine, a bile-salt binder used to treat patients with high cholesterol, and in some cases, those with jaundice. The doctor who postulates this theory thinks it should have been done years ago. He does not care about the blame game; he just thinks that this issue should be dealt with like any other problem: Help the veterans get well (Wilcox, pg.124).

In Australia, a Repatriation Tribunal has finally allowed that toxic chemicals *might* have caused the cancer that killed a Viet Nam Veteran who lived in Sydney. He died before the issue could be proven or disproven, and while the Tribunal will not admit that the cancer was caused by his exposure to AO, exposure to toxic chemicals keeps open the whole issue of all toxic chemicals possibly being the cause of other diseases: "This onus," declared the Tribunal, "is not satisfied beyond a reasonable doubt that there was insufficient grounds for granting the claim…" This, while it does open the door for future claims, is pussyfooting around the issue, and not really putting its judgement on the line (Wilcox, pg.77). The wheels of justice turn slowly… methinks, at times, too slowly for many.

At the end of World War II, toxic pollution, in the form of nuclear waste, was disposed in large metal drums buried in blocks of cement, and then buried underground so it would not leak into the water supplies. In the 1970s, with the end of the Viet Nam War, the toxic brews of AO and its cousins, sometimes of indeterminate recipes (now that it would not be used as a/an germicide/herbicide), were gathered in the most expedient ways possible, at times mixing the leftovers, and disposed in containers, put into warehouses, like Johnson Island in the Pacific, or in Gulfport, Mississippi (Wilcox, pg. 120),and sometimes forgotten, and other times, blown up!!! (Town Hall Meeting, 11/21/15). In 1972, the Mississippi Air and Pollution Control Commission ordered it removed. The Air Force could not *give* it back to the manufacturers, but it was willing to sell it to private farmers for an herbicide…no go! Finally, the EPA gave the go-ahead to store it on the German-built ship, the Vulcanus, and burn it! By the time the permit was finally granted, more than 5000 drums containing over 250,000 gallons of AO had rotted through (Wilcox, pg. 120)!

This insidious poisoning can do damage in many ways. It can break down the body's immune system, making it susceptible to all types of infection (Wilcox, pg.75). One molecule of Dioxin can take the place of a normal gene splay (phalanges, facial muscles, organs) (Wilcox, pg. 37). It accelerates the growth of a plant's cells until the plant or tree dies (Wilcox, pg.4). For the readers of this information, know that all weed killers we use today are really fertilizers, just concentrated amounts of them. If it rains during our growing season, then the water dilutes the weeds' coverage, creating the perfect growing medium for those "pesky" weeds which seem to multiply after a good soaking. If we use weed killers or bug sprays or any other chemical that is big-corporation based and manufactured, and if one can read the ingredients "dioxin," or something with a capital 'D' listed in the recipe of the product, then the toxicity of Agent Orange is being used. AO also does an acceleration of growth, be it cancer cells or the anomalous appearance of strange neurological or digestive, nervous or circulatory disorders and the horrific deformities of our veterans and their children, their grandchildren, and now their great-grandchildren. You see, dear reader, the effects of AO last for seven generations (Town Hall Meeting, 11/21/15)

{Author's Note: The VA, I feel, has become an entity almost too big to truly be objectively fair and impartial to those citizens who are to be, and have been, the beneficiaries of its largess: The veterans of military service to our country. If one looks on the Internet for information regarding the VA and how to get help, it is no wonder so many don't even try: Categories upon categories of references to hundreds of links (The "key" wording must be precise.) take one on a journey so long that sometimes one forgets the intended question or inquiry.} In an article by Rod Powers (Internet, 2016), the growth of the Veterans Administration has been recorded and has grown since our country began, one new "Veterans" eligibility law at a time, with new regulations and categories of qualification with each law. This is ridiculous! Somewhere, somehow, these laws must be unified, updated and made fairer to all veterans for all duties of service. We could argue all day about the good that the VA does for our wounded soldiers. It is true that the VA has helped millions of veterans with "medical," "surgical," and "rehabilitative" models of treatment (Powers, Internet, 2016). However, if even this website is carefully examined, the Viet Nam veterans often come out with the short end of the stick. The length of their term of service, where they served, what kind of discharge they were given and when they applied somehow leave the door for help just closed, or a commander maybe didn't have time for a proper evaluation or overlooked some detail of their quality of work, or records "cannot be found," and one of the worst, as mentioned earlier, needing to ask for their awards and medals, and then having to prove that they actually earned them!

Three practices would greatly improve the quality of care that our Viet Nam veterans receive. They are as follows:

1. When a qualifying agent interviews a veteran to determine eligibility, the questions should not be subjective… Objectivity leaves no room "for a broad interpretation" of an answer. For instance,

presently, three people can ask the same question to three different veterans seeking assistance. One veteran will be qualified for a certain disability rating with a certain percentage of disability, one veteran will have a greater or lesser rating with a greater or lesser percentage of disability, and the third veteran will get no disability rating or percentage of disability. It all depends on the mood of the agent, how he/she feels about the interviewee and interpretation of answers. Personally, if it is proven that a veteran who has been in country where a toxic substance has been used, even if it is years after the toxic substance was introduced (these toxins do not dissipate), I feel that he/she should be given eligibility for exposure and any diseases that occur from that time of service. Many times the results of the exposure do not show up until years, even decades, later. It is not the veteran's fault that the government sanctioned the use of toxins during war. It is the government's responsibility to take care of the veteran who is ill as a result.

2. If one state qualifies a veteran as needing any disability rating and a percentage of disability, then no other state should have the right to rescind or disqualify a veteran. I talked with one veteran who visibly shook; she has nerve damage and cannot work. She qualified for 95% disability in one state, and another state "zeroed" her out of any disability. See the above about "interpretation." Veteran qualification should be good no matter where it originated: in Alaska, Nebraska, Hawaii or any of the rest of the 50 states.

3. Because this is the 21st century, the western medical model of "helping" wounded or maimed veterans is quite out of date. Yes, there will always be a need for surgeries, the use of prosthetics (and they are getting better all the time), rehabilitation and counseling for handicaps that the western medical model provides. But like cancer treatment centers, it also needs to provide complementary programs like acupuncture for chronic pain, massage therapy to reduce inflammation and promote relaxation, the use of essentials oils, energy medicine and Reiki for wounded spirits, therapy dog pairing (as seen in Ed Zyer's story), the use of medical marijuana for chronic pain or migraines and even air transportation for those veterans who live several hours away from a VA medical center. Sometimes, a seriously ill veteran cannot make a several-hour-one-way car or van trip, even if a volunteer is doing the driving. This care should also be available to the homeless veteran population. Maybe housing? It would be most helpful to have local doctors working as a whole care team with the VA hospitals, sharing records, having conference calls and consultations, instead of relying on the veteran to organize and communicate treatments for each enterprise. It's called teamwork, folks.

Yes, I realize this all takes money and all hospitals as well as VA hospitals and treatment centers are short-staffed and crowded and blah, blah, blah! Many ways and means to find the money are possible. This is the crucial part of military budgeting. It is imperative that we as a nation understand and recognize the importance of caring for our veterans, especially the Viet Nam Veterans, in as many ways as can be done to assist in their care, comfort and quality of life. They protected us; now it's time to protect them, and include them in our family of community.}

{Author's Note: It is important that all veterans, their families, their children and now their grandchildren and great grandchildren, record and report any anomalies, such as cancers, the onset of diabetes at a young age, or changes like bone and cartilage deterioration as the onset of puberty occurs, to their VA office. As more information becomes known, research can be enhanced to try to discover how the DNA of a patient suffering from the effects of toxic exposure can be healed, or at least assisted in stopping replication of damage.}

Agent Orange: Illnesses

ILLNESSES/DISEASES RECOGNIZED BY THE VA AS CONNECTED TO AGENT ORANGE HERBICIDE EXPOSURE

Acute Peripheral Neuropathy: dysfunction of the nervous system: tingling/numbness in extremities

Adult Onset Type II Diabetes Mellitus: non-insulin dependent

AL Amyloidosis: abnormal deposit of protein (amyloid) in body tissue

Chloracne: acne-like eruption due to exposure of certain chlorinated compounds

Hodgkins Disease: tumor found in lymph nodes: increasing enlargement of lymph nodes, liver, spleen: anemia

Ischemic (ischaemic) Heart Disease: blocked arteries (cholesterol/plaque): most common cause of heart failure

Non-Hodgkins Lymphoma: (+chronic lymphocytic leukemia and small-cell lymphocytic lymphoma): absence of giant Reed-Sternberg cells

Parkinson's Disease: neurological disease: inability to control some muscles: loss of dopamine-manufacturing cells in the brain: accompanied by uncontrolled shaking of arms and legs.

Peripheral Neuropathy: (see Acute peripheral Neuropathy): sensory loss, atrophy, muscle weakness

Porphyria Cutanea Tarda: skin lesions on exposed portions of the body: skin pigment changes; liver disease in some cases

Spina Bifida: in children conceived after veteran first arrived in Vietnam: defective closure of spinal cord; it may be exposed and or protrude

Sub-Acute Peripheral Neuropathy: nervous system disorder: acute/temporary or chronic/long term

Cancer of the Bronchus: found in bronchus, trachea, lungs

Cancer of the Larynx: larynx/voice box

Cancer of the Prostate: prostate gland

Cancer of the Trachea: windpipe/trachea

Adult Fibrosarcoma: connective tissue

Alveolar Soft Part Sarcoma: sac-like ducts of the lungs

Angiosarcoma: breast and skin: maybe originating from blood vessels

Chronic Lymphocytic Leukemia: end of muscle where it becomes tendon

Clear Cell Sarcoma of Tendons: tendons

Congenital Fibrosarcoma: formed before birth/derived from connective tissue

Dermatofibrosarcoma: skin/one or more firm nodules

Ectomesenchymoma: certain parts of the skin

Epithelioid Malignant Leiomysarcoma: smooth muscle: covers muscle

Epithelioid Malignant Schwannoma: benign tumor: covers in-body surfaces: too many Schwann cells growing in a disorderly manner

Epithelioid Sarcoma: tumor found in membrane covering surfaces in body cavity

Extraskeletal Ewing's Sarcoma: outside of bone: small rounded cells

Haury Cell Leukemia: slow-growing blood cancer: lymphocytes have short, thin projections: hair-like: abnormal change in B lymphocytes (type of white cell)

Hemangiosarcoma: blood vessels/lining blood-filled spaces

Infantile Fibrosarcoma: found in children: fibrous connective tissue

Leiomyosarcoma: smooth muscle

Liposarcoma: irregular fat cells

Lymphangiosarcoma: blood vessels

Lymphoma: lymph nodes

Malignant Fibrous Histiocytoma: connective tissue

Malignant Giant Cell Tumor of the Tendon Sheath: tendon membranes

Malignant Glandular Schwannoma: too many cells growing in disorderly manner

Malignant Glomus Tumor: tiny nodes (glomuli) in nailbed, finger pads, toes, ears, hands, feet, and other organs

Malignant Hemangiopericytoma: rapidly growing fat cells formed in blood vessels and lining blood –filled spaces

Malignant Mesenchymoma: embryonic tissue or fluid

Malignant Schwannoma with Rhabdomyoblastic: skeletal muscle: rapid disorderly growth pattern of Schwann cells

Multiple Myeloma: bone marrow cells: bone marrow tumors in skeletal system

Proliferating Angiedotheliomatosis: increasing number of benign tumors in blood cells causing skin discoloration

RHabdomysarcoma: skeletal muscle

Sarcoma: connective tissue, bone, cartilage, muscle

Soft Tissue Sarcoma: muscles, connective tissue, body fat

Synovial Sarcoma: lubricating fluid in joints/tendons   (VVA/Self-Help: pp. 4-5)

BIRTH DEFECTS RECOGNIZED BY THE VA AS CONNECTED TO AGENT ORANGE EXPOSURE

Spina Bifida: children born to male or female Viet Nam veterans/ Spina Bifida Occulta not included

CHILDREN BORN TO FEMALE VIET NAM VETERANS

Achndroplasia: type of dwarfism

Cleft Lip and Cleft Palate

Congenital Heart Disease

Congenital Talipses Equinovarus: club foot

Esophageal and Intestinal Atresia

Hallerman-Streiff Syndrome: premature small growth/related defects

Hip Dysplasia

Hirschprung's Disease: congenital megacolon

Hydrocephalus Due to Aqueductal Stenosis

Hypospadias: abnormal opening In urethra

Imperforate Anus

Neural Tube Defects

Poland Syndrome: webbed fingers

Pyloric Stenosis

Syndactyly: fused digits

Tracheoesophagael Fistula

Undescended Testicles

Williams Syndrome: thyroid defects (VVA/Self Help: Pg.5)

NOT COVERED

Conditions that are congenital malignant neoplasms, chromosomal disorders, or developmental disorders; conditions that do not result in permanent physical or mental disability.

This list may change / has changed over time. (See also, Wilcox) (VVA/Self Help: pg.5)

Post Traumatic Stress Disorder: PTSD

Post-Traumatic Stress Disorder (PTSD) is defined as a stressfully emotional, and many times, physical and even soul, reaction to a traumatic/life-changing event. (Grassman, pp. xi-xii) In years past, this phenomenon has been called "shell shock" and "battle fatigue," in reference to affected veterans of early wars. While PTSD can affect people in all sorts of civilian experiences, (rape, physical assault, earthquakes, fire, sexual abuse, motor vehicle accidents (MVAs), death of a loved one, a fall from a horse, even a ladder or the roof of one's home), for the purposes of this book, I will address the plight of Viet Nam War Veterans and how PTSD affects them. The people whose stories have just been presented have all experienced PTSD on a scale of minimal trauma that has not really hindered their present lives to trauma so severe that it emotionally crippled them. Many of their brothers- and sisters-in-arms were so damaged they took their own lives to end their suffering. The biggest reasons why Viet Nam Veterans (and those veterans of today's wars) have not been able to heal their emotional wounds are two-fold: One, they did not have the chance or choice of deprogramming their horror upon returning home, being told to "suck it up," or to "just forget it." Two, the military traditionally considers those who seek help for emotional problems, for any reason, to be suspect in their ability to really deserve promotion into leadership positions. Incorrectly, the "silence is golden" maxim is the order of the day. Personally, I would prefer to follow a leader who considers emotional health, to be a better way to instill loyalty and trust, even in a battle situation that goes against the respect for human life (kill or be killed). The leader who has had to stuff traumatic baggage into a dark corner, could explode into behavior that endangers oneself or others, when a triggering event brings back the trauma of an earlier time. There is a movement developing to eliminate the idea that post-traumatic stress should not be described as a disorder, as if something is wrong with the sufferer. It is a purely human response to horrific events, whether it is a soldier's or a civilian's response. If television shows are to be believed, even just a little bit, police officers who have been involved in a shooting are required to sit at desk duty for a few weeks, and receive mandatory counseling before returning to duty using their firearm. I realize these scenarios fluctuate greatly in real life, but the idea is to make sure one's head is clearer, because the trauma has been defused.

Symptoms of PTSD may appear right after a horrific event, or may not surface for many years, or they may be a gradually increasing series of conditions that affect personality and the ability to live a healthy life. If one thinks PTSD is a culprit in changing health, a self-test might be in order. Answer these queries:

1. You have had nightmares about the event, thought about it even when you did not want to do so.

2. You have tried hard not to think about it, or went out of your way to avoid situations that reminded you of it.

3. You were constantly on guard, watchful, or easily startled.

4. You felt numb or detached from others, activities or your surroundings.

If one answers "yes" to any three items, one should think about seeing a doctor for an assessment.

Many people are reluctant to get help because of what others might think, or they do not want anyone to know they are in therapy. I say,"Why not?" If one breaks an arm, or has cancer, one would go to the doctor to get help. A counselor is a "doctor" for our emotions and spirit. The stigma of needing a "shrink" because people might think one is "nuts," is being lost in today's world. If one is a little scared of what the counselor might discover, take a trusted person (friend, relative, mentor, minister) to a first session. If one is a veteran, contact the local VA hospital, or Vet Center. Learn more about talking to a trusted doctor about trauma. (/public/assessment/trauma-symptom-checklist. asp)

Multiple reasons for seeking help exist to assist the person who has been traumatized:

1. Early treatment is better.

2. PTSD symptoms may get worse.

3. PTSD can change family life, not always for the better.

4. Getting help can improve family life.

5. PTSD can be related to other health problems, like heart trouble.

6. It may not be PTSD. (/public/assessment/trauma-symptom-checklist.asp) (Internet, November 3, 2016. PTSD)

Many veterans suffer survivor's guilt: "Why was I spared when another soldier next to me died?" or, "I could have saved more people than I did. I will never forget those I had to leave behind." (Hauptman, pg. 12) These feelings are real, and they are part of a soldier's life forever. However, they do not need to define one's life in every moment of every day. Soldiers, sailors and pilots will always be warriors, even when they return to civilian life. Many have led productive lives in many different career paths. Volunteerism is part of many soldiers' lives either as a part-time career, or as a retirement calling. In this way, the warriors can peacefully still be of service to others. Besides, helping is good for the soul.

In her free seminars for Opus Peace, Deborah Grassman, a nationally recognized spokeswoman for Hospice, discusses "Soul Injury." "It is a spectrum of wounds…that shrinks our sense of inner goodness and beauty, or even creates a haunting sense of feeling inadequate or defective." Soul injury differs from PTSD in that PTSD focuses on managing symptoms, but soul restoration focuses on opening up the wounds and connecting with the part of *self* that is generating pain. The process "opens the heart through grief, love, forgiveness and self-compassion." Her *Soul Restoration* workshops include education, ceremonial releasing of grief and loss for caregivers, tools for continued integration like eye movement desensitization and reprocessing (EMDR), massage therapy which helps reduce inflammation and provides relaxation, art therapy, even energy healing sessions and other community resources. PTSD treatments are enhanced, not replaced. Ms. Grassman uses acronyms like DENIAL: don't even know I am lying, to JOY: just open yourself. She reminds her listeners of fear: Fear of emotional pain is worse than the pain itself. A touchstone of her messages is found in words by Joseph Conrad: "The cave you fear to enter holds the treasure you seek." (Opus Peace. Soul Injury. Handouts/websites)

Another form of therapy is canine assistance. Similar to dogs for the blind and deaf, veteran service dogs are medicine for the veteran with PTSD. They can be calming and protective of social intrusion, with the assurance that the veteran will have a barrier between him/her and any perceived danger. Some arguments insist that service dogs make their owners dependent on them, so the need for continued therapy will never go away. (Bannow, pg. 21, 24-25) These dogs are medicine in more ways than one. They keep their owners grounded, and help with depression, instead of the owner needing to depend on anti-depressants so much. The feel-good hormone, oxytocin, is increased in both the dog and the owner in a special comradeship, especially with exchanged affection or interrupting a flashback nightmare. (Bannow, pg. 34) Canine therapy/service can help with the loneliness that all veterans of wars suffer, for instance, if they have lost limbs, or live alone, like some Viet Nam Veterans, as they age. They are companions when humans cannot be trusted with relationships, or when gatherings of large crowds of people (restaurants, theaters) can be seen as threatening. (Bannow, pg. 33) (See Ed Zyer's story.)

Can PTSD be prevented? "Trauma can produce a range of physical symptoms and may also wreck the balance between brain and immune system, contributing to feelings of anxiety, irritability, and emotional upset, as seen in PTSD." The amygdala gets ready for fight or flight, and the pituitary and adrenal glands step up cortisol production, which can suppress the immune system in the short term. Chronic stress leads to reduced cortisol, greater immune response and increased inflammation. It may also affect the areas of the brain that involve self-control and keeping emotions in check. (Valasquez-

Manoff, pg.60) It seems that the best time to treat PTSD is before it happens. If early-life trauma, such as physical/emotional abuse/neglect are part of a person's background, then they have as much as triple the risk for developing PTSD in traumatic military situations. Studies also have shown that mal-treatment is also responsible for brain areas like the amygdala, which, under extreme stress, reduces volume and functionality. If left unchecked, this condition could account for the disorder's hallmark tendency to ruminate obsessively. If these theories are right, then resisting inner voices and not being too much in one's head are important for one's recovery from trauma. The immune system and the nervous system work together, and if modified by early trauma, would have a tendency to flip quickly to PTSD in any stressful situation, whether it is from a missed car payment or finding oneself in a battle situation. Many treatments from virtual reality therapy (placing the gamer into a battle situation, in which the player's avatar is fighting a battle; the gamer knows it's just a game), anti-depressant drug therapy and food supplement therapy (foods with anti-inflammatory properties) could be given to the patient). Another future therapy could be immunizing incoming military recruits with an inoculation similar to other shots they receive when they report for induction (Velasquez-Manoff, pg. 63). {Author's Note: My question is this: Could this be helpful in helping any PTSD victim recover? Would it help future warriors who might already have the trauma in their DNA to go to war and not be as traumatized as they could possibly be without it? Would science be creating killer automatons who are trained to follow orders without getting more PTSD or soul injury? How is this situation ever justified?}

Our country and the other peace-seeking countries of the world do need to keep our military machine of soldiers, sailors and pilots trained to deploy at a moment's notice. My anger, frustration and daily plea is that when the military creates killing machines of those brave men and women who have volunteered to put themselves in harm's way, it should be mandatory, no, **Mandatory** that it deprograms them, so that they can re-integrate into civilian life with clear and healing minds, hearts and souls. The government has a duty to re-pay those who put their lives on the line, and sometimes give the ultimate sacrifice, with hospitals, care teams that combine western medicine with appropriate complementary health care choices, and rehabilitation for handicaps, as well as job training and retraining **without** cover-ups (Wilcox, Pp. 29, 43), lies presented with the excuse of "national security," and mountains of paperwork with which they have to prove that they served in a certain area for a certain amount of time. I saw the forms that one veteran had received from a Senator's office: At least 15 pages with some of the printing faded as if the printer had run out of ink, and printing just continued until the batch was finished running through the printer… duplicated? Not entirely. That's professional? Helpful? I think not.

Caregivers, such as wives or husbands, try to help with this record finding as well. Trying to complete forms, finding proof of service, collecting eyewitness statements of comrades who could be dead, or who have simply moved with no way to locate them, cause these folks as much PTSD stress as actual combat, especially considering that it can take years for the VA or DOD to answer requests with anything near helpful information. (See "A Widow's Story")

Thanks to one of the featured veterans, John Lind, who volunteers in several ways for outreach programs at the Portland, Oregon VA, a recent update from the Department of Defense and Department of Veterans Affairs, dated November 11, 2016, tells about a program that is being developed which can improve "therapeutic alliance support and effective treatment planning." It addresses the military culture. Health care professionals designed core concepts and strategies to assist those veterans with PTSD. (Internet, 02/23/16) These programs can be part of the healing that veterans need, but the word needs to be advertised loudly and often. And for the Viet Nam Veterans, it needs to be soon. Many of our Viet Nam Veterans do not know anything about these services. If one knows and loves someone with PTSD, help in any way possible needs to be offered… and sometimes, again and again. This part of the military budget is costly, but is as important as the ordnance or jet budget allocations. Solution? Idea: Some of our Congressional officials could take a pay cut, instead of voting themselves pay raises, and then having Medicare take more of a cut from Social Security every year from the general public. They could serve two terms like our Presidents do, pay Social Security and use health care programs like other citizens must do. It is time for the government, which is so fond of recordkeeping, to keep meticulous records of military service for all military personnel, from 18-year-olds just inducted to officers with 30 or 40 years of service. Our Viet Nam Veterans have many diseases, not the least of which is memory problems. They should not have to remember *where, when, or what* they did, because their records, dates of service, medals earned, and honors received should be digitally recorded and accessible when they are requested, not buried, or burned, or ignored in some dusty warehouse of forgotten paperwork. And… their time is running out!

COMMUNICATIONS DEPARTMENT REPORT

Don't Wait For An Army To Die

By Mokie Pratt Porter, Director of Communications

Significant numbers of Vietnam veterans have children and grandchildren with birth defects related to exposure to Agent Orange. A Ford Foundation public relations campaign to win the sympathy of the American people for the plight of Agent Orange victims in Vietnam does not plan to address the plight of Agent Orange victims in America.

On June 2, the Ford Foundation announced that it and the U.S.-Vietnam Dialogue Group on Agent Orange/Dioxin are hoping to mobilize resources to raise awareness about the ongoing health consequences of dioxin contamination in Vietnam resulting from the wartime spraying of Agent Orange. The end goal is to gain the support of Congress, American business, and the American people.

When VVA representatives asked at the meeting whether American veterans and their offspring also would be part of the public relations campaign, the chair of the Working Group replied: "We have given you the report."

A June 1 report, "U.S. Vietnam Veterans and Agent Orange: Understanding the Impact 40 Years Later," by the National Organization on Disability with funding from the Ford Foundation, concludes that it is not "too late to correct the lapses in the nation's treatment of veterans who were exposed to dioxin during the Vietnam War," and that "one lesson of the Agent Orange experience has been that the consequences of such chemicals are rarely easy to predict, and that the burdens they impose may well be borne for generations."

The report includes five detailed recommendations: 1) outreach to all affected veterans and their families; 2) outreach to health practitioners and disability-related service agencies; 3) medical care for affected children and grandchildren; 4) a fresh approach to research; and 5) direct service to veterans and their families.

VVA recognizes the work and commitment of the Ford Foundation Special Initiative on Agent Orange/Dioxin and the U.S.-Vietnam Dialogue Group on Agent Orange/Dioxin. Moreover, the June 1 report provides highly useful recommendations related to the unfinished business of Agent Orange/Dioxin for Vietnam veterans and their progeny.

But if the Ford Foundation's publicity campaign will focus exclusively on the plight of Vietnamese victims of Agent Orange, then Vietnam veterans need to launch their own grass-roots publicity campaign.

THE TASK AHEAD

This is not just a VVA issue. VVA members, chapters, and state councils need to reach out and work with other veterans' organizations in their communities. We cannot allow veterans to find out about their A/O exposure from the perspective of the Vietnamese victims. This is not about animosity toward Vietnamese victims of Agent Orange; it is a response to telling only one side of the story.

We need real stories about real people. We are in the process of gathering these stories. If you wish to share your family's second- and third-generation health struggles from what you believe to be due to exposure to Agent Orange/Dioxin, please send an email to mporter@vva.org or call 301-585-4000, ext. 146.

Some have suggested holding veterans' health forums at the chapter and state council levels. That's a good way to get local media attention and a perfect forum to discuss the issue of A/O, as well as the host of illnesses and maladies associated with military service.

It is useful to have a nuts-and-bolts, how-to plan for this type of health forum. What we need is something that could be shared with other states and chapters, such as a checklist for organizers of local health forums, or a document that has tips for putting on a high-interest, high-attendance, high-media-coverage veterans' health forum.

This is not just about the Vietnam War and Agent Orange; it is about all toxic exposures in all theaters of our recent wars, whether in Thailand, Eglin Air Force Base, Guam, Puerto Rico, Texas, the Gulf, Iraq, or Afghanistan. The larger lesson continues to be that the cost of war doesn't end when the guns are silent. In fact, it takes a generational toll.

This effort is just getting started. What works in one area may not work in another area. But sharing ideas, info, intel, and good stories is needed. Local initiative, local creativity, and local enthusiasm and energy will be essential.

VIETNAM VETERANS OF AMERICA
8719 Colesville Road, Suite 100
Silver Spring, MD 20910

Mokie Pratt Porter
Director of Communications

(301) 585-4000 Ext: 146
(301) 585-2691 Fax

mporter@vva.org
www.vva.org

youtube.com/user/VietnamVetsAmerica

Factoids about Vietnam Veterans

Contribution was sent by John Lind, a featured soldier in this book. John found this information on the Internet. {Author's Note: Some of the total numbers of information have dropped or added to totals in the last 19 years, as people have died, been found or continue to be missing. Not all statistics have been noted or listed on these pages, but can be found as updated material in various publications. Other updates can be found on Hugh Rowland's website: hugh@vets-helping-vets.com. Hugh's story is another feature in this book.}

These statistics were taken from a variety of sources to include: The VFW Magazine, the Public Information Office, and the HQ CP Forward Observer 1st Recon, April 12, 1997.

"In case you Vietnam Veterans haven't been paying attention these past few decades after you returned from Vietnam, the clock has been ticking."

The following contains some of the statistics that are at once depressing, yet, in a larger sense, should give some a sense of pride.

Of the 2,709,918 Americans who served in Vietnam, less than 850,000 are estimated to be alive today, with the youngest American's age approximated to be 54 years old. This number represents 9.7% of their generation.

If you are alive and reading this, how does it feel to be among the last 1/3 of all US veterans who served in Vietnam? I don't know about you, but it feels a little strange considering this is the kind of information we are used to reading about WWII and Korean War Veterans.

The last 14 years we have been dying at a faster rate than most at {about} 390 a day…too fast; only a few will survive by 2025, if any.

A total of 9,087,000 military personnel served on active duty during the Vietnam Era: August 5, 1964-May 7, 1975.

A total of 8,744,000 GIs were on active duty during the war: August 5, 1964-March 28, 1975.

A total of 3,403,000, including 514,000 offshore, personnel served in the broader Southeast Asia Theater: Vietnam, Laos, Cambodia, Thailand (flight crews) and the South China Sea waters (sailors).

Forty to sixty percent of those in country either fought directly, provided support or were regularly exposed to enemy attack.

Of the 7,484 women who served in Vietnam, 6,250, or 83.5%, were nurses.

The first man to die in Vietnam was James Davis, in 1958. He was with the 509th Radio Research Station. Davis Station in Saigon was named for him.

Total deaths were 58,202. This includes those who were formerly classified as MIA and Mayaquez casualties. {This total remains fluid, as numbers from wounded or ill personnel continue to die.}

Single-personnel deaths numbered 29,869; married-personnel deaths numbered 17,509.

Five men killed in Vietnam were only 16-years old; the oldest was 62 years old.

The state with the highest death rate was West Virginia: 84.1%. The national average was 58.9% for every 100 males in 1970.

Statistics on wounded/crippled veterans: wounded: 303,704; injured requiring no hospital care: 150,375; severely disabled: 75,000; 100% disabled: 23,204; lost or severely impaired limbs: 5,283; sustained multiple amputations: 1,081.

Amputation or crippling wounds to the lower extremities were 300% higher than in WWII, and 70% higher than in Korea (due to the expanded use of land mines)

Multiple amputations occurred at the rate of 18.4% compared to 5.7% in WWII.

Missing in Action (MIA) number 58,338; POWs number 766; 114 died in captivity. As of January 15, 2004, 1,875 Americans are still listed as "unaccounted for" from the Vietnam War. {Author's Note: See Hugh Rowland's update.}

The total military force in-country was draftees: 648,500, or 25%; Reservists: 5,977; National Guard: 6,140 served; 101 died.

Total draftees from 1965 to 1973 numbered 1,728, 344; Army: 1,685,711; Marines: 42,633; last man drafted: June 30, 1973.

Of those killed in action (KIA), 86% were Caucasian, 12% were Blacks, 2% were Hispanic, and 1% were of other races. (Of Blacks who enlisted, 34% volunteered for combat arms. Of those KIA, they suffered 12% of the deaths in Vietnam, when the percentage of Blacks of military age was 13.5% of the total population.)

Vietnam Veterans have a lower unemployment rate than the same non-veteran age groups. Vietnam Veterans' personal income exceeds that of our non-veteran age group by more than 18 percent. {Author's Note: Remember, most of these surveys were taken in the late 1900s.}

Of men sent to Vietnam, 76% of those were from the working class; 50% were from middle-income backgrounds; 75% had family incomes above the poverty level; 23% had fathers with professional, managerial or technical occupations.

Of those who served, 79% had a high school education or higher; compared to 63% of Korean Veterans, and 45% of WWII Veterans.

There is no difference in drug usage between Vietnam Veterans and non-Vietnam Veterans of the same age group. (VA study, 1995/National Association of Chiefs of Police) {Author's Note: Today, it might be higher, or even lower.}

Vietnam Veterans are far less likely to be in prison; only .5% of Vietnam Veterans have been jailed for crimes. {See above.}

In making successful transitions to civilian life, 85% of Vietnam Veterans made that claim. {Author's Note: Remember that much of what we know today about the effects of PTSD and Agent Orange exposure had not come to light. When these issues began to surface, the truth about these ugly results changed, and continues to change, these figures drastically.}

Lack of political will is the reason 82% of veterans who saw heavy combat believe we lost the war; 75% of the public agrees.

Actual Vietnam Veterans who served honorably number at 91%. Those who saw combat number at 90% say they were proud to serve their country; 74% say they would serve again, even knowing the outcome.

The public holds the Vietnam Veterans in high esteem at 87%. {Author's Note: I think it should be higher!!}

From the Army Times;

"VA Assigns Officer to Verify Claims Involving Secret Missions," by Rick Maze, staff writer *(no date given)*

For veterans claiming they can't prove a service connection for their disability because it resulted from a secret operation, the Veterans Affairs Department has assigned a liaison officer to the U.S. Special Operations Command with direct access to classified files.

The little-known program has a VA employee work closely with the command historian at the command's headquarters at MacDill Air Force Base, Fla., to review files on classified missions for special operations units in all services.

Befitting the nature of the missions involved, the program quietly launched a year ago has received scant attention. Joe Davis, spokesman for Veterans of Foreign Wars, was unaware of the initiative. "But it does make… sense, given the clandestine nature of their business," he said.

The liaison was established in December 2009 under an agreement between the Pentagon and VA.

The current VA liaison to the Special Operations Command is an Army veteran who was not part of a special operations unit but has the appropriate security clearances to review files, according to VA sources.

Lack of records access has been seen by many spec ops veterans as a roadblock to filing claims, especially for disabilities such as post-traumatic stress. There may be nothing in military health or personnel records to verify any treatment while the veteran was in uniform.

If a veteran says his claim is based on involvement in a secret mission, VA claims examiners turn files over to the liaison, who can verify the veteran's involvement, VA sources said.

If more information is needed, the claims examiner requests that the liaison search for the information by requesting it from either U.S. Special Forces Command or one of its subordinate commands.

The liaison officer then prepares sanitized information for use by the regional VA office handling the claim. Veterans have direct contact with the liaison only if more information is needed to track down records, VA sources said.

Claims from veterans who say they took part in an intelligence operation run by the Defense Intelligence Agency, Central Intelligence Agency or other governmental organization also can be researched by the AV liaison officer if a classified mission is involved, VA sources said.

The liaison officer is a full-time employee of the Veterans Benefits Administration and has access to records involving special operations units including Army Rangers, Army Special Forces, the Army's 160th Aviation Regiment, Navy SEALS, Air Force Special Operations and Marine Corps Special Operations and Reconnaissance units.

Acknowledgements

Though this book was my idea, formed in the last century, I have been blessed beyond measure by those who "traveled with me" to make this book a reality. My plan was to invite as many Viet Nam Veterans as possible to take part in this project. I created an open-ended questionnaire, and began inviting Viet Nam Veterans in Bend, Burns, La-Pine, Prineville, Redmond and Sisters, through their Band of Brothers (BoB) groups. I even invited those whose families also attended the Town Hall meeting I attended in Portland. All these cities are located in Oregon, but my journey also took me to Idaho, Illinois, and Wisconsin, via phone calls and emails, thanks to Lyle Hicks and Bob Beatty. They introduced me to Ed Zyer, Tim Schuller and Hugh Rowland. I am thankful to the BoB Presidents and the veterans who listened to my invitation and answered with the stories you have read in these pages.

Thank you to my brother and sister-in-law, Tim and Marianne McNeil, who introduced me to Gary Hartt, via his wife, Scarlett, with whom they worked in their nursing careers. Thanks to Gary, and his group of veterans who meet each year with a picnic outside of Oregon City, Oregon and the messages they sent to the Veterans Administration Medical Center, I met John Lind, who fed me information for over a year about events and news for veterans and those who love them. Thanks to John, I met my amazing publisher, Barbara Terry, and her amazing co-workers who invited me to work with them, even when I whined, to get this book into your hands, libraries, book stores, Kindles and Nooks. Barbara introduced me to Tom Peterson, another featured veteran.

Thank you to my energy healing teacher, Bear McKay of the Bear McKay School of Energy Healing, in Bozeman, Montana, for her requirement of a graduate project before graduation, and to my classmates and mentors, John and Justine Gibb, Susan Gilmore, and Beth Hattenberger, for their support. I will be writing a research paper that shows how energy healing can help with PTSD in anyone, but especially in those who have been in combat, or who have loved and lived with someone who has experienced combat. This book will be considered a companion piece to assist in the self-healing of those whose stories might bring inspiration to others who read it, like the ripples created when a stone is thrown into a pond … again, the energy of one's healing helping another's.

Thank you to all my massage clients… a huge hurrah!!! for all your support on my journey, and for those little cheers left on my phone or in a text or email just to let me know that you have *my* back! (No pun intended…)

Thank you to my teaching colleagues, Peggy and John Goodman and Leslie Colvin for referrals, Kathy Zachow, Judy Brown, Ron Rock, and Carl Robbins (who recently helped me requisition a book on grammar, so I could find a model of "Works Cited" for my Bibliography), and all my other buddies from our days in the middle school classrooms of our youth, who have always supported my literary efforts!!

Thank you to my book club ladies: Marie Glenn, Lisbet Hornung, Julie Nisley, Sue Thomas, and Courtney Turner. We have turned many pages together, and created some stories of our own!

Thank you to my oldest and dearest friend since the age of six when we met in first grade, Joanne Kennedy, and her sweetie, Emmitt Hussey, for all their love and support (and book endorsements). When it seemed like I could not go on, they were right there for me as cheerleaders who never let me quit!! A big part of their cheering squad includes long-time friends Barbara Baldwin, and her husband, Ed Johnson, Diana Barker (new vistas in Hawaii continue to amaze), Mary Bliven (the first person to invite me to speak at a book club: hers!), Diane Duke, Sally Hite, Kathy Lee, Carole Manners, Brenda McHughes, Joan Morrison (vacation planner extraordinaire and precise copy editor), Sharon Prichard, Daraleen Shales (who introduced me to Alison Perry of COVR), and Karry Thomas (excellent house and pet sitter).

Thank you to Deanna Swarthout, who is a good friend, great house cleaner, beautician and an amazing amateur photographer. She took my photo for the book cover. Thank you to Diana Hedrick, LMT, and Christina Frazier, LMT, who kept me sane with their marvelous massages. Thank you to the great folks at Postal Connections who saved the day more than once when my computer decided to overload itself. Thank you to my very necessary webmaster, Andrew Brott, Troy Ford, IT guy with computer magic when the computer did not want to cooperate, and Zoey Knorr, who brought me into the 21st century and taught me digitization of documents with a flash drive! Thank you, too, to Dr. Kyle Gillett and Dr. Eric Hayden, for their endorsement of this book, when it was still a baby.

Thank you to my husband, Harry Dawe, for his continued love and support.

Thank you to my sons, Ryan and Sean, and their spouses Amy and Frances, respectively, who live amazing lives helping our world. Through all the work I have done in this life, including this project, I have thought: If my kids can face their challenges and dangers, then I can face mine.

Thank you to all those wonderful people in my life who make my journey a blessing every day. The doors to this book opened like the pattern of carefully placed, then pushed, dominoes. When the time was right, I was given the tools to continue to the next step. I applaud career authors, as I now know that the real business of writing is solitary and lonely, at times. To create a story as a lesson, or to entertain, is to crack open one's soul and share the heart of it. There is no other work quite like it, and I am honored to be part of it.

Author Bio

Molly Burton grew up in a small Oregon town. She graduated in 1969 from Oregon College of Education (now Western Oregon College, in Monmouth, Oregon), She taught middle school language arts for 30 years. For 27 years, Ms. Burton has been a practicing licensed massage therapist and Reiki Master. Her studies in energy healing began four years ago, and she now has a growing clientele in that field as well.

Ms. Burton's interest in the Viet Nam veterans began when she first heard about the war in high school. A few years later, Lee Whitmore, a classmate, who was a neighbor, and her cousin, Don McNeil, were chopper pilots killed in the war. During her teaching career, in the 70s and 80s, she began to notice her students wearing "camo" outfits to school. These students were wearing actual uniform fatigues of their parents who had served in Viet Nam. She became even more interested when her children joined the military. Recently, a Viet Nam Veteran told his tale of being burned by Agent Orange, and that was the catalyst that began her journey in seeking the stories of the war's real heroes.

LOOK TO THIS DAY

Look to this day!

For it is the Life, the very Life of Life.

In its brief course lie all the Verities and

Realities of your Existence:

The Bliss of Growth.

The Glory of Action.

The Splendor of Beauty.

For Yesterday is but a Dream,

And Tomorrow is only a Vision;

But Today well-lived makes every

Yesterday a dream of Happiness,

And every Tomorrow a Vision of Hope.

Look well, therefore, to this Day!

From the Sanskrit
(Johnson, Pg. 55)